THE MEANING OF MARRIAGE

THE MEANING OF MARRIAGE

Family, State, Market, and Morals

Edited by

ROBERT P. GEORGE

and

JEAN BETHKE ELSHTAIN

SPENCE PUBLISHING COMPANY • DALLAS

2006

Published in the United States by
Spence Publishing Company
111 Cole Street
Dallas, Texas 75207

Library of Congress Control Number: 2005933929
ISBN 1-890626-64-3
978-1-890626-64-8

Printed in the United States of America

Contents

v

Acknowledgments

I N THE SUMMER OF 2003 a group of entrepreneurs and intellectuals
decided to establish an institution of advanced scholarship, the
Witherspoon Institute. It was given as its mission to enhance the
public understanding of the political, moral, and philosophical principles of free and virtuous societies, and to promote the application
of those principles to contemporary problems. Since then, the Witherspoon Institute has supported the scholarship of eight fellows with
projects on topics of bioethics, marriage, religion and civil society, constitutional interpretation, and natural law.

Back in early 2004, conventional wisdom had it that "the marriage debate" would be settled within months, surely by the time of
the November election. We decided nevertheless to organize a private
conference (to be held *after* the presidential election) with the title:
"Why Marriage Is in the Public Interest." The Witherspoon Institute
commissioned ten scholarly papers on the topic and brought together
intellectuals from across the academic disciplines to discuss these papers, collaborate with one another, and to take stock of the current
condition of marriage. This collection of essays—bringing the political,
moral, and philosophical principles to bear on the institution of marriage—is our first publication.

I am very grateful to the Social Trends Institute and to its president, Dr. Carlos Cavallé, for their support from the inception of the

project to its final publication. The Culture of Life Foundation, Arthur Rasmussen, Robert Myers, George Marlin, and Michael Crofton of the Philadelphia Trust Company helped make the project a reality. Much of the credit goes to Drs. James Stoner, Bradford Wilcox, and Christopher Wolfe—the conference organizing committee—for their clarity of vision and attention to detail. Our host, Princeton professor and senior fellow of the Witherspoon Institute Harold James, provided enthusiastic support from the outset.

Special thanks go to Matthew O'Brien, who drafted the first proposal for the conference, and who largely set the vision of the meeting; I am thankful for his continued help and suggestions. Ana Samuel, the executive director of the Witherspoon Institute, is to be complemented for making her first conference the unforgettable experience that it was for everyone present. Ryan Anderson had the thankless task of editing all these texts several times. While Ana is on sabbatical finishing her doctoral dissertation, Ryan has assumed the role of executive director; we are fortunate to have him with us.

I cannot adequately express my gratitude to the Smith family— Ted, Mark, Sandy, and their late mother Mary—for their support and encouragement. From the academy, Hadley Arkes, Robert P. George, Byron Johnson, and Robert Hollander have been a source of valuable counsel. Donald Drakeman, Mark O'Brien, Wiley Vaughan, Roger Naill, Michael Fragoso, and John Metzger have been helpful and generous supporters.

And finally a word about my parents, Raul and Martha. Starting a family of seven children in a small town with no running water, electricity or high schools, and suffering multiple financial setbacks, they produced children with post-graduate educations who to this day are happily living their life-long vocational commitments. Back then, there were no books about parenting; what my parents lacked in knowledge they made up in love and perseverance. It is because of the many parents like mine, and the gratitude and reverence we owe to them, that we forge ahead to promote the truth about marriage.

LUIS TELLEZ,
PRESIDENT,
THE WITHERSPOON INSTITUTE

Foreword

Jean Bethke Elshtain

T HIS BOOK ADDRESSES A DIFFICULT ISSUE, the status of the institution of marriage in twenty-first century America. Unfortunately, the topic has entered our public life at a time when the terms of our public discourse seem poorly equipped to engage in a serious and nuanced discussion concerning the nature and purpose of marriage in American (or any other) society. The political and legal maneuvers leading to the legalization of same-sex marriage in Massachusetts in the spring of 2004 forced the marriage debate into American public discourse in a broader and more divisive way than in previous decades. The polarized, "rights monist," and oftentimes over-moralized tone of American public discourse has made it difficult for intellectuals, scholars, and policy makers to model for the wider public a reasoned inquiry into the nature and purpose of marriage. At times, intellectuals seem to push for, or endorse, a breakdown of the very discourse that would enable Americans to consider this topic in all its depth and importance—as controversial and even painful as that might be.

Why is it so difficult to discuss marriage? One reason, of course, is that we all have a stake in the debate and its outcome. No one is left

* The author would like to thank Dr. Jeffrey Langan and Matthew O'Brien for their assistance.

untouched by marriage, including those who never marry, because marriage is such a pervasive institution in our society. One recent estimate indicates that 88 percent of women and 82 percent of men will marry at some point.[1] Beyond that, the problem lies in a hardening of the categories of debate. I noted "rights monism" above. This stance is one that conducts public debate exclusively in a narrow language of rights and celebrates an individualistic notion of "choice." The distinguished sociologist Robert Bellah, along with his colleagues, pointed out in the 1988 bestselling book *Habits of the Heart* that Americans have lost ways of talking about their commitments and what gives their lives meaning, except in and through a subjective kind of rights-talk. Other "languages" central to the American political tradition—civic republicanism or a rich scripturally-inspired language (here all one need do is read Abraham Lincoln's great speeches)—have faded as rights-talk has triumphed. This way of thinking and speaking tilts the debate from the outset. The benefits and burdens of traditional social relationships can be re-described only imperfectly in the language of individual choice. Therefore, anyone with doubts about same-sex marriage is often seen as "anti-choice," or even bigoted, by those who uncritically adopt the contemporary terminology of the debate. Matters frequently stall out there.

Suffice it to say, there is much lacking in current debates over marriage. This book is one attempt to remedy the problem. An underlying presupposition for the essayists featured here—who range from moderate liberals to traditional conservatives—is that if we alter the institution of marriage as it is understood in our laws, there will be profound and perhaps unintended consequences for the ways in which we think of ourselves as men and women, and for the kind of society we live in. It will have consequences for what we think of the families to which we belong, what we think of how we should organize our lives as individuals and citizens, and what kind of citizens we attempt to cultivate. It will affect quite profoundly whether we continue our long tradition of supporting mothers and their children. Given the importance of marriage as an institution for individuals and for society, the thoughtful citizen has every reason to expect, and even demand, a deep and thoughtful debate as the precondition for any change in how we understand marriage and encourage it to take shape. One need only reflect on previous alterations in the regulation of marriage in order to understand that changes in marriage law have consequences that intellectuals, politicians, and citizens alike should think through thoroughly before endorsing.

When one looks back on the debates that took place in the late 1960s and early 1970s over changing the divorce laws of this country—leading to the wide-scale institutionalization of no-fault divorce—there was much debate about the rights of women stuck in unhappy marriages. There were few serious discussions about what effects no-fault divorce would have on the institution of marriage; how social perception of marriage as a normative institution would subsequently change; how its purpose in society might be altered; what historical and philosophical roots anchored the movement; what effect widespread no-fault divorce might have on how we raise children and prepare them to become responsible citizens. Certainly people did not consider the negative impact no-fault divorce would have on women themselves! But we have now learned that divorce is strongly associated with the immiseration of women: studies indicate, for example, that between one-fifth and one-third of women fall into poverty in the wake of a divorce.[2] At the time, there were a few who argued that no-fault divorce would have significant social repercussions, but the ensuing highly-charged debate, again narrowly cast in terms of individual rights, muted their voices. Any opposition was construed as anti-feminist, despite the fact that many of the concerns expressed were precisely about the well-being of women who faced divorce.

The case of no-fault divorce reminds us of the effect that laws regulating marriage may have. At the very least, it shows that just the act of considering such changes says something profound about a society's fundamental commitments and values. Responsible social scientists and political theorists always caution that major social change—and same-sex marriage involves something more basic than no-fault divorce—*always* trails negative unintended consequences in its wake. If there are any constants or laws in political science, this is one. It follows that this recognition, for which there is a mountain of compelling evidence, should caution us to move with great care if we aim to alter the fundamental human institution that has always been the groundwork of social life.

Of course, our sense of "who" counts as family does change with the times—are big extended families the norm, or narrower, nuclear families? Some point to this variability as though it signals that marriage and the family are infinitely flexible and contingent. Not so. Marriage has always involved men and women and this has served as a *prima facie* fact of the matter. Are we prepared to jettison this? Are we that wise and well-informed? Again, these are the questions we should be debating; unfortunately, we are not. Or, at least, those who do raise such issues in this debate have been shoved into the background by all the shouting. Throughout human history societies have created many laws, customs, and institutions that have influenced the institution of marriage and the family, in ways planned and unplanned; but the overall social aim has always been to secure a safe place to rear children and establish an institution that helps to "moralize"—without necessarily being moralistic—human sexual behavior. (Marriage, in particular, should check male tendencies to wander, argued such prominent social theorists as Jane Addams. It was the women who should insist on a settled abode, she claimed.) Although the matter wasn't researched in a social scientific way for centuries, there has long been a shared recognition that a child's formative years, and his or her sense of male and female mutuality, integrity, and endurance, exercises a profound effect on what sort of adult he or she becomes. Fundamental disruptions in the home invite disrupted lives across the board.

While nearly all of the essayists in this volume draw upon the disciplines of sociology, history, and economics, social science alone is not enough to discuss—and ultimately to understand—the phenomenon of marriage. These essayists also consider marriage from the perspectives of political theory, jurisprudence, and philosophy in order to clarify the nature and purposes of marriage as an institution. Perhaps most importantly, the authors examine marriage in a context larger than the immediate same-sex marriage debates. This broader perspective helps us appreciate that debates about same-sex marriage are not mere moralistic disputes over an isolated practice. Rather, we should be considering questions about marriage's place within a delicate and dynamic web of social relationships, no one of which can be revolutionized without altering the others.

Although the essayists believe marriage's difficulties are linked to the institutionalization of same-sex unions, they do not lay blame with advocates of same-sex marriage. They acknowledge that well before the rise of the same-sex marriage debates, marriage as an institution was already under siege in American life and that children, alas, often paid the price. They recognize that on the legal, historical, philosophical, and economic fronts, the problems of marriage run much deeper than today's headlines.

THE ESSAYS

In the first essay of this collection, "Sacrilege and Sacrament," philosopher Roger Scruton addresses marriage from a far-reaching humanistic perspective, highlighting important methodological considerations in the study of human practices. Scruton begins by contrasting the external, detached stance assumed by social science, and the internal, first-person perspective of lived human experience. Considered from the viewpoint of the former, marriage provides essential social functions for perpetuating society over time, and from the viewpoint of the latter, marriage sanctifies our sexual desire by elevating and channeling it into existential commitment to another person. Scruton catalogues the tensions between these two perspectives on marriage in its literary and legal representation throughout western history. He concludes by considering our present situation, and provisionally argues that traditional marriage is vindicated both by social science and by lived experience, but that public recognition of this truth is hampered by taboos and political correctness.

Don Browning and Elizabeth Marquardt, in their essay "What About the Children? Liberal Cautions on Same-Sex Marriage," emphasize that the condition of marriage today must be understood in light of the phenomenon of modernization. The growth of technical rationality—"efficient means-ends procedures, coming from either market or state bureaucracy, that accomplish short term satisfaction"—throughout society has increasingly uprooted traditional family roles. Browning and

Marquardt proceed to offer a philosophical anthropology of marriage, exploring the similarities between the traditional views of Aristotle and Aquinas on the one hand, and contemporary evolutionary psychology on the other. These disparate sources concur on the importance of "kin altruism" for effective childrearing, an insight overlooked by most same-sex marriage proponents. Browning and Marquardt conclude by examining the concept of sexual orientation itself and articulate their own moderate position in the marriage debate, which they call "critical familism."

John Maynard Keynes famously remarked, "In the long run we are all dead anyway." True enough for us the living, but not so for society's future generations—they *are* the long run. Economists, therefore, often search for "inter-generational equity" and social mechanisms that can make reliable and legitimate transfers between generations. Economic historian Harold James, in his essay "Changing Dynamics of the Family in Recent European History," argues that the family is perhaps the only social institution capable of achieving inter-generational and inter-temporal equity. A living generation's concern for society's future stems largely from concern for the prospects of its own children. This concern provides the present generation with incentives to undertake projects and activities whose benefits they will never see, but which their descendents will enjoy. The institution of the family shapes the interests of each generation, shifting them from narrow self-regard about the present, to a more selfless concern for the future. James considers an underappreciated instance of this phenomenon in the financial world: family businesses. Against conventional analyses, James argues that the family can often be both a source of financial dynamism and market stability. Finally, he suggests that recent changes to traditional family structure could have severe unforeseen consequences for both states and markets.

Arguments against privileging traditional marriage with a network of legal supports frequently appeal to a libertarian conception of the minimal state. It is by no means apparent, however, that a minimal state is sustainable apart from a robust marriage culture—or so economist Jennifer Roback Morse contends in "Why Unilateral Divorce Has No Place in a Free Society." Morse offers an economic analysis of competing notions of marriage and the family, and assesses how they promote or diminish personal liberty in the face of state power and reach. In economic terms, contemporary progressives often treat marriage as though it were a "spot market," whereas in reality marriage is better analyzed as a long-term contract or the "team production" idea of the business firm. At any rate, where marriage is treated as a spot market, massive state subsidy and interference is required. This consequence is especially apparent in the practice of "no-fault" divorce. Although Morse focuses throughout on marriage in relation to the libertarian state, her conclusions are clearly important for any serious political vision of the left or right.

David F. Forte's essay, "The Framers' Idea of Marriage and Family", considers the place of the family in the political and social thought of America's founding generation. The founders seldom wrote explicitly about marriage and the family, but as Forte shows, this relative silence belies the important social functions that the founders thought marriage and the family must serve. Adams, Madison, Washington, and other key founders believed that successful republican self-government presupposed a virtuous citizenry. Forte argues that it is only "the school of the family" that can inculcate potential citizens with the requisite social and political virtues. Forte goes on to examine the origins of the founders' thoughts on virtue and family through the Enlightenment to classical Greece, and argues that Aristotle's conception of family and social order lie at the source.

Both law and culture are artifacts because they are brought into existence and sustained by the purposive action of human societies. But law and culture are also natural because it is part of human nature to create them. The relation between law and culture is therefore a dynamic and complicated one; it is this relation that is at the heart of Hadley Arkes' essay "The Family and the Laws." Difficult questions of moral principle cannot be avoided in the crafting of law, Arkes argues. Furthermore, once principles have been legally enshrined, their consequences tend to work themselves out whether we wish them to or not. This feature of law is crucially important in the debate over same-sex marriage. Arkes shows how the legalization of homosexual unions threatens to vitiate nearly *any* regulation of sexuality at all.

Arkes acknowledges that social scientific data provide strong reasons for being wary of alternatives to the traditional family structure, but he sets the bar higher for himself and others, claiming that debates over sexual morality must be settled at the level of principle. He begins to sketch what is required for such an account in this essay.

In "What's Sex Got to Do With It? Marriage, Morality, and Rationality," legal philosopher Robert P. George constructs an Aristotelian-Thomistic account of marriage and human sexuality, drawing on the work of Germain Grisez and John Finnis. George contends that the dominant "lifestyle liberal" views of marriage misrepresent its nature by presupposing an implausible "dualistic" conception of the human person, and by treating marriage as a purely instrumental good. Properly conceived, marriage is an intrinsic good through which human beings can find integral fulfillment, and the marital act is a two-in-one-flesh communion of persons, which is only made possible by the biological, emotional, and spiritual complementarity shared between man and woman. George concludes by arguing that political neutrality towards competing visions of marriage is impossible; the law inevitably must enshrine and support one vision or another.

In her essay "Soft Despotism and Same-Sex Marriage," political theorist Seana Sugrue identifies the market, the family, and religion as three distinct forms of social order that mediate between the individual and the state. The advent of same-sex marriage, Sugrue warns, threatens to undermine the legitimate autonomy of these "institutions of civil society" in several respects. First, same-sex marriage assimilates market-based relationships into family life, corroding the duties for the care of children which marriage traditionally enjoined. The establishment of same-sex marriage also requires introducing coercive state power into the private realm, since same-sex marriage, unlike pre-political traditional marriage, is a fragile artifact of the state which depends upon its coddling for existence. Sugrue appeals to Tocqueville in arguing that such state intrusion tends to enervate the civic virtues of a populace, rendering it dependent upon the state's "soft despotism". Finally, Sugrue examines how the legalization of same-sex marriage, far from being impartial between rival views of marriage, would marginalize and suppress religious institutions that opposed it.

Many essays in this collection draw upon or allude to social scientific data regarding marriage and the family, but in "(How) Does Marriage Protect Child Well-Being?" Maggie Gallagher directly evaluates the data. The most reputable and rigorous studies support two general conclusions about how marriage benefits children. First, a culture of legally-supported marriage creates "selection effects" that shape who becomes a parent with whom, and at what stage in life. Second, children reap unique developmental benefits when raised within the intact, married, and reasonably harmonious union of their own biological mother and father. Gallagher challenges the claims that homosexual parenting provides children with the same advantages as married heterosexual parenting. The few studies which purport to justify such claims, she argues, are methodologically flawed and incomplete. Gallagher's essay provides a valuable summary of the state of contemporary family scholarship and its developing consensus on the importance of married mothers and fathers for social well-being.

The history of family law in the United States is long and complicated, but crucial for understanding the present state of marriage and the family. In "The Current Crisis in Marriage Law, Its Origins, and Its Impact," legal scholar Katherine Shaw Spaht chronicles the development of judicial and legislative attitudes towards marriage. Spaht shows how prior to the 1960s the law protected and encouraged marriage, and how this began to change when a series of court-mandated policies refocused legal support to an individualistic conception of personal autonomy. As Spaht demonstrates, most often such innovations were not the result of popular advocacy, but rather were initiated by well-positioned judges and legal scholars. Spaht offers illuminating discussions of key court cases such as *Planned Parenthood v. Casey*, *Lawrence v. Texas*, and *Goodridge v. Massachusetts Dept. of Public Health*.

Too often contemporary debates over same-sex unions overlook the controversy's roots in the broader cultural trends of the twentieth century. In "Suffer the Little Children: Marriage, the Poor, and the Commonweal," sociologist W. Bradford Wilcox remedies this oversight by tracing the course of family breakdown over the past forty years. Wilcox shows how two innovations, the introduction of the contraceptive pill and the legalization of abortion, altered our social conception of the family. Contraception and abortion separated sex and procreation from marriage, severely weakening the social norms which previously bolstered marriage and the family. Wilcox demonstrates how the consequences of weakened marriage—out-of-wedlock childbearing and divorce—undermine the common good and disproportionately harm the poor. Wilcox's argument should dispel the common assumption that the plight of today's poor is simply a result of economic inequality and that cultural values and family structure are of secondary importance.

CONCLUSION

I shall end with a personal reminiscence. In the summer of 2005 I was one of four speakers debating—in a friendly way and to a learned and (it must be said) relatively affluent audience over the course of a week—the role of religion in public life in America. One of the speakers stated his own doubts about same-sex marriage and lamented the fact that we were not having the sort of debate about marriage as an institution we ought to be having. To my astonishment, he was booed by this respectable and mannered assembly. The hoots echoed across the audience. This left me, although I wasn't the target myself, with a rather bad taste in my mouth and a genuine sadness about the inability of such well-educated people, who are influential and accomplished in their fields of endeavor, to acknowledge the need for such a debate. Maybe it is too late and we shall never have this much needed discussion. But perhaps not. If not, this volume will make a contribution to a discussion on a higher order of intellectual rigor and specificity than we have had thus far.

THE MEANING OF MARRIAGE

— I —

Sacrilege and Sacrament

Roger Scruton

I. TWO PERSPECTIVES

A<small>N INSTITUTION CAN BE LOOKED AT FROM OUTSIDE</small>, with the eyes of an anthropologist, who observes its social function. Or it can be looked at from inside, with the eyes of a participant, whose life it transforms. And what is observable from one perspective may not be observable from the other. The anthropologist who studies the seasonal war-making of a tribe may understand this institution as a way of securing territory, a way of controlling population, and a way of reaching a renewable equilibrium with neighbors. The warrior understands the institution in quite another way. For him it is a source of brotherhood, a mystical affirmation of identity between himself and the tribe, and a call to his soul from "ancestral voices." The concepts used by the anthropologist—social function, solidarity, ideology, and so on—make no contact with the warrior's experience. If he were to make use of these concepts in describing what he feels, he would immediately cease to feel it. And the concepts that inform the warrior's self-understanding—brotherhood, destiny, sacred obligation—play no part in the anthropologist's explanation of what the warrior does.

3

This does not mean that the two people are entirely opaque to each other. Maybe, by an act of *Verstehen*, the anthropologist can enter into the experience of the man he studies and imagine what it is like to see the world as he sees it. Maybe the tribesman can stand back sufficiently from his situation to envisage how it might be understood and explained by someone who was outside the fold of membership. Nevertheless, the two assign different and incommensurable values to the institution of seasonal warfare, and criticism offered from one perspective might have no bearing on the values that inform the other. For the anthropologist the institution is justified by its function, and if it becomes dysfunctional, then it loses its rationale. For the warrior the institution is justified by the sacred obligations on which it rests, and only if those obligations are rescinded can it be allowed to decay.

This mismatch between external and internal perspectives has been frequently remarked upon, and not only in the context of anthropology. We encounter it in moral philosophy, in the conflict between consequentialism, which sees ethics as policy directed towards an external goal, and the deontological perspective that sees ethics in terms of absolute rights and duties. We encounter it in literature, in the contrast between the author's perspective and the values and motives of his characters. We encounter a version of it too in ourselves. For, as sophisticated modern people, we are in the habit of looking on our own values as though they were not ours at all, but the values of some curious stranger, who needs to be put in context and viewed from some fastidious height. We are all familiar with that Prufrock feeling, which reminds us in the midst of our warmest passions that we are perhaps wrong to presume, wrong to assume.

Indeed, it is arguable that the contrast between the two perspectives lies in the nature of things. A person is both I and he, both free subject and determined object, both rational chooser and predictable animal. We can see ourselves in either way, a possibility from which Kant derived his startling vision of our moral and metaphysical predicament. But it is perhaps a distinguishing mark of the modern condition that we are so easily tempted away from the first-person viewpoint to that other and more alienated posture that turns self into other and choice into fate.

This has a bearing, I believe, on the current debates over marriage. For marriage is one of those institutions that we spontaneously see both from outside, in terms of its social function, and from inside, in terms of the moral and spiritual condition that it creates. No honest anthropologist can fail to acknowledge the functional importance of marriage. In all observed societies some form of marriage exists, as the means whereby the work of one generation is dedicated to the well-being of the next. Marriage does not merely protect and nurture children; it is a shield against sexual jealousy and a unique form of social and economic cooperation, with a mutually supportive division of roles that more than doubles the effectiveness of each partner in their shared bid for security. Marriage fulfills this complex function because it is something more than a contract of mutual cooperation, and something more than an agreement to live together. Hence marriage enjoys—or has until recently enjoyed—a distinct social aura. A wedding is a rite of passage, in which a couple pass from one social condition to another. The ceremony is not the concern of the couple only, but of the entire community that includes them. For this is the way that children are made—made, that is, as new members of society, who will, in their turn, take on the task of social reproduction. Society has a profound interest in marriage, and changes to that institution may alter not merely relations among the living, but also the expectations of those unborn and the legacy of those who predecease them.

Wedding guests therefore symbolize the social endorsement of the union that they have assembled to witness, and the marriage is a kind of legitimization of the potentially subversive desire between the partners. Society blesses the union, but only at a price. And the price has been, in traditional Christian societies, a heavy one: sexual fidelity "till death do us part" and a responsibility for the socializing and educating of the children. As people become more and more reluctant to pay that price, weddings become more and more provisional, and the distinction between the socially endorsed union and the merely private arrangement becomes less and less absolute and less and less secure. As sociologists are beginning to observe, however, this gain in freedom for one generation implies a loss for the next. Children born within a marriage are far more likely to be socialized, outgoing, and able to form permanent relationships of their own, than children born out of wedlock.[1] For their parents have made a commitment in which the children are included and of which society approves. This fact is part of the deep phenomenology of the marital home. Children of married parents find a place in society already prepared for them, furnished by a regime of parental sacrifice, and protected by social norms. Take away marriage and you expose children to the risk of coming into the world as strangers, a condition in which they may remain for the rest of their lives.

An anthropologist will hardly be surprised, therefore, to discover that marriage is regarded, in most simple societies, as a religious condition. Rites of passage are conducted in the presence of the ancestors, and the ancestors are presided over by the gods. Religion is one way in which the long-term interests of society may animate the short-term decisions of its present members. Hence it is natural that marriage should be seen from within as something divinely ordained, with a sacred aura that reinforces the undertaken duties and elicits the support of the tribe. You don't have to be a religious believer to observe this or to see its point. You need only be aware of what is at stake when people bring children into the world and claim those children as their own.

2. CIVIL UNION

The institution of civil marriage is not a modern invention. It was already established under Roman law, which regarded marriage as a distinct legal status, protected and defined by a purely secular jurisdiction. However, the law took note of religious precedent, looked severely on those who departed from its edicts, required a kind of commitment that went well beyond any merely contractual tie involving children and property, and held both parties to their obligations. The shadow of religion fell across the Roman marriage ceremony, with its meticulous rituals and sacred words, and the household gods watched over the transition, in which they were intimately concerned. True, Roman marriages were not conceived as eternal unions: they were the legal embodiment of an intention to live monogamously together and could be ended by noting that the *affectio maritalis* had ceased. Legal recognition that the marriage was over could be obtained without difficulty, and although in later Christian times the Emperor Justinian briefly succeeded in penalizing consensual divorce, it is clear that the Roman law did not regard marriage as a radical existential change.

With the growth of the Papacy, marriage was recaptured from the secular powers, and reconsecrated as the Church's concern. And so it remained throughout the Middle Ages and the early Renaissance. An uneasy truce was struck between secular jurisdictions and ecclesiastical ceremonies, and the Church's interdiction of divorce ensured that marriage laws would enshrine the idea of a lifelong commitment. Marriage was no longer a complex and rescindable relationship, but a permanent change of status, from which there could be no real return.[2]

When Henry VIII took the English into the Reformation, it was on account of his marital problems. He wanted a divorce, and the Church would not grant one. Traditional Catholic teaching holds marriage to be an irreversible change of status, not merely within the community but also before God. Hence a marriage cannot be undone, but only annulled. An annulment does not grant release from an existing marriage but declares that the marriage never was. Naturally enough, the process of annulment has been subject to abuses; but even Henry, Defender of the Faith, could not persuade the Church to take the easy way out of their common problem. When the King took the matter into his own hands it was not in order to break the connection between marriage and the Church. On the contrary, marriage remained Holy Matrimony, and Henry solved the Church's problems by appointing himself as the head of it. It was probably not until the French Revolution that the state declared itself to be the true broker and undoer of marriages, and neither the Catholic nor the Protestant church has ever accepted this as doctrine or afforded its comforts to those who view their marriages as purely civil affairs.

Since then, however, we have experienced a steady de-sacralization of the marriage tie. It is not merely that marriage is governed now by a secular law—that has been the case since antiquity. It is that this law is constantly amended, not in order to perpetuate the idea of an existential commitment, but on the contrary to make it possible for commitments to be evaded, and agreements rescinded, by rewriting them as the terms of a contract.

From the external perspective this development must be seen as radical. What was once a socially endorsed change of status has become a private and reversible deal. The social constraints that tied husband and wife to each other through all troubles and disharmonies have been one by one removed, to the point where marriage is hardly distinct from a short-term agreement for cohabitation. This has been made more or less explicit in the American case by the prenuptial agreement, which specifies a division of property in the event of divorce. Partners now enter marriage with an escape route already mapped out.

3. CONTRACTS AND VOWS

To understand this change we should recognize that, although divorce has been permitted in Protestant cultures for some time, it has not been seen in contractual terms, even by the secular law of marriage. Divorce has been unlike annulment in recognizing that a marriage once existed and is now being undone. But it has been like annulment in recognizing that the spirit of a marriage survives its material death. There could be no return from the state of marriage, but only a transition to another state *beyond* marriage, in which as many of the marital obligations as possible would be salvaged from the ruin and reinstated as lifetime burdens on the parties. Typically the divorced husband would be charged with the maintenance of his ex-wife, the education and protection of their children, and such other liabilities as could be imposed upon a man now faced with a self-made enemy.

With the prenuptial agreement, however, divorce takes on a new meaning. It becomes in a sense the *fulfillment* of the marriage contract, which henceforth loses its force. Spouses no longer enter a marriage but, as it were, stand outside it, fully equipped to move on. Hence marriage has ceased to be what Hegel called a "substantial tie," and has become one of a lifelong series of handshakes.[3] Among the wealthy and the sexy, serial polygamy is now the norm. But the word "polygamy" already begs the most important question—which is whether such an arrangement is really a marriage. Rescindable civil unions cannot conceivably have the function of marriage as traditionally conceived. They cannot guarantee security to children, nor can they summon the willing endorsement of society, by showing the partners' preparedness to make a sacrifice on the future's behalf. The new kind of civil union exists merely to amplify the self-confidence of the partners. Children, neighbors, community, the world—all such others are strangers to the deal. Not surprisingly, when marriage is no more than an official rubber stamp affixed to a purely private contract, people cease to see the point of it. Why bother with the stamp? Whose business is it anyway?

Official policy is therefore already recognizing the effect of official policy, which is to downgrade and ultimately abolish the marriage tie. Government forms in Britain ask for details of your 'partner' where once they would have asked for details of your husband or wife. It is all but politically incorrect to declare yourself married to someone (at least to someone of the opposite sex), and many of my liberal friends now refuse to refer to their lifelong companions in terms that imply any greater commitment than that contained in an agreement to share a roof. Children are no longer part of the arrangement, which is conceived purely as a contract between consenting adults. When Kant described marriage as "a contract for the mutual use of the sexual organs" he may not have had this in mind.[4] But his words were prophetic, and proof of the extent to which his Enlightenment vision was already reshaping the world.

The contrast between marriage and the new kind of civil union is yet more striking from the internal perspective—the perspective of the partners themselves. For it is a contrast between two quite different moral positions. The traditional marriage, seen from the external perspective as a rite of passage to another social condition, is seen from within as a vow. This vow may be preceded by a promise. But it is something more than a promise. Here is how I put the point in an imaginary dialogue between Perictione, niece of Plato, and Archeanassa, alleged by Diogenes Laertius to be Plato's mistress:

"With the change in my perception of religion," Perictione went on, "came a change in my perception of marriage. For what is marriage if not a vow taken before an altar, and what remains of the vow if no god turns up to enforce it? Of course, a man and a woman can stand in front of a table and exchange promises. But I think you will agree, most honored Archeanassa, that promises and vows are quite distinct?'

Archeanassa thought for a moment.

"Is it not a question of solemnity?" she suggested. "I mean, the more solemn the promise, the more it approaches a vow."

"By no means," said Perictione, and she stared through her guest with evident satisfaction. "The difference between a vow and a promise is profound and metaphysical. For a promise is fulfilled in time. And when the promise is fulfilled it is also finished. But a vow is never fulfilled in time: it is endless and changeless, and there is no point at which the account is closed. Those bound together by vows are bound eternally; which is why the immortals must be present, to seal the vow and endow it with a more than earthly power."

"Furthermore," she went on, warming to her theme, "promises and contracts can be undone by agreement, after which no obligation remains. Whereas a vow, once knit, can never be untied, but only dishonored. Such it seems to me, is the real distinction. There is another difference too, and this deeply impressed me at the time of which I am speaking, because it helped me to understand the dilemma in which my poor mother had been placed by her husband's infidelity. Contracts, I hope you agree, are useful things. Without them, no society can endure, since there can be no security between strangers—and a modern society is a society of strangers, is it not?"

Archeanassa signified her assent to this, but could not forbear mentioning that she had heard the point argued by the great Xanthippe, whose ideas, she added, were so much more down-to-earth than those of Plato, and so much more in tune with the female temperament.

"Of course," Perictione continued, with a slight frown, "Granny introduced me, before she died, to her friend Xanthippe, and there was an exchange of ideas between us. But to return to the point. Contracts, you will admit, involve an exchange of goods and services. Nothing is given absolutely—all benefits offered depend upon benefits received. Hence the matter of a contract must be defined independently: a bag of horse-hair, say, or a waggon-load of beans. There cannot be a contract to be bound by a contract: such an agreement would be empty and senseless."

"Indeed not," said Archeanassa,. . . .

"But the subject-matter of a marriage," Perictione went on, as soon as she had recaptured Archeanassa's eyes, "what is it, if not the marriage itself? What matrimony means, by way of cost and benefit, can never be foretold by those who create it through their vows. Cares and joys, rights and duties, failures and successes—all are in the lap of Fortune, and none can be known in advance. From which it follows, as I am sure you will concede, that marriage cannot be a contract.'

"Nor," said Archeanassa, "can the vow of love.". . .

"As for that,"the girl pursued, "we must distinguish real institutions from unreal hopes. And in my father's case—since, after all, it is my father's case that we are discussing—love was no part of the deal. There was a marriage—the eternal vow which bound my mother and cut off her escape. And there was a contract—under the terms of which young Cholcis received rent and underwear, and my father expert caresses. As for the feelings—well, they take the shape of the institutions which channel them: stern duty in the one sphere, abject lust in the other. Do you follow me?"

"I wish I didn't," said Archeanassa, "for these are bitter things you speak."

"Bitter no longer," said the girl, "and hardly bitter then. For you know, I am like my uncle. When something troubles me I dissolve it in thought, and make of it an intellectual problem—which is what my parents' marriage became. I saw that marriage is not a contract but a vow, that men could not stay the course, and that in any case the immortals had faded away, leaving all vows to unravel like tapestries in which the binding thread is cut. Marriage ceased at once to be an option for me. Of course, I was intrigued by men, and tried a few experiments. But the fun occurred at a vast distance, so to speak, way below the place from which I studied it. The question came uppermost in my mind, how to live in this society of strangers—how to triumph, rather. For a descendent of Solon cannot merely live. And my first thought was this: I must replace vows by contracts, in which terms would be agreed in advance. Do you follow me still?"

"Yes," said Archeanassa, "and still, I think, your story is a sad one."[5]

The change described by Perictione is one special case of the transition "from status to contract" which was discussed, from the external perspective, by that great armchair anthropologist Sir Henry Maine.[6] But it is clear that there is more to it than that. As the story goes on to make clear, Perictione is not taking an external view of marriage, nor is she connecting marriage with child-rearing, security, or the handing on of social capital—vital though it may be, for the effective performance of those functions, that people think of marriage in the terms that she suggests. Perictione is reporting a change in the phenomenology of sexual union, a retreat from the world of vows and "substantial ties" to a world of contracts, promises and negotiated deals. And, as she implies, the world of vows is a world of sacred things, in which holy and indefeasible obligations stand athwart our lives and command us along certain paths, whether we will or not. It is this experience that the Church has always tried to safeguard, and it is one that has been jeopardized by the state, in its efforts to refashion marriage for a secular age.

4. THE VOW OF LOVE

Vows and oaths automatically transport us to the realm of the sacred. You can see this from the Homeric poems, from Virgil's *Aeneid*, from the Icelandic sagas, *Beowulf*, the *Niebelungenlied* and all the other stories of people immersed in the urgencies of tribal life. When the Church first declared marriage to be a sacrament, to be administered before the altar in the presence of God, it was attempting to give institutional form to a vow. From the inner perspective, however, this vow preceded the Church's endorsement. And the theory of marriage as a sacrament captures a prior sense that something similar is true of erotic love. Whence does this sense of the sacred arise? Anthropologists can tell us why the vow of love is useful to us and why it has been selected by our social evolution. But they have no special ability to trace its roots in human experience, or to enable us to understand what happens to the moral life when the vow disappears and erotic commitment is replaced by the sexual handshake. Indeed, anthropologists may be even more tempted than the rest of us to read their own internal perspective into the behavior of the people whom they study: witness the now notorious case of Margaret Mead, who travelled all the way to Samoa in order to witness the sexual culture of New York.[7]

The supposed sanctity of the erotic tie, the connection with chastity, celibacy, and the vow of love—these themes animated medieval literature and came to the fore at the time when the Ecclesiastical view of marriage as a sacrament was beginning to take a hold on the law and the imagination of medieval Europe. The literature of courtly love, as it came to be known, was an attempt to raise the erotic from the realm of animal passion to that of rational choice.[8] This literature was inspired by neo-Platonist theories which had already exerted considerable influence over Islamic and Hispano-Arabic literature, and which were distilled in the works of Avicenna (Ibn Sinna), the Persian physician and Sufi philosopher who had provided so many of the metaphysical conceptions that shaped the theology of the medieval Church. Much of what is proposed by the poets and philosophers of courtly love is apt to seem absurd. The extraordinary legalism of *Le roman de la rose* and the fictitious "courts of love" described by Andreas Capellanus and others strikes us now as a vain attempt to deny the obvious truth, which is that sexual desire is not a choice or a judgment but a passion.[9] The medievals were themselves aware of this, and side by side with the courtly literature we find the tales of Tristan and Isolde and Troilus and Cressida, which emphasize the untameable power of sexual longing and its ability to subvert all that we might erect by way of legal, conventional, and institutional restraints.

But it is in these very dramas of passion that we find an explanation for the vow of love and for the aura of sanctity that surrounds it. The vow is not imposed on lovers by custom, nor required of them by law. It is present in the very experience of desire: such is the burden of the medieval tales. Isolde's desire for Tristan subverts her marriage vows, but only so as to prove that her true vows were not to King Mark but to Tristan. The sin of Cressida is not that she defies the laws of marriage, but that she betrays the vow of love that arose in her first desire, and which dedicated her to Troilus.

Well yes, you say, that may have been true of those particular fictions. But what bearing does it have on life as it is lived by the rest of us? We are not heroes of passion, nor given to these catastrophic commitments from which there is no turning back. We are content to live at a lower level, accepting sexual desire as a source of pleasure, but wary of the obsessive attachments that it can generate and which leave us perpetually unassuaged.

That response is apt to be supported by a weight of cultural history. It will be said that the vow of love—conceived one way by the courtly literature, and another way by the subversive response to it—is in both versions a piece of ideology. It is an attempt to present as a permanent and metaphysical truth what is in fact no more than a passing social fashion, useful in securing the property relations of a vanished leisure class, but with no claim to be the enduring truth of the human condition. The myth of the love-vow had a lasting influence on Western culture, leading to the great celebrations of man-woman love in Shakespeare and Milton, to the heroic passions explored by Racine, to the literature of romantic love and to the operas of Bellini, Verdi, and Wagner. But all this is culture, not nature. Other societies have viewed love, desire, and marriage in other terms, and the idea of marriage as rooted in a personal choice and an existential commitment is as foreign to oriental traditions as the love of counterpoint, the belief in the Incarnation, or a taste for *confit d'oie*.

It is hard to disagree with all that. Yet there is something that it overlooks, something which is at the heart of the medieval conception of the love-vow, and of the marital practices that it has been used to authorize. This thing is the peculiar intentionality of human sexual emotion. Sexual desire is not a desire for sensations. It is a desire for a person: and I mean a *person*, not his or her body, conceived as an object in the physical world, but the person conceived as an incarnate subject, in whom the light of self-consciousness shines and who confronts me eye to eye, and I to I. True desire is also a kind of petition: it demands reciprocity, mutuality, and a shared surrender. It is therefore compromising, and also threatening. No pursuit of a mere sensation could be compromising or threatening in this way.

I have tried to defend those claims elsewhere.[10] They are not claims about culture, nor are they claims about the way in which desire has been rationalized, idealized, or constrained by institutions. They are claims about a particular state of mind, one that only rational beings can experience, and which nevertheless has its roots in our embodiment as members of the human species. There are other states of mind that have a passing resemblance to sexual desire, but which do not share its intentionality—for example, the sexual excitement aroused by pornography, or the excitement that finds relief in fetishism and in necrophilia. There is a whole gamut of perversions, the object of which is not to possess another person in a state of mutual surrender, but to relieve oneself on someone's body, to enslave or humiliate, to treat the other as an instrument through which to achieve some sensory excitement, and so on. But in calling these things perversions we indicate a defect in the intentionality from which they spring. They are no more to be seen as expressions of sexual desire than the desire to eat your child is to be seen as an expression of love or the desire to humble yourself before your enemy is to be seen as an expression of anger. Such is the complexity of the human condition that the mental forces that erupt in us can find just such peculiar outlets. But in describing them as perversions we convey the idea that a state of mind has a normal object, a normal fulfilment, and a normal course towards its goal. In the case of sexual desire, the norm can be seen externally, in terms of its social function, and also internally, as a feature of the intentional object and of the description under which he or she is desired.

5. POSTMODERN SEX

Now many people will question what I have said about desire. There is a picture of human sexuality that is propagated by the media, by popular culture and by much sex education in our schools, which tries both to discount the differences between us and the other animals and also to remove every hint of the forbidden, the dangerous, and the sacred. It is a picture that makes no place for shame, save as a lingering disability, and which describes the experience of sex as a kind of bodily sensation. Sexual initiation, according to this picture, means learning to overcome guilt and shame, to put aside our hesitations, and to enjoy what is described in the literature as "good sex." The function of sex education in schools—and especially in those schools controlled by the state—is to rescue children from the commitments that have been attached to desire by displaying sex as a matter of cost-free pleasure. Even to describe desire as I have done in the foregoing paragraphs is regarded, by many educationists, as an offence—a way of cluttering the minds of children with unmanageable guilt. Such educationists regard the free play of sexual titillation as a far healthier option than the death-encompassing passions associated with the old conception of erotic love.[11] Most parents, however, encountering this attitude to sex and the literature used to implant it in the adolescent mind, experience a surge of revulsion, even going so far as to question the right of the state so to poison the hearts of their children. Indeed, sex education has become one of the principal battlegrounds between the family and the state. There is a reason for this, to which I return.

Before the advent of modern sex education, the object of desire was represented through concepts of purity and pollution, sanctity and desecration, and it is the transition between these states that is dramatized in the story of Troilus and Cressida. It is because the object of desire has been perceived in this way that jealousy can take the murderous form in human beings that Shakespeare puts before us in *Othello*. Desdemona, in Othello's eyes, has been ransacked, polluted, like a violated temple, and only her death can extinguish this sacrilege and restore the pre-existing holiness. What Shakespeare is describing here is precisely not a local form of erotic passion, but a human universal, a predicament that we are involved in by the very fact of sexual desire. That sexual desire is directed towards an existential commitment is the unwritten assumption of the literature of erotic love, from *Daphnis and Chloë* to the puppet plays of Chikamatsu, and from *Arcassin et Nicolette* to *Lady Chatterley's Lover*.

This existential aspect of desire makes it dangerous. Rape is a crime not because it involves force, but because it is a desecration, a spoiling and polluting of that which it is in a woman's nature to hold in reserve until it can be given freely. If sexual desire were merely the desire for sexual sensations, this ransacking of the body could not occur: to be raped would then be no worse than to be spat upon. It is precisely the existential seizure that humiliates and destroys. For it is a kind of murder, a reducing of the embodied person to a corpse.

Again, however, we must confront the modern sceptic. Even if people once understood the sexual act through those quasi-religious conceptions, the sceptic will argue, they do so no longer. There is now neither pollution nor taboo, but an easy-going market in sexual commodities: a market which can be entered without shame and left without damage. And maybe the growth of this market, and its extension, through sex education, to an ever-growing number of participants, is a real contribution to human freedom and to the undistinguished contentment of the postmodern herd.

It seems to me, however, that desire freed from moral constraints, and from the ethic of pollution and taboo, is a new and highly artificial state of mind. It can be maintained in being only by forms of discourse that wilfully disenchant the sexual act and the human body: in other words, which are wilfully obscene. This partly explains the gradual invasion of popular culture by explicit sexual images, and the consequent shift in focus from the human subject to the dehumanized object. These cultural developments are not random: they have a function, and this function can be clearly seen when we contrast the old Hollywood approach to romance with the modern cult of explicit images.

When the erotic kiss first became obligatory on the cinema screen it was construed as a coming together of faces, each fully personalized through dialogue. The two faces had carried the burden of a developing drama, and were inseparable in thought from the individuals whose faces they were. When, in the last seconds of the Hollywood movie, the faces tremblingly approached each other, to be clichéd together in a clinch, the characters sank away from us into their mutual desire. This desire was their own affair, a kind of avenue out of the story, that took them quickly off the screen and into marriage.

Pornography is the opposite of that: the face is more or less ignored, and in any case is endowed with no personality and made party to no human dialogue. Only the sexual organs, construed not as agents but as patients, or rather impatients, carry the burden of contact. Sexual organs, unlike faces, can be treated as instruments; they are rival means to the common end of friction, and therefore essentially substitutable. Pornography refocuses desire, not on the other who is desired, but on the sexual act itself, viewed as a meeting of bodies. The intentionality of the sexual act, conceived in this disenchanted way, is radically changed. It ceases to be an expression of interpersonal longing, still less of the desire to hold, to possess, to be filled with love. It becomes a kind of sacrilege—a wiping away of freedom, personality and transcendence, to reveal the passionless contortions of what is merely flesh. Pornography is therefore functional in relation to a society of uncommitted partnerships. It serves to desecrate and thereby neutralize our sense that the object of desire is made sacred and irreplaceable by our longing. By shifting the focus downwards, from the end to the means, from the subject to the object, pornography diverts sexual feeling away from its normal course which is commitment, and empties it of its existential seriousness. Pornography is sex education for life, as it were.

6. STATE AND FAMILY

To what point does this bring us, in the contemporary discussions over marriage? My tentative conclusion is this: that the view of marriage as a sacrament is an accurate, if theologically loaded, account of how marriage has been experienced, of why it is wanted, and of what it inwardly does to those who enter it. Marriage is not a contract of cohabitation, but a vow of togetherness. Its foundation is erotic, not in the sense that all marriages begin in or exist through desire, but in the sense that, without desire, the institution would rest on nothing in the human condition. At the same time, looked at from outside, with the eye of the anthropologist, marriage has a function, which is to ensure social reproduction, the socializing of children and the passing on of social capital. Without marriage it is doubtful that those processes would occur, but when they occur they provide both a fulfillment of sexual union and a way to transcend its scant imperatives, into a realm of duty, love, and pride. The inner, sacramental, character of marriage is therefore reinforced by its external function. Together they endow marriage with its distinctive character, as an institution that is normal and sublime in equal measure.

When the state usurped the rite of matrimony, and reshaped what had once been holy law, it was inevitable that it should loosen the marital tie. For the state does not represent the Eternal, nor does it have so much regard for future generations that it can disregard the whims of the merely living. The state is always and inevitably the instrument of its current members; it will respond to their pressures and try to satisfy their demands. It has therefore found it expedient to undo the sacrament, to permit easy divorce, to reduce marriage from a vow to a contract, and—in the most recent act of liberalization—to permit marriage between people of the same sex. None of this has been done with evil motives, and always there has been, in the back of people's minds, a memory of the sacred and existential ties that distinguish people from animals and enduring societies from madding crowds. The desire has been to retain the distinctiveness of marriage, as the best that we can hope for by way of a lasting commitment, while escaping from its more onerous demands—demands that people are no longer prepared to recognize. As a result, marriage has ceased to be a rite of passage into another and higher life and become a bureaucratic stamp with which to endorse our temporary choices. I would not call this a gain in freedom—for those choices have never been denied to us, and by dignifying them with the name of marriage we merely place another obstacle before the option to which humanity has devoted so much of its idealizing fervor. Of course, we are still free to dedicate our lives to each other, to our home and to our children. But this act is rendered the more difficult, the less society recognizes the uniqueness, the value, and the sacrificial character of what we do. Just as people are less disposed to assume the burdens of high office when society withholds the dignities and privileges which those offices have previously signified, so are they less disposed to enter real marriages when society acknowledges no distinction between marriages that deserve the name and relationships that merely borrow the title.

Ordinary conjugal people, who marry and raise children in the traditional way, and who believe that these acts point beyond the present moment to an indefinite future and a transcendental law, have a voice in law-making and will tend to vote for legislators who uphold the sacramental view of marriage and who pass laws endorsing the normal way of marital sacrifice. From the external point of view, that is what an anthropologist would expect. For societies endure only when they are devoted to future generations, and they collapse like the Roman Empire when the pleasures and fancies of the living usurp the inheritance of those unborn. Here in the United States, however, there is another way to legislation, through the Supreme Court, and this way is the way of the state and of the elites who control it. And because the Supreme Court can override any merely democratically elected body, and will—as the case of *Roe v. Wade* amply demonstrates—use any measure of sophistical argument if it sees the need to do so, Americans are increasingly aware that—in many of the most important matters, the matters that govern the life and death of society—it is the state, not the people, that decides. The attitude of the state to marriage should therefore be set beside its attitude to sex education and the bearing of children. The burden of state-sponsored sex education, I have suggested, is to turn the sexual urge away from erotic passion, marital commitment, and dutiful child-bearing towards disposable pleasures. This attitude is reinforced by the state's support for abortion, and its "discovery," in *Roe v. Wade*, that the unborn have no rights under the Constitution and therefore no rights at all. Put all this together with the state's constant tendency to erode the tie of marriage, and you will be tempted to believe that the state has set itself against the goal of reproduction. This has not been a conscious decision. Nevertheless it reflects a vast movement in the modern world towards the confiscation of hereditary rights.

Some will see this attitude as involving a kind of collective infanticide: such, I suspect, is the response of the Roman Catholic Church. Others, however, welcome it, even under the somewhat bleak description that I have offered. Thus Richard Rorty, in *Achieving Our Country*, ostensibly a critique of the anti-patriotism of the left establishment, sees the emergence of the easygoing culture of promiscuity, and the political correctness which is well on the way to censoring out every alternative, as positive steps towards the only thing that matters, which is an "Enlightenment utopia" in which complete equality of condition will have at last been achieved.[12] To get there you need the Supreme Court, if only to extinguish those exclusive passions and loyalties which are the source of local privilege. The fact that the resulting Utopia will be unable to reproduce itself is not a fact that pragmatists like Rorty are equipped to notice. And what a pragmatist doesn't notice is in any case not a fact.[13]

7. THE FUNCTION OF IDEOLOGY

It is here that we should step back from the discussion of marriage in order to visit a distinction fundamental to the Marxist vision of human institutions: the distinction between ideology and science. A scientific theory is part of our search for truth, and it endures because it has not been refuted. An ideology is part of our search for stability, and it endures because it fulfills a social function, shoring up customs, practices, and institutions that require just this if they are to provide their benefits. We can see the point from the initial example that I took of seasonal warfare. The warrior's belief that this is a sacred duty, an obligation to the ancestors, and a solemn gesture of brotherhood is ideological. His belief is to be explained in terms of its function, rather than its explanatory power. Its function, roughly, is to commit the warrior to his dangerous exploits, in a way that he could be committed by no merely dispassionate analysis of the cost and benefit of pursuing them. From the external point of view seasonal warfare too must be explained by its function: it is a way of securing territory, controlling populations, and achieving equilibrium in the search for scarce resources. The external view is scientific: it explains the behavior of the tribe, but does not justify it. The internal view is ideological: it justifies the behavior, but does not explain it. The true explanation of the behavior is also an explanation of the ideology, and in both cases the explanation refers to a social function.

You might wish to apply Marx's distinction to what I have said about sex and marriage. The external viewpoint offers an explanation of marriage in terms of its social function. It is because it facilitates social reproduction that marriage exists and endures. If marriage became dysfunctional it would disappear, just as seasonal warfare has disappeared from modern societies. This external explanation can also form the starting point for a justification, by showing that the consequences attached to marriage are socially beneficial, and the consequences of destroying marriage socially disastrous. I believe that this kind of consequentialist justification of marriage has already been made by Charles Murray, James Q. Wilson, and others. But there is also an internal justification of marriage in terms of the sanctity of the erotic tie. The Marxist anthropologist might say of this internal justification that it is "mere ideology," meaning that it is to be explained in terms of its function in securing marital commitment, but has no rational basis in the erotic tie itself. To explain the institution of marriage from the external perspective is also to expose the internal perspective as a kind of illusion, which records no independent fact of the matter, being merely an aura cast by the institution in the minds of those over whom it holds sway.

Although not all debunkers of "bourgeois" society make use of Marx's distinction between ideology and science, the idea that our dearest beliefs and most precious values are merely ideological constructs, destined to disappear with the institutions and the power relations that temporarily require them, is now a common assumption in the social science and humanities departments of our universities. It is assumed by feminism of the Judith Butler kind, by Foucault in his theory of the *episteme*, by Edward Said in his critique of the "Orientalist" posture, by Fredric Jameson in his postmodern Marxist criticism, and by most of those exposed by Alan Sokal and Jean Bricmont in *Intellectual Impostures* and satirized by Frederick Crews in *Postmodern Pooh*.[14]

Applied to the case of marriage it would very quickly deliver interesting results. It would tell us, for example, that the view of marriage as a sacrament, and the associated experience of erotic love as involving a vow, a commitment, and an existential tie, are all part of the ideology of marriage. When marriage loses its function so too does the ideology; and since the ideology rests on no independent ground, it will disappear like a dream in the waking conditions of modernity. Moreover, the Foucauldian will say, societies no longer require bourgeois marriage in order to generate children and endow them with social capital. On the contrary, bourgeois marriage stands in the way of the new forms of social reproduction, which are all in the hands of the state. Through welfare benefits and social initiatives the state takes charge not only of the education of children, but also of their production. Modern sex education is not concerned to convey the facts about sex any more than was the old apprenticeship in chastity. Sex education too is ideology, functional in relation to the new form of social reproduction, in which the parties are the single mother and the state, and in which exclusive and lifelong attachments threaten the state's control over the reproductive process. By desacralizing the sexual bond and removing the existential danger, the new ideology prepares the way for a process of social reproduction in which sexual desire and sexual excitement play only a transitory and non-constitutive part.

My response to that argument is twofold. Although (as I suggested above) modern sex education is functional in relation to the society that it seeks to produce, I do not believe that the function of traditional marriage can be effectively performed by the welfare state or by any other institution in which love is not the principal foundation. Empirical observation is beginning to confirm what should have been obvious a priori, which is that societies in which the vow of marriage is giving way to the contract for sexual pleasure are also rapidly ceasing to reproduce themselves.

Second, and more important, the theory of ideology is incomplete and depends on a contrast between the merely functional and the scientific that is neither exhaustive nor exclusive. The belief that murder is wrong is not a scientific belief: it is not based on evidence, nor can it be refuted. No society could survive without this belief, and in that sense it serves a social function. But it is also true, objective, capable of justification in ways that are spelled out by Kant in the second *Critique* and which are familiar to all of us in some simpler and less metaphysical version.

Similarly, our beliefs about the bindingness of erotic love and the existential change that it inflicts on us are objective, based in a true apprehension of what is at stake in our sexual adventures, and what is needed for our fulfilment. To spell out the justification may be hard, and the full reality of sexual emotion will always be more readily presented by a work of art, such as *Troilus and Criseyde*, *Tristan und Isolde*, or *Mansfield Park* than by a metaphysical discourse. Nevertheless, it is true of erotic feelings as it is of moral values, that their functionality does not undermine the vision that they impart.

8. SAME-SEX MARRIAGE

How does all that bear on the debate over "same-sex marriage"? For a religious person, who regards marriage as a sacrament, the matter is (or ought to be) urgent in the extreme. This is because people who abuse a sacrament, who turn a sacrament against itself, as in the Black Mass, commit an act of sacrilege, which is an offence against God. Such people must therefore ask themselves whether the distinction of sex between the spouses is essential to the sacrament of marriage, or merely accidental. I suppose that if God has pronounced it essential, then the believer must accept this as a revelation. But appeals to authority don't go down so well these days, not even in those institutions, such as the Christian Churches, which are founded on appeals to authority. Believers are apt to look, therefore, for secular guidance, if only so as to understand how the word of God must be reinterpreted to fit our changing circumstances.

It seems to me that the external perspective is hardly likely to countenance gay marriage. Not that the external perspective is inherently conservative; rather, that it puts social function before individual happiness. To treat marriage simply as the seal set upon a (possibly fleeting) sexual relationship, rather than a mutual assumption of the burden of social reproduction, is to deprive the institution of its rationale.

That argument tells heavily against accepting the idea of gay marriage. But it tells heavily against accepting just about everything else that people have come to take for granted, from no-fault divorce to prenuptial agreements, and from welfare support to single parents to libertarian sex education in schools. If the function of marriage has already been destroyed, why not extend what has become only a name to any other relationship that seeks the charm of it?

From the internal perspective, however, matters are more troublesome. Even if homosexual men are more given to promiscuity than

those of the other persuasion, few people doubt the possibility of faithful homosexual attachment or of lifelong domestic harmony achieved
from the starting point of a homosexual affair. The vow of love does
not, in itself, demand that the partners be of separate sex: think of the
Sacred Band of Thebes, in which men went side by side with their
lovers into battle, sworn to die for each other.

To mention such cases, however, is not to address the central issue, which is the place of sexual difference in desire and in all that is
built on desire. Heterosexual union is imbued with the sense that your
partner's sexual nature is strange to you, a territory into which you
intrude without prior knowledge and in which the other and not the
self is the only reliable guide. This experience has profound repercussions for our sense of the danger and the mystery of sexual union, and
these repercussions are surely part of what people have had in mind, in
clothing marriage as a sacrament and in the ceremony of marriage as a
rite of passage from one form of safety to another. Traditional marriage
was not only a rite of passage from adolescence to adulthood; nor was
it only a way of endorsing and guaranteeing the raising of children. It
was also a dramatization of sexual difference. Marriage kept the sexes
at such a distance from each other that their coming together became
an existential leap, rather than a passing experiment. The intentionality
of desire was shaped by this, and even if the shaping was—at some deep
level—a cultural and not a human universal, it endowed desire with
its intrinsic nuptiality, and marriage with its transformatory goal. To
regard gay marriage as simply another option within the institution is
to ignore the fact that an institution shapes the motive for joining it.

Marriage has grown around the idea of sexual difference and all
that sexual difference means. To make this feature accidental rather
than essential is to change marriage beyond recognition. Homosexuals
want marriage because they want the social endorsement that it sig-
nifies; but by admitting same-sex marriage we deprive marriage of its
social meaning, as the blessing conferred by the unborn on the living.
The pressure for same-sex marriage is therefore in a certain measure
self-defeating. It resembles Henry VIII's move to gain ecclesiastical

endorsement for his divorce by making himself head of the Church. The Church that endorsed his divorce thereby ceased to be the Church whose endorsement he was seeking.

That does not alter the fact that same-sex marriage furthers the hidden tendency of the postmodern state, which is to exclude future generations from the legal order and to rewrite all commitments as contracts between the living. It is a near certainty, therefore, that the state, acting through the Supreme Court, will "discover" a constitutional right to same-sex marriage just as it discovered constitutional rights to abortion and pornography and just as it will discover, when asked, a right to no-fault divorce. Moreover, the state will use all its weapons, and in particular the new forms of censorship, to make resistance futile.

Those who are troubled by the matters that I have been discussing in this paper must take note of this censorship. It is a remarkable fact, and proof of the preconscious and collective emotions that are propelling liberal democracies, that public debate about the most important things is now more or less impossible. Already it is widely assumed that opposition to same-sex marriage is proof of "homophobia." As we know from the history of political name-calling, once the name is called it sticks. We have already seen the effect of this in the adoption of feminism as the unquestionable premise of what is jokingly called liberal education in the American academy. To believe in the reality of sexual differences is to be a "sexist," and "sexism" comes next to racism in the litany of crimes. There is no defence, since the charge is too vague and too all-encompassing to permit one. As a result, few people will take the risk, in an American university, of questioning the fundamental tenets of feminism, even if these tenets are (as I think they are) transparently false.

The same is true concerning the normalization of homosexual desire. Just as the person who publicly expresses doubts about the feminist assumptions is dismissed as a sexist, so will the person who dissents from what is fast becoming orthodoxy in the matter of gay rights be accused of "homophobia." Maybe I have proved myself guilty of the crime in this essay, so risking my future career, were there any likelihood that I had one. All over America there are appointment committees intent on examining candidates for suspected homophobia and summarily dismissing them once the accusation has been made: "you can't have that woman pleading at the Bar, she is a Christian fundamentalist and a homophobe"; "no, even if he is the world's authority on second dynasty hieroglyphs, you can't give him tenure, after that homophobic outburst last Friday." This censorship will advance the cause of those who have made it their business to "normalize" the idea of homosexual union. It will not be possible to resist it, any more than it has proved possible to resist the feminist censorship of the truth about sexual difference. But maybe it will be possible to entertain, between consenting adults in private, the thought that homosexual marriage is really no such thing.[15]

What About the Children?

Liberal Cautions on Same-Sex Marriage

Don Browning and Elizabeth Marquardt

THE QUESTION OF SAME-SEX MARRIAGE IS DIFFICULT. There are strong arguments that can be advanced in support of same-sex marriage that must be taken seriously. But before considering what can be said for or against gay marriage, we must first pose as carefully as possible the question to be addressed. Here is our formulation of the issue. Should our present society allow persons who believe that they have a homosexual orientation the privileges and responsibilities of civil marriage? This formulation raises three issues that will be addressed in this essay—the character of our present society (the question of modernity), the meaning of civil marriage, and the nature of same-sex attraction.

All three of these issues have often been ignored in recent debates on same-sex marriage. First, the question of the nature of modernization and its impact on the field of intimate relations is almost completely invisible in public deliberations about gay marriage. Second, many people who are for or against same-sex marriage seldom advance careful definitions of marriage, particularly civil or legal marriage in contrast to marriage solemnized by a religious community. Finally, the question of the meaning and nature of homosexual orientation also has nearly vanished from the contemporary discussion, yet assumptions about the concept are constantly being made by all sides in the controversy.

We approach these issues as religious and political liberals. In both fields of human endeavor, we value justice and critical reflection. Although we honor tradition, we believe that the wisdom of the past must submit to a variety of critical tests. Nonetheless, these commitments, in contrast to many of our liberal colleagues, lead us to believe that same-sex marriage is unjust in many ways and that liberals should be cautious about endorsing it. We will argue that it is most particularly an infringement on the rights of children, whose voices, it should be noted, are often neglected on this issue.

THE MULTIPLE SEPARATIONS OF MODERNITY

We will examine these three issues more carefully. First, the question of same-sex marriage should not be approached as a single issue isolated from a wide range of social trends. To be for or against extending civil marriage to gay and lesbian couples is to be tacitly for or against, or at least critically reflective about, a range of other social trends. We think these trends are nicely summarized under the phenomenon of modernization. Both the demand for same-sex marriage and many of the best arguments on its behalf can be understood fully only within the context of the social and cultural transformations wrought by the processes of modernization. We define modernization, following both Max Weber and Jürgen Habermas, as the spread of technical rationality. This is the drive to bring more and more of life under the control of efficient means-end procedures, coming from either market or state bureaucracy, that accomplish short-term satisfactions.[1] This process, as we presently will see, tends to shift time-tested patterns of mutual dependency from husband-wife and parent-child relationships to increasing dependency on market, state, formal education, and peer groups. The spread of technical rationality also is fueled in Western societies by individualistic cultural values, but it can be motivated almost as easily by more corporate ideals, as is the case in Eastern societies such as the People's Republic of China, South Korea, and Singapore.[2]

The processes of modernization have greatly changed the meaning of marriage. They have influenced the rise of publicly visible homosexuality and possibly certain cultural manifestations of the phenomenon as well. The subtle changes brought by modernization to the broad field of human sexuality have so transformed the meaning and dynamics of marriage in the popular mind as to render the idea of same-sex marital unions far more plausible than was the case earlier.

Modernization has influenced our experience and understanding of marriage through many social and cultural avenues. The summary result of these influences has been the introduction of a variety of separations or disjunctions into the complex range of goods that the institution of marriage legally and religiously has *intended* to integrate and hold together. The result of these multiple separations has been to reduce the idea and reality of marriage in the minds of many people to little more than an affectionate sexual relationship (the lucky finding of a soulmate) of tentative commitment and uncertain duration.[3] The market, the areas of medicine and reproductive technology, and the sphere of law (especially family law and constitutional law) have, in different ways, mediated both technical rationality and individualism into the realms of sex, marriage, and the family. These three spheres have injected a range of disconnections among certain goods that they once worked together to integrate into the institution of marriage.

Take the world of business. Economists point out that the move in the nineteenth century from the farm to the wage economy disconnected the conjugal couple from the larger extended family.[4] In the second half of the twentieth century, women moved into the wage economy, gained new economic independence from men, and partially, in some cases completely, separated their financial well-being from the institution of marriage. In addition, since technical and functional skills have become the main qualification for job competence in the modern corporation, companies increasingly have deemphasized the marital status of employees and competed for skilled workers by extending marriage-type benefits to unmarried and same-sex couples. These moves in market and industry were paralleled by government's entrance into the family welfare field, further making women less dependent on marriage and family stability.[5] Although these economic and bureaucratic trends have had some positive effects, they also have injected marriage and family with the cost-benefit and efficiency logics of both market and government bureaucracy, weakened patterns of mutual dependency between husband and wife, and contributed to the rise of a culture of divorce, cohabitation, and nonmarriage.[6]

But these trends have been further aggravated by other modernizing developments. Take the field of reproductive technology. Reliable contraception, legal abortion, artificial insemination, in vitro fertilization, surrogacy, gamete intrafallopian transfer, zygote intrafallopian transfer, and the possibility of cloning all inject new separations into the delicate, historically marital integration of sexuality, love, childbirth, socialization of children, and mutual dependency. Although many, but not all, of these procedures can be used within the institution of marriage to enhance these integrations, many are increasingly used outside of marriage. Furthermore, some of them will doubtless be used more and more to promote childbirth by singles and same-sex couples. In fact, legalized same-sex marriage will likely spur demands for greater legal and social support for same-sex couples to have access to reproductive technologies, since only by using these technologies can they have their "own" children.

Law has contributed to these separations as well. From the 1950s and to the present, American family law has replaced the central principles supporting marriage and monogamy with new ones supporting the concepts of consent and privacy. Although most people would be sympathetic to the U.S. Supreme Court's decision in *Griswold v. Connecticut* (1965) that "freed birth control for married couples from state interference," the decision did soon set the precedent for *Eisenstadt v. Baird* (1972) that "struck down a Massachusetts law that prohibited the prescription or sale of contraceptives to unmarried people."[7] As historian Nancy Cott has written, "Rather than tying privacy in reproductive

decision-making to marital intimacy the *Eisenstadt* decision made it
a more portable, individual right: 'the right of the individual, married
or single, to be free from unwarranted governmental intrusion into
matters so fundamentally affecting a person as the decision whether
to bear or beget a child.'"[8]

As harmless as the *Eisenstadt* decision must have seemed at the
time, it simultaneously made marriage less central to the law, set the
stage for the eventual treatment of marital and nonmarital sexual and
reproductive acts as equivalent before the law, and robbed the law of
the grounds for restricting certain reproductive technologies to their
use within marriage. The emerging emphasis on privacy and consent
led to the erosion of an institutional understanding of marriage, making
it a private intimate association with little public significance, yet one
still deserving of the protection and legitimation of the law. Although
these decisions might possibly have been justified on grounds of the
impossibility of enforcing laws applying to such private behavior, the
mode of legal reasoning clearly functioned to make law a leading contributor to the multiple separations of the goods of marriage that have
occurred in recent decades. These disconnections also contributed to
the precedents needed to increase the legal plausibility of same-sex
civil marriage and the significant cultural redefinition of marriage that
same-sex marriage entails.[9]

FOUR STRATEGIES

Marriage is a complex social phenomenon and has been perceived as
such throughout history in all cultures. As legal historian John Witte
has pointed out, through most of the history of marriage in the West,
it simultaneously has been perceived as a material institution giving
expression to many natural needs and tendencies, a contractual institution requiring social control, a public institution contributing to the
common good, and a religious institution seen as covenant or sacrament
and witnessed and sanctioned by God.[10] Different periods of history
have emphasized one or the other of these dimensions of marriage,

but most of them were visible in one way or another at all times. We would add that marriage as affection, sexual exchange, and intersubjective communication—what the Roman Catholic tradition has called the "unitive" goods of marriage—were also visible.[11] The history of marriage can be seen as the growing ascendancy of the unitive values of marriage in relation to the procreative. The present controversy over same-sex marriage is in some respects about whether the so-called unitive aspects should now become almost completely separated from the procreative and yet still enjoy the legal privileges and protections of traditional marriage that held the unitive and procreative in some kind of balance. The question has become, should marriage be seen primarily as an interpersonal "close relationship" between consenting adults, with considerations such as material dependency, the conception of children, and child-rearing responsibilities being viewed as contingent and incidental?[12]

The dynamics of modernization have forced this question. Any solution to the problem of same-sex marriage inevitably raises additional issues about modernity's desirability and the possibility of constraining or redirecting some of its social and cultural consequences. We have identified four grand strategies for coping with the tensions between marriage and modernization. We list them now and discuss them from time to time in the remainder of the paper.

First, is the strategy of retrenchment, which idealizes the divided spheres of the nineteenth century between home and paid employment and would use both religion and law to reinforce the monogamous, marriage-centered, and child-centered family built around a pronounced differentiation between the roles of men and women.[13]

A second view, advanced by legal scholar Martha Fineman, holds that modernization has already rendered the family of the married mother and father raising children a thing of the past and that marriage therefore should be delegalized. She would then have law and public policy directed to the support of arrangements where the care of dependents is the central task—single mothers with children being the chief example.[14]

Then there is the view powerfully associated with Jonathan Rauch's argument in his *Gay Marriage* (2004). He proposes fighting the disruptions of modernization by creating a new marriage culture that would eliminate domestic partnerships and cohabitation by convincing everyone—gays and straights alike—to align affection, sex, and commitment within the institution of marriage.[15]

Finally, there is the position that we represent called "critical familism." This position tries to retain the historic alignment of sex, affection, generativity, child care, and mutual assistance accomplished by the institution of marriage. It does this, however, by advocating for a *reconstructed* view of gender and work-family relations in modern marriage, as well as an aggressive curtailment of the negative impact of modernization on the integrity and stability of the conjugal couple raising children. We hold that this position best grasps the weight of tradition on the primary purposes of marriage, best protects the interests and rights of children, best serves the common good, and best preserves the integrity of the law.

A BRIEF ARCHEOLOGY OF MARRIAGE

We now turn to the second neglected issue listed above—the meaning of marriage. It is widely thought that the history of the institution of marriage is about what religious forces, especially Judaism and Christianity, have taught and imposed on the whole of society. Nothing could be further from the truth. The theory of marriage in the West has had a religious dimension, but beneath and within the symbolism of religion can be found a variety of additional features. One can find naturalistic assumptions about human nature; Greek, Roman, and German legal theories about marriage; and philosophical perspectives from Plato, Aristotle, Kant, Locke, and Rousseau. We claim that powerful philosophical and naturalistic views of marriage can be found within the contours of what often appears to be primarily theological thinking and that this inner core of Western marriage theory is worth retaining, even as it is amended in some respects.

We argue that Western marriage theory brought both religious and legal support to the consolidation of what evolutionary psychologists today call "kin altruism." This term refers to the care that natural parents are inclined to give to their children because they have labored to give them birth and have come to recognize them as a part of themselves that should be preserved and extended. The idea of kin altruism also implies a reciprocal identification of children with natural parents because of this labor and because children perceive the bodily continuity with those who give them life. The other goods of marriage—sexual exchange, affection, and mutual assistance—are goods in themselves but also gain their larger meaning from their integration into childbearing and childrearing. The covenantal and sacramental aspects of marriage provided by religion gave sacred weight and approval to these integrations as centered in the solidarities of kin altruism. In addition, the Abrahamic religions of Judaism, Christianity, and Islam added the idea that parents should love their children not only because they are extensions of themselves but also because of the deeper reason that they are also children of God and objects of God's unconditioned love.

It is a matter of cultural variability as to whether families are patriarchal, polygynous, monogamous, extended, joint, or nuclear. But within all this pluralism of family forms, there is a persistent core value that is widely cherished and protected around the world. *This is the importance of the people who give life to the infant also being, as nearly as possible, the ones who care for it.* This principle is based on the widely held assumption that people who conceive a child, when they recognize their relation to it, will on average be the most invested in its nurture and well-being. It is also based on the observation that, when other things are equal, children themselves want—indeed, often *long*—to be raised by those who gave them life.

There are various languages designed to communicate this truth. Religious and theological languages in Judaism, Christianity, and Islam used the language of divine creation and divine command. Some philosophical systems have employed a combination of biological and philosophical arguments. Then there were a surprising number of instances in which a dual language combining both religious revelation and naturalistic philosophy came together to create powerful synthetic arguments supporting the integration of kin altruism into the reinforcements of marriage.

Aristotle provided much of the naturalistic and philosophical language for the centrality of kin altruism in family theory found in Western philosophy, law, and religion. His insights were used to reinforce folk observations in Christianity, Judaism, and Islam. He had insight into what contemporary evolutionary psychologists describe as our tendency to invest ourselves more in those individuals to whom we are biologically related—those individuals who carry our genes.[16] In his *Politics*, Aristotle writes, "in common with other animals and with plants, mankind have a natural desire to leave behind them an image of themselves."[17] It was simple comparative observation that formed Aristotle's belief that humans share this impulse with other animals and that this tendency constitutes a basic framework within which behavior proceeds.

We see this idea developed more in Aristotle's critique of Plato's *Republic*. Plato tells us that Socrates believed that nepotism (the preferential treatment of kin by blood relatives) was the fundamental cause of divisiveness within a city. This factionalism could be eliminated, he believed, if the city required elite men to have offspring with women who were held in common, then having state nurses raise the infants with neither parents nor children knowing their biological ties with one another. In such a state, Plato believed that everyone would "apply the terms 'mine' and 'not mine' in the same way to the same thing"—especially to children, thereby undercutting the divisive consequences of nepotism.[18]

Aristotle, however, believed that Plato was wrong. In developing his case, we see Aristotle's theory of kin altruism amplified even more fully: "Whereas in a state having women and children in common, love will be watery; and the father will certainly not say 'my son,' or the son 'my father.' As a little sweet wine mingled with a great deal of water is imperceptible in the mixture, so, in this sort of community, the idea of relationship which is based upon these names will be lost; there is no reason why the so-called father should care about the son, or the son about the father, or brothers about one another. Of the two qualities which chiefly inspire regard and affection—that a thing is your own and that it is your only one—neither can exist in such a state as this."[19] Aristotle believed that such a society would water down and undermine parental recognition and investment. Furthermore, he believed it would unleash violence because people will no longer "be afraid of committing any crimes by reason of consanguinity."[20]

The great Roman Catholic theologian Thomas Aquinas synthesized Aristotle's insights on kin altruism with the theology of creation from Judaism and Christianity. He developed a double language on marriage that was simultaneously philosophical and religious, secular and sacred, naturalistic and sacramental. It constituted the core ideas supporting one of the most powerful theories of the relation of family to the state that is available, namely, the theory of subsidiarity as it functions in Roman Catholic social teachings and the secular family law of several modern nations, most notably Germany.

Aquinas called marriage in its primordial form an "office of nature." It was a matter of natural reason and natural law that both children and adults flourish better if supported by the power of marriage to integrate procreation, the socialization of children, love and commitment, and the regulation of sexual desire.[21] At this level marriage could be illuminated by the natural law, especially that aspect of it that identifies those natural inclinations that are further guided by interventions of "the free will" and "acts of virtue."[22] But marriage for Aquinas also was revealed in scripture, specifically in the Genesis account of creation. In the "Supplement" to the *Summa Theologica*, he quotes Matthew 29:4, "Have ye not read that He Who made man from the beginning 'made them male and female,'" a verse which itself refers back to Genesis 1:27. Nearby he refers to Genesis 2:21 and claims that from the foundations of Creation and before the emergence of sin among humans, God "fashioned a help-mate for man out of his rib."[23] This implies what the full Genesis passage makes explicit, "It is not good that the man should be alone; I will make a helper as his partner" (Genesis 2:18).

Scripture deepens and gives ontological significance to Aquinas' philosophical view of marriage, *but his full argument does not stay at the level of scriptural interpretation*. This observation is extremely important. Religious perspectives are not always advanced on narrowly religious grounds, just as so-called secular arguments often contain in their horizons quasi-religious assumptions about the depth of human experience.[24]

Thomas Aquinas was one of the architects of the sacramental view of marriage that has so much influenced marriage theory in Christian nations in recent centuries. Yet, despite this, we should not blind ourselves to his naturalistic theory of family formation and marriage, especially in view of how similar it is to modern scientific views found in the emerging field of evolutionary psychology. Aquinas defined matrimony as the joining of the male to the primordial mother-infant family. He saw this happening for four natural reasons. First, the long period of human infant dependency makes it very difficult for mothers at the human level to raise infants by themselves. Hence, they turn for help to their male consorts.[25] Second, the fathers are much more likely to attach to their infants if they have a high degree of certainty that the infant is actually theirs and hence continuous with their own biological existence.[26] Third, males attach to their infants and consorts because of the mutual assistance and affection that they receive from the infant's mother.[27] Finally, even Aquinas realized that sexual exchange between mother and father (even though he talked about it as paying "the marital debt") helped to integrate the male to the mother-infant dyad.

Of course, Aquinas could not support his bio-philosophical theories with the scientific explanations that are available today. We should note, however, that these four conditions are almost perfectly parallel to those that the fields of evolutionary psychology and anthropology believe led humans, in contrast to most other mammals, to form families and long-term attachments between fathers and mothers for the care of their offspring.[28]

Kin altruism was at the heart of this naturalistic model of family formation. When Aquinas said that the human male "naturally desires to be assured of his offspring and this assurance would be altogether nullified in the case of promiscuous copulation,"[29] he was echoing Aristotle's belief that parental investment is more intense and durable between natural parents and their offspring. We see that belief again when Aquinas offers naturalistic reasons for the permanence of marriage by referring to the long period of care that is required to raise to maturity the child who is, as well, "something" of the parent.[30]

Aquinas' naturalistic theory of family formation gains consolidation and reinforcements from his theology of creation and sacrament, but can stand independently of them. Indeed, this Aristotelian-Thomistic naturalism has been a powerful force in subsequent legal and religious developments for centuries after Thomas gave them such compelling articulation in the double language of theology and philosophy. The idea that the institution of marriage should channel the investments of kin altruism for the good of both children and their parents is the grounding assumption of the Roman Catholic theory of subsidiarity—the principle that governments and markets should support (*subsidum*) the family solidarities motivated by kin altruism, but should do nothing to undermine or replace them.[31] We believe that this basic concept is one that contemporary law should recall, fine-tune for present-day circumstances, and appropriate.

It is important to notice the flexibility of Aquinas's naturalistic argument. He was fully aware that humans have conflicting natural tendencies with no single fixed aim. The world of nature is full of proximate causes. But when human sexuality is guided by the needs of child rearing, then the inclinations toward kin altruism, reinforced by culture and religion, should have a commanding role in ordering our unstable natural tendencies. Hence, Aquinas gave us a flexible natural law argument, not a rigid one.

Aquinas's view is consistent with the images of natural law developing in the thought of contemporary philosophers and theologians, such as Mary Midgley,[32] Jean Porter,[33] Stephen Pope,[34] Larry Arnhart,[35] and Lisa Cahill.[36] Mary Midgley says it well when she writes that in spite of our plural and flexible human desires and needs, "The central factors in us must be accepted, and the right line of human conduct must lie somewhere within the range they allow."[37] It is clear that for Aristotle, Aquinas, and much of contemporary evolutionary thought, kin altruism is a central tendency that both biology and moral sensibilities have honored as being one of these "central factors." It is our argument that it also should be the *intention of law* to honor kin altruism in its understanding of marriage.

To say this, of course, does not mean that either law or religion should allow the kin solidarities of one family to harm other families. Plato's concern with nepotism and unjust family preferences had a point. Nor do we intend to diminish the special, pro-child role of adoption in finding willing parents for children who need them. Our argument is simply that justice between families includes the idea of supporting and enhancing their kin investments, even as it resists absolutizing our kin investments to the point of harming other families. The good of marriage—whether seen as a philosophically conceived intrinsic good or a religious sacrament or covenant—is crucially preserved by the mutual investments of kin altruism.

MARRIAGE FOR ALL

Until recently, it has been the intention of law to support both marriage and kin altruism. Until the 1960s and 1970s, divorce was difficult to obtain, nonmarital sex was sometimes penalized, and certain legal privileges extended only to married couples. But as Cott points out, since that time law has relativized and decentered marriage and granted legal protections to a variety of nonmarital sexual and reproductive behaviors, all in the name of enhancing liberty and individual freedom. The journalist Jonathan Rauch agrees that the directions of modernizing societies and their family-law trends may be highly problematic. He is pro-marriage, through and through. In fact, he wants marriage for everyone—straights and homosexuals alike. And, as the subtitle of his book *Gay Marriage* suggests, he claims it will be "good for gays, good for straights, and good for society." Rauch wants to develop a new marriage culture to resist the individualizing and isolating forces of modernization. He wants to reintegrate sexual behavior—all sexual behavior—back into marriage.[38] Furthermore, he would eliminate domestic partnerships and civil unions, not only for opposite-sex partners but same-sex partners as well. The real enemy of marriage is not, he tells us, same-sex marriage; rather it is those marital substitutes that give legal privileges and protections to new forms of "marriage-lite."[39]

Marriage, for Rauch, is primarily about mutual dependency, commitment, and intimacy. From the standpoint of the classic goods of marriage spoken about by Augustine and Aquinas, Rauch puts the accent on mutual dependency and commitment (*fideles*).[40] Marriage is about two consenting adults committing themselves to take care of each other—in sickness or in health, whether rich or poor, whether young or old. Marriage is also, for Rauch, about kinship—about married couples becoming integrated into extended families and enjoying shared celebrations, holidays, and, once again, mutual care. His view of kinship should, however, be distinguished from the Aristotelian-evolutionary psychological view of kin altruism. His idea is not primarily about parental investment in children but, rather, the emotional enrichment and communal involvement of adults in family-like networks.

Nonetheless, Rauch does address those who believe that the institution of marriage is primarily about having and raising children. Rauch agrees: children are a fine thing. However, the goods of sexual pleasure, love, commitment, and mutual dependency are, for Rauch, plenty enough reasons for marriage. These goods can be enhanced by the good of children; the children just don't necessarily need to be one's own offspring.[41] Nor does the presence of children need to be a defining element of marriage. Same-sex marriage is like sterility. He writes, "Biologically speaking, a homosexual union is nothing but one variety of sterile union, and no different even in principle: a woman without a uterus is no more open to procreation than a man without a uterus."[42] He points out that society does not prevent infertile couples from marrying. Nor does it prohibit the elderly from marrying nor those heterosexual couples who simply do not intend to have children at all. So, he asks, why restrict gays and lesbians from marrying? The nonprocreative reasons to marry are reason enough, he says, especially the good of mutual dependency.

Rauch's understanding of marriage is serious and requires critical response. It also gives us an opportunity to tighten the definition of marriage that we will advance in this paper. Rauch would agree with the majority opinion of the Massachusetts *Goodridge v. Department of Public Health* decision mandating same-sex marriage in that state. It defines marriage as primarily a "private," "intimate," "committed," and "exclusive" union that is "among life's momentous acts of self-definition."[43] The majority opinion in *Goodridge* says that it is "incorrect" to claim that having children is the primary purpose of marriage. Although the majority admits that, "it is certainly true that many, perhaps most, married couples have children together (assisted or unassisted)," it nonetheless asserts that "the exclusive and permanent commitment of the marriage partners to one another, not the begetting of children, . . . is the sine qua non of civil marriage."[44] The heavy-duty generative purposes of the large majority of married couples is set aside and replaced with the idea of marriage as a sexual and affectionate friendship. The *Goodridge* majority acknowledges, in ways that Rauch does not, that this is a change in the definition of the institution of marriage, but asserts, in total contradiction to the historic principle of subsidiarity, that the state "creates civil marriage." The majority admits that its final definition of marriage as the "voluntary union of two persons as spouses, to the exclusion of all others" is a "reformulation" of the historic, dare we say, classic definition.[45] But it assumes that the Supreme Judicial Court, in its role as the authoritative interpreter of the Massachusetts Constitution, has the right to contradict history, the *jus gentium*, common law definitions of marriage, and even past legal assumptions of the State of Massachusetts. In short, the court's justifications for decentering marriage from generativity constitute an unreflective and naïve affirmation of the blind forces of modernization and the various changes in intimate life that it has shaped.

For example, the *Goodridge* majority first invokes the de facto demographic decline of households with children. It then cites trends in Massachusetts law to respond "supportively to the changing reality of the American family" and to "strengthen the modern family in its many variations."[46] Hence, the sociological fact that Massachusetts *already* in its many family policies has blurred the distinction between marriage and nonmarriage and *already* has drifted toward taking lightly the childbearing features of marriage becomes the excuse to continue riding the wave, taking the final step of intentionally redefining marriage at the level of law, with all of the normative, cultural, and channeling implications that this act implies.

The difficulties with the position of Rauch and the *Goodridge* majority (shared by other articulate advocates of same-sex marriage such as Evan Wolfson and Andrew Sullivan) are multiple.[47] First, this position intentionally aims to undermine, with the force of law, understandings of marriage and family that have already been fragmented by the modernizing forces summarized at the beginning of the paper. In fact, their position assumes that the struggle to balance modernization with marriage is over—modernity has won. *Goodridge* is full of statements taking for granted that the law has already swung to the side of what Daniel Cere has called the "close relationship" theory of marriage.[48] Its reading of the Massachusetts Constitution is filtered through lenses of interpretation that assume the permanence of some of the current drifts in demography, reproductive practices, and the pluralism of family forms. The decision follows the logic that since these social realities have already evolved, then same-sex marriage is all the more justified. It never occurs to either Rauch or the *Goodridge* majority to question these trends or to envision the use of law to reinforce those forces in civil society intent on reconstructing marriage to better cope with the forces of modernity.

The *intention* of the law is the issue at stake here. It is one thing for law not to question the capacity of opposite-sex couples to have children, be they infertile, too old, uncertain, or disinterested. In the name of privacy, the law rightfully does not pry, partially because things change (infertility is sometimes corrected, people sometimes change their minds), and the elderly traditionally have married to honor the child-centered view of marriage and the need to symbolically reinforce the norm of integrating sex, love, dependency, childbirth, and childrearing into the institution of marriage. So, it is the classic intentionality of law that the *Goodridge* majority rejects—the intention to guide and channel the integration of this list of goods as nearly as possible. The problem with the final decision of *Goodridge* and the inclusive marriage program of Rauch is that they both intend a form and model of marriage that breaks the integrative goals of the institution. They both make sexual exchange, affection, and mutual dependency the center of the institution with its generative goals secondary, incidental, and even ignored.

Second, this redefinition of marriage raises to the level of public policy the rejection of the historic relation between marriage and kin altruism. It dispenses with the principle that the individuals who give life to children should be the ones who raise them in a bonded and enduring relation. We believe that the reasons implicit in this tradition, when properly identified and brought to light as we attempted to do in the middle sections of this paper, pass the rationality standard requested by the Judicial Supreme Court of Massachusetts. Dismissing this core relation between kin altruism and marriage constitutes the ultimate injustice to children. Children have a right not only to parents and families, as the United Nations Convention on the Rights of the Child has asserted.[49] They also have the right to expect to be raised in a society whose legal and cultural institutions attempt to maximize the possibility that they will be raised by the parents who conceived them.

The positions of the *Goodridge* majority and Rauch are adultocentric. They are both correct in holding that there are goods other than procreation that marriage celebrates and protects. They both fail, however, to take or even consider the point of view of children—their need and right to be raised in a society whose legal, religious, and cultural institutions intentionally promote, and do nothing to compromise, the principle that children should be raised, as nearly as possible, by the parents who conceive them.

Marquardt has studied children of divorce whose experience was almost entirely ignored as the no-fault divorce revolution took hold.[50] In the three decades during which a high divorce rate has come to be seen by many as an unavoidable fact of contemporary society, legal theorists have continued to overlook and deny the injustice forced on these children. They are required to divide their time and affections between two homes or to lose contact with their mother or father, too often in the name of the happiness of their parents. While some divorces are necessary, the fact that the majority of divorces end low-conflict marriages reinforces this question as one of social justice.

Just as no-fault divorce was ushered in with virtually no regard for the children's needs, the *Goodridge* decision that legalized same-sex marriage in Massachusetts brushes aside the now-large body of social science data which indicates that children raised by their married biological parents do better, on average, than those raised by single parents or stepparents.[51] Although data sets are not sufficiently large to demonstrate anything definitive about the strengths or weaknesses of same-sex couples for childrearing, our society's experience with other alternative family forms suggests that these families will not, on average, be able to reduplicate the investments and consolidations of marriage built on the energies of kin altruism, the consolidation of which has been in the past the primary goal of marriage.[52] To disregard the needs of children, the traditions that have understood these needs, and contemporary social science evidence offends natural justice. That is, this wholesale dismissal offends both what is fair and what contributes to human flourishing by meeting the unique needs of the individuals in question. If our earlier summary of the discon-nections introduced by modernizations into the field of generativity is correct, the legalization of same-sex marriage would not be just one more example of the drift, but the culmination that finally shifts the institutional logic of marriage and further marginalizes children from its basic meaning.

Third, the legalization of same-sex marriage is not only unjust to children, it is unjust to a wide range of other human arrangements that attempt to meet the dependency needs of the vulnerable, including those who are old, ill, or disabled. The feminist legal scholar Martha Fineman has observed that same-sex marriage extends the protections of marriage to one type of sexual family while excluding nonsexual arrangements organized around the care of dependents. These examples include single parents with children, brother caring for ailing brother, daughter taking care of aging mother, friend caring for dying neighbor, and more.[53] She believes that the forces of modernity have so radically transformed society that the "sexual family"—whether married or unmarried, gay or straight—should in the name of justice be delegalized.[54] The benefits traditionally associated with marriage should now be distributed to actual caregivers and their dependents. Although Fineman has no prejudice against homosexual couples, it is real and grave dependency that she wants to draw attention to and protect. She does not believe that the robust benefits that once went to marriage should go to the many able-bodied heterosexual and homosexual couples who are healthy, employed, and have few actual dependency needs. She thinks the new, thin, affectionate-sexual relationships at the heart of the legal norms intended by *Goodridge* and Rauch should be protected, at best, by privately drawn legal contracts—not the status-granting powers of actual marriage.[55]

Fineman's position has the virtue of showing how same-sex marriage, rather than being unambiguously just, actually can lead to new perceived injustices. We believe, however, that her proposal has additional, potentially graver problems. First, her position is a still more radical capitulation to the fragmenting forces on families of modernity and technical rationality. She assumes that the conjugal couple with children is nearly a thing of the past.[56] Her suggestion that we remove the legal protections of marriage from the sexual family will, in the end, further undermine the integration of sexual behavior, birth, and care by natural parents. She assumes that in the future neither law nor individuals need aspire to integrate these various goods. If couples want to form sexual families, they can marry as they wish, develop private contracts, and perhaps solemnize their relation before a religious body, but not receive legal marriage. Her confidence in the ability of adults to forge meaningful, long-term, child-centered bonds with only minimal social and legal supports is much greater than ours.

Instead, we would embrace a two-part solution. The first part would retain the historic child-centered view of marriage at the center of law and public policy, requiring not only the denial of legalized same-sex marriage but the consideration of other legal and cultural changes to help support marriage. The second part of our solution is the proposal to meet the dependency needs of other classes of individuals, including single parents, the ill and old, gays and lesbians, and other needy persons, through appropriately targeted legal contracts and social programs, including welfare programs, as well as child supports and adoption in cases where these instruments are relevant. Neither the radical extension of marriage as Rauch proposes nor its eradication as a legal category as Fineman advocates meet the standard of those forms of justice that aspire to promote the common good, especially for children.

THE CONCEPT OF ORIENTATION

A few words need to be added on the concept of homosexual orientation. Critical analysis of this concept is notably absent in recent discussions about same-sex marriage. *Goodridge* totally avoids the subject. Rauch advances what is commonly called an "essentialistic" definition of orientation.[57] This view holds that sexual orientation is a given, perhaps biologically determined, inclination that cannot be changed short of grave damage to the psyche and personhood of people with such feelings. This view is strikingly different from another powerful perspective—the "social constructivist" view that holds human sexuality is plastic and flexible. According to this view, one learns to think of oneself as gay or lesbian depending on the social context, opportunities, and language games available to read one's sexual feelings.[58] Rauch's inclusive marriage project is buttressed by his assumptions that there are basically two kinds of people, gays and straights. He is fond of repeating the statement that "homosexuality really exists."[59] He gives that statement the weight of philosophical realism by saying that for gays, homosexuality is "natural," meaning, we take it, that this is just how they are by birth or some other unchangeable reason.[60]

We do not plan to get embroiled in an assessment of the contradictory evidence from the social sciences on the nature and cause of orientation. Nor do we believe, at all, that society should try to change those who define themselves as gay or lesbian. Nor do we want persons who attribute consistent homosexual feelings to themselves to be persecuted, shunned, stigmatized, or in other ways oppressed. In fact, we want them to live in a society that fully respects them, and we know our society has not yet reached that point.

We only want to make a few points relevant to the role of law in changing the definition of marriage. First, it should be noticed that homosexual orientation is a self-attribution. In contrast to race or gender, upon which unjust discriminations have been made, homosexuality is a definition that people place on their own subjective feelings, often struggling to read them correctly and even changing their self-definitions several times throughout the life cycle.

Furthermore, the homosexual community itself is quite torn about the concept of orientation and about the advisability of legalizing gay marriage. Regarding orientation, many hold the constructivist view and advocate getting beyond the distinction between gay and straight, forming a new, liberated, sexually fluid bisexuality.[61] It is also important to realize that a significant number of influential voices on the gay left reject the idea of same-sex marriage, finding it oppressive, and tolerating it only as a transitional moment toward the eventual abolition of marriage.[62] We mention these debates internal to the gay community not to take sides but to insist that legal positions such as *Goodridge* or programs such as Rauch's must not act as if these debates do not exist. (The mainstream media, for instance, choose to ignore them almost entirely, routinely featuring advocates of same-sex marriage who aspire to a bourgeois, more-or-less middle-class vision of marriage.)

Acknowledging these debates within the gay community is relevant to an accurate understanding of what is happening to marriage now and what could happen in the near future. Is society being asked to include within marriage an oppressed minority whose sexual orientation is some unchanging essence, or is it being asked to change not only its definition of marriage but its entire understanding of the organization of the sexual life cycle—a change that could usher in a new flexible bisexuality that would transcend the poles of homosexual and heterosexual? Perhaps it is far too simple to say that there are two kinds of people with differing, fixed sexual orientations and that what happens to one group has no implications for the other. In view of the strong impact that legal same-sex marriage would doubtless have on the major socializing institutions of our society—elementary and secondary schools, colleges and universities, social-service organizations, and even religious institutions—this question is all the more justified. Out of justice not only to children but to their parents and other adults, this discussion that tries to clarify what is actually being asked for—Marriage like straights have it? Or marriage on the way to something else?—should not be prematurely stifled by the rapid creation and enforcement of same-sex marriage. Are we being asked to reject the classic definition of marriage as a public institution that integrates sexual desire and affection into the heavy-duty tasks of generativity and kin-based intergenerational child care, with exceptions to this general rule built in for the contingencies of infertility and the inevitability of aging? And are we then being asked to replace this view with one that makes interpersonal sexual affection the core of marriage with the exceptions becoming the classic view, that is, the public integration of sex and love into kin-based intergenerational child care?

CRITICAL FAMILISM AND MODERNITY

In conclusion, we reject handling the challenges of modernization to marriage by either radically changing its meaning (as do Rauch and

Goodridge) or eliminating marriage as a legal category, as does Fineman. Both strategies, in the end, are uncritical capitulations to these modernizing social forces. Nor, however, should our position be confused with a traditionalism that seeks no reconstruction of traditional marriage or no redirection of modernity. We believe human beings can learn to live with the modernization process, affirm its benefits for physical health and prosperity, learn to limit its excesses, and finally take steps to reconstruct marriage to more successfully cope with the dynamics of modernity. We would do this by retaining the core meaning of marriage built around generativity, increase gender justice both in domestic and public spheres, and redirect and constrain the forces of modernity to make these two goals more feasible.

We call this position "critical familism."[63] It is familistic in that it is a pro-marriage strategy built around the equal-regard partnership between husband and wife in both the public world of employment and politics and the domestic sphere of child care and daily chores.[64] We envision marriage in the future to be more flexible on gender roles, but we do not assume all differentiations will disappear, especially those relevant to the vulnerabilities of pregnancy, birth, and caring for small children.[65] In fact, we advocate a life-cycle view of equal regard that recognizes that there are different rhythms of work and parenting dictated by childbirth and childrearing that both couples and societies must recognize and accommodate in the name of justice and personal fulfillment. For example, we believe that husband and wife should both have free access to the benefits and responsibilities of participation in the wage economy, but we would limit its reach into marriage and family by encouraging—perhaps mandating—the availability of more thirty-hour workweeks for parents with children, more flex time, higher tax exemptions and credits for minor children, elimination of all marriage tax penalties, and creating supports similar to the GI bill for parents who leave the wage economy for a period to care for children.[66]

We believe that marriage—its definition, renewal, and reconstruction—should be primarily in the hands of the institutions of civil society. These include voluntary organizations, religious organizations, and the open legislative process permeable to the influences of people at the grassroots. A growing and increasingly more powerful marriage education movement now teaches young people, minorities, and even the poor—in schools, the military, and in churches—new communication skills and fresh understandings necessary for the strengthening of marriage in a dynamic modern society. Law and government should support, and do nothing to undercut, such initiatives rising from civil society.

Law and government must regulate marriage, but they do not create the meaning of marriage any more than they create the substance of the institutions of education or business. Critical familism is fully aware that civil marriage is based on public principles that can be rationally reviewed and tested, and we have tried to present some of these in this essay. Although religious traditions contain religious narratives that empower and consolidate their views of marriage, critical familism holds that they also contain an inner core of rationality that can contribute to public discourse and deliberation. Hence, critical familism tries to invigorate the critical retrieval of religious traditions, not only Judaism and Christianity which have contributed so much to Western views of marriage, but other great traditions such as Islam, Buddhism, Hinduism, and Confucianism that increasingly will and should become a part of public discourse about marriage and family.[67] The law has an important part to play in systematizing and codifying these public discussions, but it is not, and must never be permitted to become, the creator of the conversation and the only player that counts.

But a full exposition of the meaning of critical familism is beyond the scope of this paper. Much has been written about it already, and we hope the progressive, egalitarian, pro-child, and pro-marriage position we propose becomes more visible in the current national conversation about same-sex marriage.

— 3 —

Changing Dynamics of the Family
in Recent European History

Harold James

T
HE AFFAIR OF THE NOMINATION and then the withdrawal of
Rocco Buttiglione as European Union Commissioner with
responsibility for Justice, Freedom, and Security touched one
of Europe's sorest spots. He was opposed because of a hearing before a
committee of the European parliament in which he had been maneu-
vered by his interrogators into agreeing to a description of homosexuality as "sinful," but also because he argued that the purpose of marriage
was to give women "the right to have children and the protection of a
man." On the first point, relating to homosexuality, which he specifically
identified as a personal view which would not affect his official actions
(a similar stance to that taken by Senator John Kerry on abortion) he
may well have been wrong, and as a Catholic he might have appreciated
that his Church's teaching is not that homosexuality is sinful, but that
sexual acts outside of marriage are wrong. On the second point, relating
to marriage, however, he was articulating a view which is at the heart of
the legal view of marriage in many European countries. The protection
of women in marriage as mothers is in fact a part of public policy and
is the rationale, for instance, of tax privileges. Buttiglione's opponents,
who successfully pressed the President-designate of the Commission,

José Manuel Barroso, to withdraw his nomination, clearly felt that existing law and the norms that it embodies no longer corresponded to new social "realities." The implication was clear that the law needed to be changed in order to reflect a new social order. The debate is quite characteristic of a new critique, which largely ignores the public policy reasons for a special position of the family.

A great deal of the story of the last two or three centuries can be described in terms of the interaction of three major social organizations: family, state, and market. All of these have undergone quite remarkable changes over the past two centuries, and the changes have produced confusions and uncertainties. Recently a great deal of literature has been devoted to demonstrating that there is no simple opposition between state and market: in particular, that a well-functioning market needs a secure institutional framework that can only be provided by well-functioning states. With a complete absence of a state, there is no way of enforcing contracts, which are at the heart of the market process. Where states become abusive, arbitrary, or corrupt, the scope for rent-seeking increases, and the agents in the market, instead of looking for technical improvements or innovations as a way of expanding their activity, try to capture the state so as to be able to reshape contracts.

The proposition that the state requires the market is perhaps more controversial, but it really should not be so. The extreme example of the malfunctioning of communist systems demonstrated how when states become arbitrary and seek to replace markets, they lose legitimacy because they have extended themselves into too many areas in which individuals have not only strong feelings but also dignity and rights.

The third element of the interactions has been surprisingly missing in many discussions. A great deal of examination of the way in which an efficient and just operation of markets and states can proceed ignores the contribution of the family to the functioning of markets and states. This is an odd omission, because the family can be understood as providing a link across generations, and with this a perspective on time and the competing relative claims of different generations. The process of building institutions and markets is one that demands a long-term, not a short-term perspective, and becomes dysfunctional if there is no long-term outlook.

One common theme in dealing with economic change, which is often painfully disruptive, is that the pain only makes sense in a long-term horizon. A skilled worker in middle age who is laid off because of technical change, or foreign competition, has no real hope for the immediate future; the only hope lies in a perspective which demonstrates that the changes will produce advantages for children and grandchildren. Suppose there are no children? Then the willingness to tolerate present sacrifices will be sharply reduced. We could also look at this as an investment issue: investments in new technologies that have a long time horizon will no longer make sense or be attractive.

Economists are often looking for what they call inter-generational equity and for mechanisms for making inter-generational transfers that have the most acceptance and legitimacy. Questions such as the optimal use of natural resources, the way we deal with waste and pollution, our dependence on water and air all depend on the way in which we assess the rights and the utility preferences of people who are not yet born. These are rights that exist in respect to beings not yet in existence. Yet they arise out of our sense of a need to provide for a future that is not just our own. Children are an investment in the future, and societies that do not adequately reproduce themselves have great problems in other areas that demand equity and justice.

The claim of this paper is that the family is the central, and indeed only, social institution that is capable of assuring inter-generational and inter-temporal equity. The family is not only a source of stability, but also of dynamism, creativity and innovation; and its capacity to produce or stimulate innovation depends on its stability-generating functions. The paper tries to explain why this is the case.

I

One of the least well known or understood ways in which families provide a longer term basis is to be found in the link between family and enterprise. I start with an examination of family firms, which still represent, across many different national cultures, the most common form of enterprise; if I concentrate on some examples of large family firms, it is simply because the history of these is much better documented than that of micro-enterprises. The story of family capitalism is still generally presented as fundamentally a negative one that brakes development and instills corrupt practices. People turn up their nose at family business, and think it has a taste of Parmalat. The concept is often used, particularly in the United States, to explain deviation from some notion of an ideal-typical American path, of the kind best described by the business historian Alfred Chandler.[1]

Management is rational in this view, while family firms are emotion-driven. In this prescriptive and normative tradition of analysis, firms should move smoothly from an entrepreneurial to a managerial type of organization, with the movement to the multi-divisional firm being taken as the key indicator that such a transition to business modernity has been achieved. The dominance of family business has historically been used to explain, for instance, poor French economic performance until the second half of the twentieth century, when the deficiencies of such organizations were overcome by a transition to planning in which technically trained business elites replaced dynastic control. The financial limitations which keep family firms small is also generally held to explain why Italian modernization remained incomplete and polarized in a dualism between a large and until recently state-dominated industry and myriad small producers. The idea of the family firm is thus at the heart of a debate over the costs of the divergence of a continental European model of capitalism from the "Anglo-Saxon" one. According to this view, path dependence locked continental economies on a sub-optimal institutional track.[2]

One variant of the gloomy depiction of family business holds that such firms may play a useful role in resolving the problems of trust that arise in small-scale local economies, but that large family firms still carry a heavy price.[3] The penalty of the family is thus far heavier for larger sized enterprises. Such an interpretation escapes from the simple mechanism of Chandler's account of family firms being a childlike stage in the path to the mature managerial enterprise. It allows interpretations in which economies thrive on the interplay of a dualism between a small family-based sector and large modern enterprise, where Italian micro-firms produce innovative textile designs.

On the other hand, this picture does not take into account the amazing range of family business. It is obviously rather hard to claim that German or Japanese business life was generally sluggish in the century after 1870, although there were family firms that dominated large as well as smaller-scale business. Nor were family firms particularly undynamic. Jeffrey Fear has recently used the impressive development of August Thyssen's firm in the late nineteenth century to challenge the Chandlerian tradition, and to show how innovative and responsive personal capitalism could be.[4] In the late nineteenth and early twentieth century U.S. "gilded era," owner-dominated firms like Singer or Carnegie Steel were often more gung-ho on growth than managerial enterprises, including the large company formed by a merger in 1901 which absorbed Carnegie steel, namely U.S. Steel.[5]

Perhaps surprisingly, however, it is not economists or economic historians but rather anthropologists, notably Jack Goody, who have mounted a sustained challenge to the simple idea of family capitalism being simply and inevitably replaced by a modern rational individualistic managerial capitalism. Goody concludes: "The aspect of the managerial approach that sees the evolutionary replacement of the family firm by impersonal forms of economic organization has little empirical justification and neglects the continuing role of the family not only in smaller enterprises but also in many larger ones. Firstly it gives insufficient weight to the growth of new businesses that are bound to be centered on the family . . . Secondly, even where control may be transmitted in a bureaucratic way, the property people possess at death normally passes to family members, whether this consists of jewellery, a house or shares." In short, across the world, from Ahmadabad and Toulouse to Bradford, "the structure of the enterprise tended to duplicate the structure of the family."[6]

Most scholars will happily accept that this was broadly true before the French Revolution. The European *ancien regime* was certainly a family affair, at every level of society. The most obvious embodiment of the dynastic principle was the hereditary divine right monarchy; but poor peasant farmers also treated their activity as a household enterprise. At every level, families looked to dynastic marriage strategies to find greater wealth and power. A Bourbon prince marrying a Habsburg princess was only the highest level exemplification of the logic of family existence; farmers could try to marry additional land. (Analogies between the world of business and the world of royalty continue today: the Queen of England apparently habitually refers to the monarchy as "the firm.")

Family values meshed especially well with craft traditions in manufacturing. Iron-working or textiles abounded in all sorts of arcane techniques and secret tricks that needed to be carefully guarded from competitors. Businesses were continually prying and trying to lure skilled workers away from their rivals, and industrial espionage evolved into a major *ancien regime* activity. The best defense mechanism against defecting craftsmen was to restrict the most important secrets to sons or even daughters: the sons would be locked into the business, and the daughters would be a useful bargaining chip in the strategic game of dynastic marriage.

For some people in the eighteenth century, however, the collectivism and anti-individualism of their family-dominated world looked strange and irrational. It was also at odds with the relatively new idea that states had identities that went beyond the person of the ruler and that an Enlightened ruler should be, as Frederick the Great memorably put it, the first servant of the state. To take the example of the royal marriages: was not Louis xvi's Habsburg wife, Marie-Antoinette, an affront to French national interest, national honor, and the reason of state?

During and after the French Revolution, a cult of romantic individualism released men and women from family ties, which were reinterpreted as being conventional and restrictive. In economic life, the territorial changes, the upheavals of markets, the search for new technologies that would yield military advantage, all helped to shape an image of a creative individual entrepreneur driven by a demon. The new man both created and destroyed: he was a sort of Napoleon of the business world. But there was an irony in all of this Napoleonic emulation: as has repeatedly been observed, Napoleon depended on his family for influence and power and became an archetypal dynast.[7] And far from being destroyed by the political turmoil of the French Revolution, family firms were actually strengthened.

Resilience is especially evident at moments of political and social strain. In France, family enterprises such as that of the pioneering iron and steel firm de Wendel reconstituted themselves under the threat and challenge of the French Revolution, when property relations were challenged and transformed. The firm was nationalized, sold off at auction, and then eventually bought under the Empire by the son of the persecuted original owner. Ignace de Wendel had fled to Germany and ended up at the court of Saxony-Weimar, where he was pitied by the minister and poet Goethe, who observed his decline: "His sorrow was so great that neither the support of the prince nor the charitable activity of the princely advisers who had been instructed to help could restore him. Far removed from his fatherland, in a quiet corner of the Thuringian forest, he too fell as a victim to a revolution without frontiers."[8] In April 1795, de Wendel took a high dose of opium, and drew up a brief will, addressing his children: "Reputation is what is dearest to us. Goodbye, my children, may you not be so unhappy as was your father during his life."[9] François de Wendel then saw it as his life's mission to rescue his father's work and reputation from the legacy of Revolution. The children would be able to realize opportunities, but these depended not just on monetary capital (which didn't matter all that much because the Revolution expropriated and debauched money) but more importantly on honor and reputation, in short on what modern analysts call social capital.

In the twentieth century, there are analogous developments in great upheavals such as the transition from totalitarian to representative

democratic rule in Germany and Italy. The great era of family capitalism in Germany came after 1945: in part when some old firms—often
controlled by bitterly divided families—remade themselves and took
on a new entrepreneurial dynamism, in part with new dynasties such
as the Quandts or the Burdas. There are obvious analogies in Japan,
where after 1945 the U.S. occupation dissolved the *zaibatsu* and purged
fifty-six members of *zaibatsu* families. Within ten years the family
groupings had effectively reconstituted themselves.[10]

In general, the story of the changing role of the family in the classic
story of the western model of industrialization is impossible to separate
from the process of organizational development of enterprises. The
evolution of a strong sense of family is a crucial part of the creation
of the nineteenth-century bourgeoisie, a class whose social formation
has been the subject of many well-organized and large-scale national
and sometimes international research projects.[11] The family in fact
provided networks of relationships, which expanded as time passed.
The information gains provided by such networks can be described as
a social capital that complemented financial capital. They contribute
to the efficiency of the firm by lowering transaction costs.[12]

Family capitalism has thus been particularly important in countries
and societies with profound shocks and discontinuities. It is a way
of managing risk in a high-risk environment. This historical role is
confirmed by recent work which suggests that in developing countries
undergoing economic transition family firms play a major role. They
can generate a better access to market capital, because they create a
degree of trust that offers a response to market failure. They provide a
higher degree of human or social capital. Thus with the liberalization
of the Indian economy since 1991, family groups (which many predicted
should disappear over the course of development) have become more
important.[13] Francis Fukuyama has emphasized the importance of trust
in the case of Asian capitalism: the central institution in this regard is
the extended family, and it is family networks which have transferred
capital and skill to China from the "greater China" of the Chinese
emigration in Asia but also in the United States. The European expe-

rience, which was highly politically turbulent until relatively recently (the mid-twentieth century), offers some important lessons here. It is directly relevant to the problems of developing resilient companies and robust corporate governance through most of the world.

Over three quarters of registered companies in the industrialized world are family businesses, and—especially in continental Europe— they include some very large companies. Scholars of the subject are often surprised by the extent that the phenomenon has survived into present day business existence.[14] According to one recent calculation, seventeen of the largest hundred companies in Germany are in family hands, twenty-six in France, and forty-three in Italy.[15] France and Italy still consider themselves to be the "champions of family capitalism."[16] In France, at the beginning of the twenty-first century, 33.8 percent of the total market value of listed corporate assets was controlled by just fifteen families (and 22.0 percent by five families). For Italy, the equivalent figures are 21.9 percent and 16.8 percent, and for Germany 25.0 percent and 15.7 percent. By contrast, in the United Kingdom, the equivalent figures are just 6.6 percent and 4.1 percent.[17] That is not to say that there are no long-lived family firms in the United States and Canada—the often eccentric Duponts and the highly secretive Cargills would be obvious examples. But many of the most outstanding North American family dynasties are relatively recent.

The main controversy however revolves around the qualitative evaluation of the implications of statistics about how widespread are family firms. In Asian capitalism, the special trust that exists among members of very extended families is often interpreted as a source of greater resilience. In a similar vein, the mid-nineteenth century conservative French social theorist Fréderic Le Play argued that industrial success was a reflection of the spirit of the family. At the beginning of the twenty-first century, an emphasis on the positive sides of family business returned, especially in debates outside the United States and Great Britain.

Family ownership has the advantage of being visible and identifiable, in contrast to the anonymous capitalism of large numbers of individual investors or the facelessness of institutional investors. If ownership is an important or even the defining feature of the capitalist process, it may be desirable that it is transparent. The greater difficulties that arise when disposing of ownership in consequence offer a guarantee of continuity and make property part of a stakeholding and relatively permanent pattern of institutional arrangements in which there are higher levels of commitment. This means that it may be easier to motivate managers and workers in a setting when they do not know whether tomorrow the (faceless) owners will walk away. Families in business recently responded to this sort of analysis by developing a concept of "professional ownership." The family and its long-term vision thus offered a striking and reassuring alternative to the emphasis on "shareholder value" that had been so fashionable in the 1990s, and had been linked with the "Americanization" of business conduct.

One way of understanding how family firms managed such dramatic transitions of social systems is to think how the families conceived of themselves and their role. Large enterprise families (as opposed to small-scale artisanal family firms) frequently and explicitly compared themselves to monarchs of the *ancien regime*: they preserved into modernity the dynastic principle and what it represented. In Germany, the Krupps saw themselves as monarchs. The economic historian Knut Borchardt concluded that the way in which the family's functions became increasingly representative replicated the dynamic of the princely court of the *ancien regime*.[18] After the Italian electorate rejected the monarchy, Gianni Agnelli became "the uncrowned king of the nation," with intense press interest in the succession struggles and difficulties. The family and its organization in a company could offer a self-consciously aristocratic or even royal vision. At the beginning of the twentieth century, an influential German handbook referred to the corporation as having to that day an "aristocratic molding."[19]

Many large family-owned firms are still unusually dynamic and creative, and have a particular advantage over joint-stock companies which have to pay greater attention to short-term stock market valuations. Some examples of the greater success of family firms can be found in European automobiles, where BMW (owned by the Quandt family) has been much nimbler than larger companies; or the German Haniel company, which in the 1960s made an early move into systems technology in retail and wholesale trade, using managers hired away from IBM in order to introduce a new approach to a traditionally rather conservative sector.

At one level, then, the family seems to offer an alternative pole of loyalty to political allegiances—in other words, to the state. At another level, it can substitute for the anonymous abstractions of the market and perform very well. That is a function that companies in general have: they are—following the classical analysis of Ronald Coase—ways of substituting control for market operations in a climate of information uncertainty. Family firms offer a particularly clear logic of control. The story of economic development is thus best understood as the narrative of the interplay of families, states, and markets, and of the differing ways in which they understood themselves and each other.

A central concept in explaining this interplay is that of property. Critics from Karl Marx and Friedrich Engels onward have attacked the family as an economic rather than an emotional construct: the bourgeois family was kept in place by a sense of property rather than by romantic love or tender paternal and maternal feelings. The intangible assets and networks of the family thus became quite material and tangible. Pierre Bourdieu in this tradition (in an article illustrated incidentally by a photograph of members of the de Wendel family lined up at the family funeral of the dynastic patriarch), concluded that "the family spirit and even the affection which creates family cohesion are transfigured and sublimated forms of the interest specifically attached to the membership in a family group, or the participation in a capital whose integrity is guaranteed by family integration. By this sort of writing error, which is in principle a collective alchemy, the membership in an integrated family assures every individual the symbolic profits corresponding to the cumulative connections of all members of the group."[20]

The supposed incompatibility between love and rationality then produced continuous psychic crisis and made the institution of the family firm emotionally and in the end psychologically dysfunctional. The family did change, however, in response to changed ideas about affection, with the result that the twentieth century experience was quite different to that of the nineteenth century. Just to take the examples of the three European business dynasties that I examine in a forthcoming book on family business,[21] cousin marriage was extremely common in the nineteenth century, but quite rare after the First World War. There is an economic reason for this, as well as a question of generally changing cultural norms. Without a joint stock company as a way of organizing and limiting family owners' control of the company, the family members need to be tightly controlled in some other way. Parental choice of marriage partners avoids the dissipation of wealth through the marriage of heiresses to aristocrats, wastrels, or charming adventurers. Thus it is actually not a coincidence that when joint stock companies with limited liability became generally available on the European continent in the 1860s and 1870s, some of the necessity for parental discipline disappeared. Bad behavior by heirs no longer had the capacity to wreck the whole family unit so comprehensively as in the old order. In consequence young men became free to spend their inherited fortunes on racehorses, and young women could have exciting and financially unsolid husbands.

The family firm played an absolutely central role in the early stages of the story of European industrialization, before the institutional innovations associated with the joint stock limited liability corporation (generally a feature only of the mid-nineteenth century and later). At first, there was little alternative to the family as a way of establishing a link based on trust between individuals. There was no way legally of enforcing trust, so it had to depend on family piety and duty. Piety is to be taken seriously as a word here: religiously pious families often did much better in commerce because they established trust more easily.

But even after the availability of the joint stock company as a way of establishing a solid long-term business relationship between people with potentially divergent interests, families still remained important. The cynic might have said, if you have a company why do you need a family that behaves like a company. But the old models of behavior were deeply entrenched in the European psyche. At the beginning of the novel *The Man of Property*, John Galsworthy describes the Forsytes, a British dynasty:

> Those privileged to be present at a family festival of the Forsytes have seen that charming and instructive sight—an upper middle-class family in full plumage. But whosoever of these favored persons has possessed the gift of psychological analysis (a talent without monetary value and properly ignored by the Forsytes), has witnessed a spectacle, not only delightful in itself, but illustrative of an obscure human problem. In plainer words, he has gleaned from the gathering of this family—no branch of which had a liking for any other, between no three members of whom existed anything worthy of the name of sympathy—evidence of that mysterious concrete tenacity which renders a family so formidable a unit of society, so clear a reproduction of society in miniature. He has been admitted to a vision of the dim roads of social progress, has understood something of the patriarchal life, of the swarmings of savage hordes, of the rise and fall of nations.

In the family enterprise, the close relationship of family members solved a number of problems, which would otherwise have impeded the process of economic growth. In an age of great demographic uncertainty, with high mortality rates, it offered a way of securing the future of an enterprise. Relatives who were brought into the firm could give security, lend money, and provide reliable business contacts in distant cities. Daughters could be used in the same way they were treated by the royal families (also a sort of business) that governed Europe: to make strategic alliances between firms on a secure and long term basis. Marriage remained, long into the age of romantic love (and longer than for other social classes), a business transaction. In the twentieth century, André Michelin was still urging his family to preserve wealth by marrying their cousins (a strategy common in such long-lived dynasties as de Rothschilds, Haniels, and de Wendels).

Families are of course not always harmonious, and, as Tolstoy reminds us at the opening of *Anna Karenina,* can be unhappy in quite different and ingenious ways. In a business context, family quarrels required some sort of legal management and institutional solution in order to stop feckless or irresponsible or simply irrepressibly entrepreneurial members of the family endangering the whole enterprise. The family disputes of the de Wendels produced two highly complicated and long-drawn law cases in the early nineteenth century. The brothers Haniel at the same time were infuriated by the scroungingly parasitical behavior of their brother-in-law, to whom they were bound in a joint business venture. At the end of the twentieth century, after a series of business setbacks, the Falcks in Italy split their family enterprise between two branches.

Keeping the family together was not an easy exercise before the creation of the legal concept of a limited liability corporation. Then, when limited liability offered a new way of protecting wealth, it also endangered the ideal of family control, in that family members might sell their shares in a publicly quoted corporation. The more legal certainty there was, the less the family seemed necessary.

II

It was the greater certainty in other areas of life that allowed the full blossoming of the romantic cult. Life became increasingly subject to planning through contracting. Something profound now changed in the notion of marriage.

We can best follow this discussion of new meanings of marriage through an examination of the changing reputation of one of the most important writers on demography and the family. In the 1790s, the Anglican minister and amateur economist Thomas Malthus believed that the family and marriage constituted the best—indeed the only "non-vicious"—way of regulating the relationship between population and resources. He used the generational argument as part of an attempt to refute the Enlightenment idea—propagated by Condorcet and in

England by William Godwin—of the perfectibility of man. He begins by the statement that "the great question now at issue" was "whether man shall henceforth start forwards with accelerated velocity towards illimitable, and hitherto unconceived improvement, or be condemned to a perpetual oscillation between happiness and misery, and after every effort remain still at an immeasurable distance from the wished for goal." When people bettered themselves too much, and prosperity increased, they would marry earlier and reproduce more. But the additional population would put pressure on available resources, and could only be checked by catastrophe (famines, or domestic and international wars which would be more likely as a consequence of an intensified struggle for resources). Alternatively, the population might be reduced by vice: by which Malthus understood infanticide, and unproductive sexual relations (i.e., the application of birth control). Indeed, Malthus castigates Condorcet's belief that one element of perfectibility involved casting off "the ridiculous prejudices of superstition," and a movement "either to a promiscuous concubinage, which would prevent breeding, so to something else as unnatural."[22]

Malthus saw marriage as the only virtuous way of controlling population size, in that poor societies (like those of most of early modern Europe) would have late marriage, and in this way escape from the impact of the more obvious and potent scourges of war and famine. "Famine," he added, "seems to be the last, the most dreadful resource of nature." Marriage and property in his eyes were the twin pillars of a civilized society.[23] It is important to note that Malthus did not believe that these were the same, or that men held a property in their wives (as many interpretations of the old world now suggest). Property belongs to the domain of contract, while marriage in Malthus' eyes, was something else.

Most twentieth century analysts were dismissive of Malthus, largely because they believe that western societies have successfully avoided the malthusian trap. Major elements of Malthus' calculation now appeared to be unrealistic, in that in his picture children are the more or less costless product of "the passion between the sexes," while their costs are felt in labor market shifts in subsequent time. In advanced industrial societies, we have come to a situation remarkably different from that sketched out by Malthus. We have thrown out Malthusian demographics, and with them we are also inclined to ignore Malthus' reflections on the beneficial effects of marriage.

Modern societies are facing dramatic and threatening demographic imbalances. From 1995 to 2015, the population in the EU over age sixty-five is estimated to increase by 30 percent, and that over age eighty by 39 percent. The greying of Europe results from changed calculations about the utility of family life. We are more prone to see the costs of bringing up a family, in terms of outlays, and also of the opportunity cost of lost income; we don't see the gains of a family in securing infirmity and old age because the costs of this aging have been apparently socialized. In many European societies, the risks of aging are collectivized through state-run pension schemes, and elsewhere private sector pension schemes provide a similar safety net. We don't think in making this calculation about long-term demographic imbalances, which are more unfavorable in Europe (and Japan) in the early twenty-first century than in other parts of the world. The actuarial provisions of state pension schemes are only now being rethought in Europe to take account of the aging of the population. Economists are profoundly uncertain about the private sector schemes, but there is an obvious vulnerability in that the stock market returns of the past twenty years were raised by the inflow of funds to pension schemes in a way that is unlikely to be repeated. The result of big macroeconomic miscalculations is that we value the costs of children too highly and the benefits too lightly. We are thus plunging into an opposite version of the trap that Malthus had attempted to predict.

III

The modern calculus of family life thus differs radically from that offered by Malthus, with children appearing as an immediate burden. Another way of thinking about the change is that the cohesion of the various relationships that make up the family has eroded. When we look at families, we are now less interested in generational questions, and more interested in the affection (or the lack of it) between spouses.

Marriage has changed primarily because of the intrusion of the idea that it is about the search for happiness. This is the quintessential Enlightenment theory—indeed it is the one that Malthus set out to combat in Godwin and Condorcet. In its extreme version, the modern view treats marriage as simply an extension of a search for consumer satisfaction. If I buy a good at a store, I am party to a contract, which I participate in because it enhances my satisfaction at that moment. There is no obligation to treat it in a particular way. If I get pleasure from buying an expensive watch and then smashing it on the ground, the worst that I can be accused of is eccentricity or perhaps tastelessness. And we perfectly well expect that over the course of time, a watch will wear out and need to be replaced.

This view of marriage as a search for satisfaction is now more or less prevalent. It is attached as an initial, indisputable premise to modern arguments. Recently, the new Hungarian Prime Minister Ferenc Gyurcsany, a forty-three-year-old multimillionaire who has been married three times and whose present wife is in her early thirties, said that his Socialist party, which dismissed his predecessor Peter Medgyessy, was entitled to do so, just as "anyone whose wife is getting old deserves a younger one."[24] The great Princeton historian of marriage, Lawrence Stone, observed that "If Thomas Jefferson today was asked to rewrite the Declaration of Independence he would certainly have to add total sexual fulfillment to 'Life, Liberty and Human Happiness' as one of the basic natural rights of every member of society."[25] The result as far as the family is concerned is that children are seen as a nuisance, because the key relationship is that of the married partners. Recently, for instance, the National Marriage Project at Rutgers University concluded that "Children seem to be a growing impediment for the happiness of marriages."[26]

Some go as far as to suggest that any other picture of marriage must be a sign of insanity. According to the Princeton historian Hendrik Hartog, "Today everyone understands marriage as an individual life choice, and as an event within an individual life. Though marriage continues to offer the fantasy of continuity and permanence (till death do us part), all sane people who enter into it know that it represents a choice to marry this person at this time and that if living with this person at a later time no longer suggests the possibility of happiness, that you are entitled (have a right) to leave and to try again."[27]

But this interpretation fails to notice or take seriously two features about marriage which were at the core of the traditional view, and which were inextricably linked with each other. The first is that marriage is a particular kind of relationship, which is not affected by the current or subsequent feelings or emotions of the partners, but which lasts until death. The second is that marriage is concerned with reproduction.

The relationship in the center of marriage is in its eternal or unchanging character identical to the relationships created by reproduction. In the same way as I am someone's son or someone's father, and cannot stop being a son or father simply by an act of will, I am someone's husband. This does not necessarily mean that I am a good husband or that my wife is happy, any more than it means that I am a good son or a good father. Indeed it is quite conceivable that in a marriage I might do something so horrible that my spouse might never want to associate with me again, and fathers and sons can quarrel with each other in the same way. But a son who refuses to see his father does not stop being a son, and fathers and sons do not stop having particular responsibilities to each other.

The recognition of this truth is at the heart of two of the most famous literary depictions of the problematical character of filial affection. When Cordelia tells her father in the opening scene of *King Lear* that "I love your majesty according to my bond, no more or less," she outraged and puzzled many subsequent critics, especially modern ones, who on this ground find the play incomprehensible. Is she peculiarly stubborn or insensitive, or is she maniacally and irresponsibly devoted to truth-telling at whatever cost? The idea that she is confronting is that filial love should be rewarded by showers of presents; the truth that she is expressing is that filial love arises out of a bond of obligation.

The flashy and eventually counterproductive Defense Counsel for Dmitri Karamozov, Fetyukovich, tries to reason that "such a father as the murdered old Karamazov cannot and does not deserve to be called a father. The love for a father who does not deserve such love is an absurdity, an impossibility. One cannot create love out of nothing, only God can create something out of nothing."[28] As with the elder daughters of King Lear, what is presented here is a fallacious view of the filial relationship. Dmitri, on the other had, recognizes that though he did not kill his eminently detestable father, he would have liked to kill him and thus bears a guilt.

The permanence that a family relationship produces—it is important to note that it is an involuntary permanence—produces feelings that are deep and indeed are part of what makes us human. They intrinsically extend to some still remaining ideas of marriage. No less than filial love, conjugal love arises out of obligation. Even at a time when the consumerist view of marriage is prevalent, we are quite shocked by Britney Spears' apparently frivolous decision to marry and then immediately leave an old childhood friend. Many secular marriage services still include from the Anglican Prayer Book some secularized version of the minister's admonition that marriage "is commended of Saint Paul to be honourable among all men: and therefore is not by any to be enterprised, nor taken in hand, unadvisedly, lightly, or wantonly, to satisfy men's carnal lusts and appetites, like brute beasts that have no understanding; but reverently, discreetly, advisedly, soberly, and in the fear of God; duly considering the causes for which Matrimony was ordained."

The seriousness of marriage goes beyond a simple contractual relationship. It is this that gives reliability—to return to the link of the family and enterprise—to the business that is built on the family foundation. The considerations about how family firms operate and how prevalent they actually are—quite in contrast to the appalled expectations of theorists of efficient capital markets, show how important are parent-child relations, and child-parent relations, as well as the relations between spouses.

There is an analogy here from Christian theology, which is profoundly helpful. The early Church was most divided over the doctrine of the Trinity, which seemed to many unnecessarily complicated, a fuzzy holdover from hellenic philosophy. The Trinity is also the doctrine that sharply distinguished Christian from Jewish and Islamic theologies. If we think about the relationship of Our Lady with the Trinity, we have a theology of the family. She is the Mother of Jesus, the immaculate and obedient daughter of God, and the bride of the Holy Spirit. These three relationships depend on each other.

Since parent-child relations are not a matter of choice, they cause the greatest problems for the modern personality. The modern mentality because of its orientation toward personal freedom indeed wants to make them also subject to human choice: to make us capable of choosing our offspring as if from a catalogue, to make parents able to select a dark-haired daughter, or a blue-eyed son, with high intelligence and athletic abilities. So far such choices have not been easily possible. The relation of parent and child is for exactly this reason a crucial reminder that the important relationships that define our being are not a matter of us choosing.

Since we are not able to select our offspring or our parents, there has been a tendency to place more and more importance on the relationship that—in the modern world—we can choose. Choice is absent from other parts of family existence, but is inserted into the marriage relationship. The remarkable fact is that there is no evidence that choice makes for increased happiness in marriages. There are plenty of examples of misery and unsuitability in arranged marriages, but there is also an abundance of despair and incongruity in voluntary ones. Indeed it is easy to see why an argument could be made that choice makes the situation more difficult. In a pre-modern arranged marriage, if I am very unhappy, I can blame my parents or whoever else made the match; but I need not and should not blame myself or my wife. In a marriage of choice, the search for who is to blame runs much more deeply and destructively: either I made a fundamental error, in which case I am wrestling with a flaw in myself, or my partner deceived me in some way, in which case I wrestle with the aftermath of deception. This is not to make a plea for a return to arranged marriages, but rather an exemplary story of how when we privilege one particular relationship that is in reality embedded in a deeply complex social fabric, we raise expectations to an extent that they cannot subsequently be realized, that they produce bitter disappointment, and may then damage the other relations.

If we imagine that every relationship is simply contractual, and can be broken at will—at a price to be paid for the renunciation of the contract—we will find ourselves in a position where the bedrock of certainty on which contracts depend melts away. Families showed their greatest strength as a social mechanism when markets and states faltered. The nineteenth and twentieth century shifts in attitude to the family were a reflection of a great confidence that states and markets can do more. The element of hubris in this claim in relation to the state became very clear in some of the perverted state-centric experiences of Europe's twentieth century, and by the end of the twentieth century there was much greater degree of skepticism about the capacity of the state to deliver. But the collapse of communism was accompanied by a great (and excessive) faith in the capacity of markets to undertake every kind of adjustment. We know that when markets fail they can breed very powerful and destructive anti-market reactions. A more nuanced view of markets sees them in terms of an institutional setting, in which their efficacy depends on their interactions with other types of institutions.

It is here that the family holds a central position, but one that has become very vulnerable. An intrusion of the characteristic way of thinking about a state or a market, namely that they rest on contracts which can be broken, into the domain of family life, will undermine not just families, but also states and markets.

4

Why Unilateral Divorce
Has No Place in a Free Society

Jennifer Roback Morse

D IVORCE IS A CRUCIAL SOCIAL ISSUE in at least two ways. First, the high divorce rate contributes to any number of social problems and pathologies. Each one of these social problems has fiscal implications. Second, divorce is in the background of the same-sex marriage debate because same-sex marriage is the end of the trend that no-fault divorce began. The legal innovation of unilateral divorce began to reduce marriage to nothing but a temporary association of individuals. If marriage is merely a free association of individuals, there is no principled reason to exclude same-sex couples, or even larger groupings of sexual partners. The permanence of marriage was one of the key features that distinguished it from an ordinary contract.

This paper will demonstrate that unilateral divorce is not consistent with a free society in the libertarian, minimal government sense of the term. A society which allows the dissolution of marriage for any reason or no reason will not be a minimal government society for very long. This is the chief reason why libertarians must discard the "laissez-faire" strand of argument in favor of unilateral divorce. I shall show that the application of "laissez-faire" to marriage and divorce is misplaced, a distortion of the genuine meaning of laissez-faire. Once this argument is dispatched, it will be relatively easy to sweep away the free choice argument in favor of gay marriage, though it is beyond the scope of this paper to do so.

The importance of this argument goes far beyond the small group of people who describe themselves as libertarian. The "leave us alone" posture has been one of the most successful rhetorical moves of the advocates of the deconstruction of marriage. I believe this is because minimum government has traditionally had deep roots in the American psyche and continues to have a deep hold on the American imagination. But the redefinition of marriage is part of the left's attempt to redefine freedom to mean a combination of having your own way and being completely unencumbered by human relationships. This understanding of freedom will not, and cannot, lead to a smaller, less intrusive government.

To put it another way, the consistent libertarian position combines features from both the right and the left. Libertarians want to combine the "fiscal right," which wants minimal government taxation, spending, and regulation, with the "lifestyle left," which wants minimal governmental definition of proper sexual, marital, and family behavior. I will show that it is not possible for a society to be both fiscally conservative and lifestyle liberal. It sounds good on paper, but in practice it simply is not possible. It is a bit like trying to have a prosperous society that has no property rights.

I. MARRIAGE IS A PRE-POLITICAL, ORGANIC SOCIAL INSTITUTION

I define marriage as a society's normative institution for both sexual activity and childrearing. Marriage is an organic, pre-political institution that emerges spontaneously from society.[1] People of the opposite sex are naturally attracted to one another, couple with each other, co-create children, and raise those children. The little society of the family replenishes and sustains itself. Humanity's natural sociability expresses itself most vibrantly within the family. A minimum-government libertarian can view this self-sustaining system with unadulterated awe.

Government does not create marriage any more than government creates jobs. Just as people have a natural "propensity to truck, barter and exchange one thing for another," in Adam Smith's famous words from the second chapter of *The Wealth of Nations*,[2] we likewise have a natural propensity to couple, procreate, and rear children. People instinctively create marriage, both as couples and as a culture, without any support from the government whatsoever.

The sexual urge is an engine of human sociability. Our desire for sexual satisfaction draws us out of our natural self-centeredness and into connection with other people. Just as the desire to make money induces business owners to try to please their customers, so too the desire to copulate induces men to try to please women and women to try to attract men. The attachment of mothers to their babies, and women to their sex partners, tends to keep this little society together.[3] The man's possessiveness of his sexual turf and of his offspring offset his natural tendency toward promiscuity.[4] These desires and attachments emerge naturally from the very biology of sexual complementarity, with no assistance from the state.

This is not the only sense in which the institution of marriage arises spontaneously. In every known society, communities around the couple develop customs and norms that define the parameters of socially acceptable sexual, spousal, and parental behavior. These parameters differ across culture, and they have changed over time even within cultures. But these variations should not blind us to the more basic fact: every society places limits on the sexual and parental behavior that it is willing to tolerate among its members.

This culture around marriage may have some legal or governmental elements. But in most times and places, the greater part of that cultural machinery is more informal than legal and is based more on kinship than on law. We do things this way because our parents did things this way; our friends and neighbors look at us funny if we go too far outside the norm. The formal legal and political structures provide some support and enforcement for the norms, but by far, the bulk of the daily enforcement of the social expectations about marriage takes place informally.

The modern alternative idea about marriage is that society does not need such an institution: no particular arrangement should be legally or culturally privileged as the ideal context for sex or childbearing.[5] This, by definition, means the end of marriage. The institution formerly known as marriage is to be replaced by a legalistic concept of a bundle of benefits granted by the state.[6] Instead of marriage as an organic social institution, we will have marriage as a creation of the state.

The supposedly libertarian subtext of this idea is that people should be as free as possible to make their personal choices. But the very non-libertarian consequence of this new idea is that it obliterates the informal methods of enforcement. Parents can't raise their eyebrows and expect children to conform to the socially accepted norms of behavior, because there are no socially accepted norms of behavior. Raised eyebrows and dirty looks no longer operate as sanctions on behavior slightly or even grossly outside the norm. The modern culture of sexual and parental tolerance ruthlessly enforces a code of silence, banishing anything remotely critical of personal choice. A parent or peer who tries to tell a young person that they are about to do something incredibly stupid, runs into the brick wall of the non-judgmental social norm.

This shift from marriage as an organic social institution to marriage as a legalistic institution will be a disaster for the cause of limited government. Disputes that could be settled by custom will have to be settled in court. Support that could be provided by a stable family must be provided by taxpayers. Standards of good conduct that could be enforced informally must be enforced by law.

State Impartiality

The spontaneous emergence of marriage does not imply that any laws the state happens to pass will work out just fine. And it certainly does not follow that any cultural institutions surrounding sexual behavior, permanence of relationships, and the rearing of children will work out just fine. The state may still need to protect, encourage, or support permanence in procreational couplings, just as the state may need to protect the sanctity of contracts.

No libertarian would claim that the presumption of economic laissez-faire means that the government can ignore violations of property rights, contracts, and fair exchange. Apart from the occasional anarcho-capitalist, all libertarians agree that enforcing these is one of the basic functions of government. With these standards for economic behavior in place, individuals can create wealth and pursue their own interests with little or no additional assistance from the state. Likewise, formal and informal standards and sanctions create the context in which couples can create marriage, with minimal assistance from the state.

Nor would a libertarian claim that people should be indifferent between living in a centrally-planned economy and a market-ordered economy. No one disputes the free speech rights of socialists to distribute the *Daily Worker*. It does not follow that impartiality requires the economy to reflect socialism and capitalism equally. It simply can't be done. An economy built on the ideas in *The Communist Manifesto* will necessarily look quite different from an economy built on the ideas in *The Wealth of Nations*. The debate between socialism and capitalism is not a debate over how to accommodate different opinions, but over how the economy actually works. Everything from the law of contracts to anti-trust law to commercial law will be a reflection of some basic understanding of how the economy works in fact.

There are analogous truths about human sexuality. I claim the sexual urge is a natural engine of sociability, which solidifies the relationship between spouses and brings children into being. Others claim that human sexuality is a private recreational good, with neither intrinsic moral nor social significance.[7] I claim that the hormone oxytocin floods a woman's body during sex and tends to attach her to her sex partner, quite apart from her wishes or our cultural norms.[8] Others claim that women and men alike can engage in uncommitted sex, with no ill effects. I claim that children have the best life chances when they are raised by married, biological parents.[9] Others believe children are so adaptable that having unmarried parents presents no significant problems. Some people believe marriage is a special case of free association of individuals.[10] I say the details of this particular form of free association are so distinctive as to make marriage a unique social institution that deserves to be defended on its own terms, and not as a special case of something else.

One side in this dispute is mistaken. There is enormous room for debate, but there ultimately is no room for compromise. The legal institutions, social expectations, and cultural norms will all reflect some view or other about the meaning of human sexuality. We will be happier if we try to discover the truth and accommodate ourselves to it, rather than try to recreate the world according to our wishes.

Equality

A minimum government depends on people creating most of the machinery of the society for themselves. One of the attractive features of the market as a social institution is its self-regulating character. Set up a society with property rights, contract law, and a court and police system; populate it with people who have a functioning conscience and sense of reciprocity; give the system a push—and it runs itself. The government performs limited, but important functions. The ordinary people of society vote once in a while, pay a few taxes, and go home to do all the rest of the social business without the state.

Most free market economists tend to speak in generalities about civil society or mediating structures or the private sector. But all that other social business does have to get done. Without somebody taking care of the human business, a free society simply can't function. Actual people have to have babies, raise them, and educate them. Some actual people have to start schools and hospitals and charities and symphonies and clubs. If ordinary people don't take care of this activity, it either won't get done, or the state will have to do it. If a society literally has no mediating structures, we might well ask whether we can even properly call it a society. We might have business and economic institutions. People could earn a living and produce material things. But the whole social, cultural and moral part of life would be neglected. Such a situation would be more like a collection of individuals than a real society.

The alternative to people creating these organic social institutions is that the state performs these functions. The state will have to fill in the blanks left by the absence of civil society. We therefore conclude that the formation of social institutions is extremely important, even necessary, to the functioning of a minimal government society. Without social institutions, there is either no society at all, or there is a society completely dominated by the state.

By contrast, there is nothing fundamental about state guarantees of equality, in any sphere other than its own, very limited sphere of enforcing contracts and providing justice. Freedom does not require people to have equal incomes, equal educations, equal life chances, equal numbers of friends, or an equal chance at happiness. The government in a free society needs to be a referee, but it need not and in fact cannot be a guarantor that anyone will be equal to anyone else in any particular dimension. The idea that every individual is entitled to be equally respected by every other individual is an impossible ideal.

The modern idea about marriage is based on a demand for equality in a sphere that need not, and in fact cannot accommodate equality. The idea is that society should be impartial among all alternative arrangements for bearing and raising children, and among all alternative contexts in which sexual activity takes place. No particular arrangements should be legally or culturally privileged as the ideal context for sex or childbearing. In short, the modern alternative to marriage is a series of random couplings, more or less permanent. If people should choose a more permanent union, for whatever reason, that is of course acceptable. But the modern idea holds that there is no particular reason to hope for or celebrate long-term relationships over short-term ones, or sexual exclusivity over sexual promiscuity.

This kind of equality is really not consistent with a free society as conventionally understood. It is not possible to achieve equality in this context and still have anything like a minimal state.

To demonstrate this point, let me paint a picture of sex and child-rearing in an environment with complete social and legal neutrality among family forms. We do not have to use our imaginations. The scenario I am about to describe is all too common. This scenario has become common precisely because American society is trying to create a world in which the government maintains an official posture of neutrality among contexts for both sexual activity and the rearing of children.

II. RANDOM COUPLINGS ARE NOT CONSISTENT
WITH MINIMUM GOVERNMENT

A man and woman have a child. The mother and father have no permanent relationship to each other and no desire to form one. When the relationship ceases to function to their satisfaction, it dissolves. The mother sues the father for child support.

The couple argues through the court system over how much he should pay. The woman wants him to pay more than he wants to pay. The court ultimately orders him to pay a particular amount. He insists on continuing visitation rights with his child. She resists. They argue in court and finally settle on a periodic visitation schedule to which he is entitled.

The agreement works smoothly at first. Then the parents quarrel. At visitation time, the mother is not home. He calls and leaves a nasty message on the answering machine. They quarrel some more. She says his behavior is not appropriate. He smokes too much and over-indulges the child in sweets. She says the child, who is now a toddler, is impossible to deal with after visits. He quits paying child support. The court garnishes his wages to force him to pay. He goes to court to try to get his visitation agreement honored. The court appoints a mediator to help the couple work out a solution. The mother announces that she plans to move out of state. He goes to court and gets a temporary order to restrain her from moving. She invents a charge of child abuse and gets a restraining order forbidding him from seeing the child.[11]

Say what you like about this sort of case. You may think this is the best mere mortals can do. You may think this contentiousness is the necessary price people pay for their adult independence. You may blame the mother or the father or both. Or perhaps you think this is a nightmare for both adults as well as for children. But on one point we can all agree: this is not a libertarian society.

Some libertarians might focus on the specific activities of the family court, regarding them as grotesque infringements of both parties' privacy. Agents of the government actively inquire into, pass judgment upon, and intervene in the most intimate details of this couple's life. Or we might view the entire existence of the court system as an outrageous subsidy to this couple, paid by the rest of society. When the woman asks for the state's help collecting child support, the state provides this service at no charge to her. When she makes a charge of child abuse, the state keeps the man away from her and her child. If the charge is proven to be unfounded or frivolous, the state does not require her to pay compensation for its expenses, or the man for his losses.

This is not the posture of a night-watchman state. You need not be a libertarian to be troubled by this scenario, both by the power exercised by the state and the ugliness of the personal relationships.

The state solicitude for the mother and her child is a direct result of father absence. Without a father's assistance, this woman and her child are more likely to become dependents of the state. The state believes, quite reasonably, that it is more cost-effective to help the mother extract assistance from the father, than to provide taxpayer-funded financial assistance. Aggressive programs for tracking down "dead-beat dads" become a substitute for providing direct payments through the welfare system as conventionally understood.

A radical individualist might argue that the state should allow this couple to sink or swim on its own. If the man abandons her, tough luck for her and her child. If she kicks the man out, for good reason or no reason, tough luck for him. The individualist might argue (quite correctly, in my view) that the social order cannot afford to indulge people who can't get along with their closest and most intimate family members. If the state would get out of the family business, or charge people the full cost for the use of its services, fewer people would get into these contentious situations. People would be more careful in forming their intimate childbearing unions.

But our current ideological environment makes this position impossible, however much it might appeal to the radical individualist. The political pressures for the state to intervene on behalf of the unmarried mother are simply overwhelming. The welfare state is so entrenched that singling out unmarried mothers at this late date is not plausible. Given that reality, it is not realistic to expect the state to cease and desist from all the activities of the family court, no matter how intrusive or highly subsidized they may be.

Nor does the sense of financial entitlement exhaust the entitlement mentality. Unlimited sexual activity is now considered an entitlement.[12] Marriage is no longer the only socially acceptable outlet for sexual activity or for the rearing of children. It is now considered an unacceptable infringement on the modern person's liberty to insist that the necessary context of sexual activity is marriage, with rights and responsibilities, both implicit and explicit. It is equally unacceptable to argue that having children outside of marriage is irresponsible. Women are entitled to have as many children as they choose in any context they choose. In this sense, children have become a kind of consumer good. Choosing to have a child is a necessary and sufficient condition for being entitled to have one. Given this social and cultural environment, it is completely unrealistic to think that we can muster the political will to deprive unmarried parents of the use of the courts to prosecute their claims against one another.

Contrast this scenario with intact married couples. Not deliriously happy married couples, with stars in their eyes at all times. Just ordinary, everyday, run of the mill, married couples.

No one from the state forces them to pool their incomes, if they both work. If they have the traditional gender-based division of household labor, no one forces the husband to hand over his paycheck to his wife to run the household. No one makes the wife allow him to take the kids out for the afternoon. No one has to come and supervise their negotiations over how to discipline the children. When he's too tough, she might chew him out privately, or kick him under the table. When she lets them off the hook too easily, he might have some private signal for her to leave so he can do what needs to be done.

The typical married couple has regular disagreements over money, childrearing, the allocation of household chores, how to spend leisure time, and a hundred other things. Every once in a while, even a stable married couple will have a knock-down, drag-out, (usually) private quarrel. But they resolve their disagreements, large and small, perhaps a dozen a day, completely on their own, with neither supervision nor subsidy from any court.

Social Costs of Private Conflicts

Whether a couple loses the ability to negotiate, or whether they never had it in the first place, the dissolution of their union has significant spillover effects. The instability in their relationship is likely to be detrimental to their child. The children of unmarried or divorced parents are more likely than other children to have emotional, behavioral and health problems.[13] The children of unmarried parents are more likely than other children to be abused by their own parents, or by step-parents or parents' boyfriends or girlfriends.[14] As these children become old enough to go to school, they absorb more educational resources than other children, because the school has to deal with lowered school achievement, poor school attendance, and discipline problems.[15] As these children mature, they are more likely to get into trouble with the law, commit crimes, abuse drugs and end up in jail.[16] And they are more likely to have difficulties forming their own stable families.[17]

These costs are more than purely private costs to the mother and father. The costs of healthcare, schooling, and mental health care are not entirely private in this society, no matter how much libertarians might wish they were. In modern America, a child who cannot behave in school is a cost to the local school district as well as to all the other children in the classroom. A seriously depressed person, or a drug addicted person is likely to make demands on the public health sector. If the child ends up in the criminal justice system, as the children of unmarried parents are significantly more likely to do, they will be a significant cost to the state.

The demand that the government be neutral among family forms is unreasonable. The reality is that married-couple families and child-less people are providing subsidies to those parents who dissolve their marriages or who never form marriages. Libertarians recognize that a free market needs a culture of law-abidingness, promise-keeping, and respect for contracts. Similarly, a free society needs a culture that supports and sustains marriage as the normative institution for the begetting, bearing, and rearing of children. A culture full of people who violate their contracts at every possible opportunity cannot be held together by legal institutions, as the experience of post-communist Russia plainly shows. Likewise, a society full of people who treat sex as a purely recreational activity, a child as a consumer good, and mar-riage as a glorified roommate relationship, will not be able to resist the pressures for a vast social-assistance state. The state will irresistibly be drawn into parental quarrels and into providing a variety of services for the well-being of the children.

The Libertarian Individual or the Naked Individual?

The alternative to my view that marriage is a naturally occurring, pre-political institution, is that marriage is strictly a creation of the state. The Supreme Court of Massachusetts notoriously asserted this posi-tion.[18] If this is true, then the state can recreate marriage in any form it chooses. Implicit in this view is the decidedly non-libertarian view that the state is the ultimate source of social order.

Listen to a self-described progressive bring the implicit connection between the expansive state and the deconstruction of marriage out of the shadows. New York University Queer Studies professor Lisa Dug-gan critiques the marriage promotion portion of welfare reform:

Women and children, . . . [according to the welfare reform model] should depend on men for basic economic support, while women care for dependents—children, elderly parents, disabled family members, etc. Under such a model, married-couple households might "relieve" the state of the expense of helping to support single-parent households, and of the cost of a wide range of social services, from childcare and disability services to home nursing. Marriage thus becomes a privatization scheme: Individual married-couple households give women and children access to higher men's wages, and also "privately" provide many services once offered through social welfare agencies. More specifically, the unpaid labor of married women fills the gap created by government service cuts.[19]

This statement brings the statist world view out of the closet: the most basic relationships are not between husband and wife, parent and child, but between individual citizens and the state. The family is not the natural unit of society. The most basic unit of society is not even the libertarian individual, embedded within a complex web of family, business, and social relationships. Rather, the natural unit of the society is the naked individual, the isolated individual, standing alone before the state, beholden to the state, dependent upon the state.

The libertarian approach to caring for the dependent is usually described in terse form as "let families and private charity take care of it, and get the government out of the way." This position is sometimes ridiculed as unrealistic or attacked as harsh. But the libertarian position, once fully fleshed out, is both humane and realistic.

The libertarian preference for non-governmental provision of care for dependents is based upon the realization that people take better care of those they know and love than they do of complete strangers. It is no secret that people take better care of their own stuff than of other people's. Economists conclude that private property will produce better results than collectivization schemes. But a libertarian preference for stable married-couple families is built upon more than a simple analogy with private property. The ordinary rhythm of the family creates a cycle of dependence and independence that any sensible social order ought to harness rather than resist.

We are all born as helpless infants in need of constant care. But we are not born alone. If we are lucky enough to be born into a family that includes an adult married couple, they sustain us through our years of dependence. They do not get paid for the work they do: they do it because they love us. Their love for us keeps them motivated to carry on, even when we are undeserving, ungrateful, snot-nosed brats. Their love for each other keeps them working together as a team, with whatever division of labor works for them.

As we become old enough to be independent, we become attracted to other people. Our bodies practically scream at us to reproduce and do for our children what our parents did for us. In the meantime, our parents grow older. When we are at the peak of our strength, stamina and earning power, we make provision to help those who helped us in our youth.

For this minimal-government approach to work, there has to be a family in the first place. The family must sustain itself over the course of the lives of its members. If too many members spin off into complete isolation, if too many members are unwilling to cooperate with others, the family will not be able to support itself. A woman trying to raise children without their father is unlikely to contribute much to the care of her parents. In fact, unmarried parents are more likely to need help from their parents than to provide it.

Enemies of Marriage, Enemies of the Market [20]

In contrast to the libertarian approach, "progressives" view government provision of social services as the first resort, not the last. Describing marriage as a "privatization scheme" implies that the most desirable way to care for the dependent is for the state to provide care. An appreciation of voluntary cooperation between men and women, young and old, weak and strong, so natural to libertarians and the majority of economists, is completely absent from this statist world view.

This is why it is no accident that the advocates of sexual laissez-faire are among the most vociferous opponents of economic laissez-faire. Advocates of gay marriage are fond of pointing out that civil marriage confers more than 1,049 automatic federal and additional state protections, benefits and responsibilities, according to the federal government's General Accounting Office.[21] If these governmentally-bestowed benefits and responsibilities are indeed the core of marriage, then this package should be equally available to all citizens. It follows that these benefits of marriage should be available to any grouping of individuals, of any size or combination of genders, of any degree of permanence.

But why should libertarians, of all people, accept the opening premise at face value? Marriage is the socially preferred institution for sexual activity and childrearing, in every known human society. The modern claim that there need not be and should not be any social or legal preference among sexual or childrearing contexts is, by definition, the abolition of marriage as an institution.

Libertarians do not believe that what the government chooses to bestow or withhold is the essence of any social institution. When we hear students from third world countries naively ask, "If the government doesn't create jobs, how will we ever have any jobs?" we know how to respond. Just because the government employs people and gives away tax money does not mean it "created" those jobs. Likewise, the fact that the government gives away bundles of goodies to married couples does not prove that the government created marriage.

III. WHATEVER HAPPENED TO THE SANCTITY OF CONTRACT?

One common assertion about marriage, made by libertarians and leftists alike, is that marriage is something like a contract. As long as both parties agree to its terms, no outside party has any right to interfere, or even to express a critical opinion. I have argued elsewhere that comparing marriage to a contract is an incomplete view at best.[22] But let's take the contract argument seriously for a moment. In fact, let's take it seriously not just at the moment that people are deciding whether to get married or live together, whether to marry a person of the opposite sex or of the same sex, whether to marry one person or a group of people. Let's treat the contract analogy seriously at the moment of the breakup of marriage as well.

If we took the marriage-as-contract view seriously, we would not have a legal rule allowing one party to breach unilaterally with no penalty. Far from supporting a "no-fault" position, the marriage-as-contract argument specifically rejects no-fault. If one party breached the marriage contract, that party could be held accountable to the other party. If one party wants to end the marriage contract and the other party doesn't, that fact does not create a legal presumption that the marriage should end. And it certainly doesn't imply that the person who wants to break the contract would automatically face no penalty or cost.

On the contrary, in ordinary contracts the court inquires which party, if either, was at fault. If marriage contracts were enforced in the same way as other contracts, the court would be very interested in who breached and why. The court would levy penalties on the defaulting party. Neither husband nor wife could assume that their wishes would prevail over transparent legal standards of contract compliance.

The case that inspired the so-called no-fault divorce revolution was the case in which both parties agreed the marriage should end. Advocates of the no-fault innovation argued that the state had no compelling interest in forcing loveless marriages to continue. Under the fault-based system, someone had to claim that a fault had been committed, and someone had to take the rap for having committed that fault. The rationale for the no-fault system was that this whole process was demeaning and unnecessary. If both parties agreed to the divorce, why should they be required to go through the charade of staging a phony adultery or making a false accusation of abuse?[23]

This line of argument did not fully appreciate the magnitude and scope of the changes that no-fault divorce would put into motion. No-fault advocates assumed that there were a fixed number of divorces that were likely to take place, and the state ought to reduce the cost of those divorces as much as possible. But the institution of no-fault divorce changed the calculations around the divorce decision in many different dimensions.

The number of divorces is not fixed, but can be changed by changes in incentives created by changes in public policy. No-fault treats every divorce as if it were an uncontested divorce, and sees the state's role as minimizing the costs of divorce so people can break up smoothly and cleanly and go about their lives. What is unstated is that the no-fault institution essentially removes the ability to contest the divorce. If one person wants a divorce, for any reason or no reason, they can have their divorce. They can breach the marriage contract without penalty or explanation.

That is why the term "no-fault" is misleading. The more accurate, descriptive term would be "unilateral divorce."[24] One person can unilaterally end the marriage. If the other person wants the marriage to continue, and is willing to work to keep it alive, that doesn't matter. This legal arrangement favors the person who wants to end the marriage, not the person who wants to work at keeping it together. No doubt there are still divorces that occur by mutual consent. But even among those divorces, there are probably some marriages that could have been saved with more effort and encouragement.

Imagine the impact on the economy if this type of contract were standard in the business world. It would be difficult to do business if the law of contract made no distinctions among those who kept the terms of the contract and those who did not. It would be particularly difficult to make plans involving large expenditures of capital over long periods of time, if no one were held accountable for breach.

Here is a concrete example. A building contractor engages a concrete contractor to come and pour concrete on a particular day, under particular circumstances agreed to by both parties. Both contractors have plenty of competition at the time they make their agreement. The concrete company could choose to work with other builders; the builder could choose a different concrete company. The reputation of each company is very important, because once they have made an agreement, they have much less opportunity to find a suitable competitor.

So suppose on the day scheduled to pour concrete, the builder has everything ready. All his workers are in place. The builder has done all he agreed to do. He is waiting at the site for the cement trucks to arrive. They don't show up.

When he calls, the dispatcher says, the driver didn't feel like showing up. It's a free country. He's not your slave. He doesn't have to show up. The builder is understandably angry. His workers could have been doing something else on the project besides waiting for the cement truck. He has lost a day's work. His project may be thrown off schedule.

The situation isn't much better if the builder breaches. The cement company shows up with the cement trucks filled and rolling, but the builder hasn't done what he was supposed to do, or hasn't shown up. If the concrete isn't poured at that site, the trucks have to keep rolling until they can pour it somewhere else. Turn off the rotating drums in those trucks and the concrete solidifies in place. Those trucks filled with concrete could have gone somewhere else, and done something else: very expensive, anyway you look at it.

Or the builder could show up and say, in effect, "Hey buddy, you are vulnerable right now with those trucks filled and drums rotating. How about we renegotiate the price?" In other words, the breaching party could hold out for greater benefits to himself.

The point is that once their mutual agreement progresses to a certain point, both companies are vulnerable to each other and need each other. There are not close substitutes available at reasonable cost within an appropriate amount of time. Opportunistic behavior and hold-out problems reduce the overall efficiency of the market. It would be very expensive to do business in a legal environment in which either party could breach without cost. There would be fewer buildings built, of lower quality, and at higher cost, than would otherwise be the case.

Marriage and childrearing have significant similarities with the cement company and the builder. Each party has significant competition for mates before entering into the marriage. Marriage produces a product that takes a long time and a lot of investment, namely, children. Once you've entered into the child-making and childrearing process, there aren't good substitutes for the partner you have. Social science research shows that step-parents are imperfect substitutes, at best, for the original parents. Kids usually want their birth parents and tend to be extremely loyal to them. The party that initiates divorce can extract greater resources from the other party.

In economics, a long-term contract is one tool for managing these problems. Marriage is a situation with "transaction specific capital," where at least one party has an asset that is of far more value in this particular transaction than in any other transaction. The children of the marriage are more valuable to their particular parents than to any other adults. In marriage, investments in specific capital take place over long periods of time. And the flow of "payments," implicit and explicit, between the parties is staggered over intervals. All of this adds up to a situation tailor-made for enforceable long term contracts, as a device for increasing the efficiency of producing the ultimate product, children. Reducing the permanence of the marriage contract has done exactly what an economist would expect: fewer children, lower quality, at higher cost.[25]

Long-term contracts lie midway between two extremes of relationship duration. The most immediate kind of economic relationship is one in which the entire exchange takes place at a given point in time: no staggered payments, no relationship-specific capital, and no particular expectation of a long-term relationship. This kind of market, the kind usually studied in elementary economics, is called a spot-market. You might say that the sexual revolution claimed that sexual activity could be, and ought to be, handled as if it were a spot-market.

The other end of the spectrum is that the relationship is so intimate, so enduring, and possibilities for mutual exploitation so great, that even a long-term contract is not adequate to protect all the parties. In cases like these, the market creates a different institution: the business firm. The firm brings all the transactions under one roof, so to speak. The firm internalizes many of the negotiating and decision-making costs associated with opportunistic behavior.

Instead of trying to negotiate and enforce contracts with people who could find ways to subvert the contract, the firm creates its own internal mechanisms to handle the problem. The firm has employees instead of contractors: the firm buys instead of rents. This way, the decision-making is concentrated and costs of breach can be avoided by being internalized. A successful firm is one that creates an internal culture that solves the problems of opportunistic behavior, on the job shirking, and holding-out more effectively than a comparable set of contracts could do. Successful firms have ways of building team loyalty, reducing internal friction, and minimizing opportunistic behavior by the unscrupulous. The firm has an identity, independently of its individual members.

There are two different ways this idea can apply to marriage. One way is to treat the marriage as a functioning social unit. Inside the marriage, people learn to work together to function as a team, for the good of the team and its product, children. The world outside the marriage views it for some purposes, as an entity independent of the two members. Problem-solving within the context of the team is valued as a good in itself, both by the team members and by the surrounding community. You could interpret the modern crisis of marriage as a break-down in this problem-solving ability inside marriage. Just as too much individualism inside a company can disrupt the firm's ability to operate as an economic unit, too much self-absorption inside a marriage can undermine the couple's ability to work together for the good of the family.

The other way to apply the "team production" idea of the business firm is literally to reduce the "team" to one member. If there is only one decision-maker, then by definition, there can be no conflict, no opportunism, no holding out. This is the modern direction of marriage. A family is only a woman and her children. Other parties are peripheral or superfluous. The problems of group decision-making are solved by having one person completely internalize all the costs and benefits for herself. This would be a complete "privatization" of childrearing. The mother privately "owns" the children.[26]

Of these possible models for marriage, which is the most in harmony with the realities of childrearing? Which is most consistent with maximizing personal liberty, broadly understood, to include reasonable provision for the unique features of raising children? The "spot market" model of marriage fails the reality test. Marriage has too many long-term features that have to be accommodated. The complete privatization model fails as well. It does not give due weight to the fact that making babies takes two people, genetically for sure, and socially and morally as well. Social science has demonstrated that children need their father. Fairness and common sense demand that fathers be given some participation rights in the upbringing of their children. There is nothing humane about treating men as if they were nothing but sperm banks or wallets.

Either the long-term contract view of marriage or the "team production" view of marriage is more in harmony with the biological and social facts about the bearing and rearing of children. I have argued elsewhere for the superiority of the team view over the contract view, and I will not repeat those arguments here. But neither of these views of marriage is consistent with a legal regime of unilateral divorce. Far from supporting the current regime, economic analysis suggests that the no-fault divorce is the least efficient and the least likely to make people happy.

IV. WHY WOMEN CHOOSE DIVORCE

It is a little known, but well-established fact that most divorces are initiated by women. This has been true through most of American history. The proportion of divorce cases filed by wives ranged from around 60 percent for most of the nineteenth century to more than 70 percent in some states immediately after the introduction of no-fault divorce. The percentage seems to have stabilized around two-thirds.[27] In the 1998 book, *Divorced Dads*, Sanford Braver cites numerous studies conducted in the 1990s, showing that women initiate about two-thirds of divorces. These studies focused on couples with children still at home.[28] More recently, the American Association of Retired Persons conducted a study of divorce among people over forty. They also found that women initiated about 60 percent of the divorces.[29] If we hope to lower the divorce rate, we have to deal with women.

Alexis de Tocqueville observed that the women of America were the guardians of its morals, and therefore in a certain sense of democracy. He attributed this, in part, to the American appreciation of marriage:

"Religion reigns supreme in the souls of women and it is women who shape mores. Certainly of all countries in the world, America is the one in which the marriage tie is most respected and where the highest and truest conception of conjugal happiness has been conceived."[30]

We must address both public policies and the social climate that steer women toward divorce. Are there public policies that seem to encourage women to choose divorce? And we need to address the dreams and aspirations of women that also encourage them to believe that divorce is a solution to their problems, or a step toward larger goals. I believe it is possible to make substantial progress both on the public policy front and in the realm of personal goals and desires.

The Red Herring: Domestic Violence

What are some possible reasons that women choose divorce? First, let's rule out the obvious: domestic violence. Some feminists claim that women need the option of divorce at will as a protection against domestics violence. These feminists resist any change in divorce law that reduces the likelihood of divorce or increases the costs of divorce, arguing that women will be trapped in abusive relationships.

The domestic violence argument is a red herring for several reasons. First, studies that examine the factors that contributed to divorce consistently find domestic violence to be a factor in only a small percentage of divorces. Braver's study, referenced above, finds domestic violence ranked sixteenth in order of importance as a reason women cited for divorce. Only 20 percent of those women divorcing said that domestic violence was "very important" as a factor contributing to divorce.[31] Another study examined records for divorcing couples in Virginia. A mere 6 percent of those actually getting divorced even mentioned violence as a contributing cause.[32] We conclude that the vast majority of divorces have little or nothing to do with domestic violence.

The second reason domestic violence is a red herring is that violence has always been considered a legitimate cause for divorce. The feminists want us to forget that under the fault-based divorce systems of previous generations, people could get divorced for cause. Physical abuse counted as a cause. In other words, you could always get divorced for cause, namely for abuse, even during the darkest days of the Eisenhower Administration. Placing reasonable restrictions on the divorce process will not presumably change this basic practice.

Finally, domestic violence is a red herring because marriage is the safest context for sexual activity. For most women, the alternative to marriage is to be sexually active with someone to whom they are not married. Cohabitation is the most likely alternative to marriage. But a woman is much less likely to be abused by a man to whom she is married, than by a man she is merely living with.[33] Denigrating marriage increases the likelihood of women choosing cohabitation, which is much more dangerous than marriage.

With the red herring of domestic violence out of the way, let us consider some other possible explanations for why women choose to end their marriages. As we do so, we must keep in mind that many different explanations can possibly be true, even for a particular person. We need not discover the One True Reason women initiate divorces. Rather, we need to be looking for a series of plausible reasons that can account for large numbers of divorces. If we can isolate a few important causes and work to reduce the frequency of those causes, we may be able to make substantial progress in reducing the divorce rate. We should look both for public policies that can be changed by government and for changes in social and cultural expectations that all of us could participate in bringing about.

Sole Custody: Changing the Costs and Benefits of Divorce.

One possible explanation has to do with custody rules. The most important asset of most marriages is the children. Unlike financial capital which can be easily divided between the parties, the ability to divide up the kids is obviously limited. A high probability of the woman obtaining sole custody of the children is correlated with an increased probability of women initiating the divorce. The woman can have the enjoyment of her children, and possibly some financial support from the father, while reducing the difficulty of negotiating with their father over the children's care. To see the point more clearly, ask yourself this: suppose a woman knew with certainty that her husband would have sole custody of the children after divorce. That would certainly decrease the probability that she would initiate an end to the marriage. According to one study, switching the award of custody from the mother to the father would decrease the probability that the mother files for divorce by about half.[34] The public policy implication of these findings is that changes in custody rules may be a mechanism for reducing the probability of women choosing divorce. Even if "no-fault" rules continue in force, making the custody outcome more uncertain would change the calculations surrounding the decision to stay married or try to work on the relationship.

Psychological and Physiological Factors

There may be other reasons women initiate divorce more often than men, a set of possible explanations that have nothing to do with public policy. It is a stereotype that women are more concerned with relationships and relationship quality than are men. If this common image is true, then it stands to reason that women would be more distressed when the relationship goes sour. Greater distress over something that matters a lot might very well lead women to try and remove themselves from the troubling situation. If this hypothesis is true, it would explain the observation that women's higher propensity to file for divorce pre-dates changes in divorce law that allowed no-fault. The problem, then, of women-initiated divorce will be less amenable to public policy changes. We would have to focus much more attention on the cultural and social pressures that support women in choosing either divorce or continued marriage.

There is very provocative evidence that women actually are more distressed by arguments and disagreements within marriage. A group of researchers at the Ohio State University studied ninety newly-married couples who described themselves as happy. The researchers from the departments of psychiatry, medical microbiology, and immunology, psychology, and medicine, checked the couples into a hospital research unit for a twenty-four-hour stay. The researchers essentially provoked the couples to quarrel under controlled conditions and took observations on their behavior and their stress hormone levels.[35] Here are some of the findings.

First, negative or hostile behaviors such as sarcasm or put-downs, increased the levels of stress hormones. No surprise. However, they also found variations in the amount of increase in stress hormones, and in the persistence of those hormones after the quarrel or negative inter-action. Women, on average, showed a greater physiological change in response to the quarrel than men. Moreover, women were more likely to have elevated levels of stress hormones throughout the day, and even the next morning. Finally, the researchers found that these increases in stress hormone levels were a good predictor of divorce ten years later. Although the literature suggests that negative behavior would be a good predictor of divorce, the researchers found that the hormone levels that are partially a response to negative behavior actually predicted divorce better than the behavior itself.

These physiological findings support the observation that women do get more upset about relationship problems than do men. Women hold onto their stress longer, and probably rehearse their quarrels and grievances. The researchers actually found that women have elevated stress hormones even the morning after a fight.[36]

This may be why a wife gets up in the morning with a new round of complaints and arguments, while the husband gets up and wonders what's for breakfast. We women add insult to injury by blaming the men for being insensitive and clueless. But it might sometimes be more accurate to say that we are being overly sensitive. Sometimes our husbands are doing the relationship a favor by changing the subject or dropping a quarrel. Not every argument is worth winning, or even pursuing.

The culture can play a major role in this area by helping couples find the will to stay married. Women have been taught by the feminist movement, and by the culture as a whole, that self-assertion is the key to high self-esteem, and that self-esteem, in turn, is the key to happiness. But this is not necessarily true. If your self-esteem depends on always prevailing in a quarrel, or on always getting your own way, then your self-esteem will always be fragile.

Women have been taught to bear all kinds of costs for the sake of education, career, and professional status. We delay all kinds of gratification to get our degrees and keep our high-status jobs. Not only do we work hard and forgo immediate pleasure, we sometimes sacrifice the opportunity to get married, or postpone childbearing, or leave the kids in daycare far more than we really want to. If we are willing to bear those costs for the sake of economic status, why should we be ashamed to bear some costs for the sake of getting married and staying married?

CONCLUSION

One urgent business for the culture of life-long marriage is that women need new dreams. Marriage needs to seem like more than a drudgery. Give women different dreams and aspirations, so that life-long marriage seems to her a worthwhile goal in itself, rather than something that is instrumental to other goals like career and children. Instead of seeing each quarrel as an occasion for self-assertion, we could see managing the stress as a source of pride. Women need to stop seeing marriage as dispensable and men as disposable.

Life-long love is an adventure, not for the faint-hearted. We enter into our married lives without knowing for certain how it will turn out. We may have every prospect of living happily with our mate for a lifetime, and something could happen entirely beyond our control. Someone could become seriously ill, or injured. One of us could choose to do serious wrong. We might have major disappointments with our careers, communities, or children. Sustaining our love for each other under these circumstances will require every ounce of our strength, all of our talents and all of our stamina. And yet it is intrinsically worth doing. Men and women alike have a way of rising to the challenge of a difficulty worth bearing. We need once again to instill a sense of the value of our marriage vows. That is a goal to which everyone can contribute, with or without the assistance of government.

5

The Framers' Idea
of Marriage and Family

David F. Forte

I

LEO TOLSTOY begins the story of his fated *Anna Karenina* by declaring, "Happy families are all alike; every unhappy family is unhappy in its own way."

Tolstoy may have it backwards. If we listen to the conversation of two happily married women, for example, we hear pictures of drastically different families. Each one has its own set of unique individuals with particular interactions, gifts, problems, failures, and triumphs. One has a son who is gifted in hockey (though getting him to study is a chore). Another has a daughter who has a learning disability (but they have found a school that seems to be helping her). One has a husband who is out of work (but a new opportunity seems around the corner). Another has an aunt who has just died from cancer (though she was beloved by all). One is pregnant (with her fourth child). The other hopes to take her family on a cruise (but offers to help until baby arrives).

And so it goes. Quarrels, reconciliations, jokes, tears, intimacy and distance, too many tasks, too little time, the need for prayer, the worries over money, the parties, illness, the new driver's license, the leak in the basement, the new plantings, the car repair bill. Each "happy" family is a texture of problems and solutions, opportunities taken and wasted, sickness and recovery, points of joy and spikes of frustrations. It is not, in the unrealizable image of many, effortless bliss.

So, you might say, is every unhappy family. What is the difference? Clearly, the difference is that the happy family has developed complex interactive mechanisms to resolve conflicts and nurture the growth of each individual within the family. The unhappy family is unable to cope with the very same dissonances; it draws down the individuality of each member in the unsuccessful attempt to contain the conflicts, and often breaks under the stress of irresolution.

The question, therefore, is how the "happy" family comes to be. In talking about a happy or unhappy family, we can begin by determining just what we mean by "happiness." For Tolstoy, it was harmony, the leisure to enjoy the higher pleasures, undoubtedly including an efficient and complaisant set of servants, a comfortable dwelling, a passionate cathexis of body and soul, and an existential connection with the deepest movements of being.

It was thoroughly Romantic—and necessarily tragic.

Tolstoy was right about one central element of happiness, however. It is experienced. False is the old saw, "Happiness is not experienced, but remembered." Happiness remembered is at worst, mere nostalgia, at best, gratitude. It either case, it is a memory of what was a real experience. The experience of living in a happy family is in the doing of the tasks, among people who are emotionally, socially, and legally bonded in a singular enterprise, every member of which is needed for its success. Families are as much about "doing" as "being."

The wise lights of the founding of the American polity understood the necessary connection between the successful enterprise of the family and the successful enterprise of a free and representative republic. In the midst of the dark days of the Revolution, John Adams wrote, "The foundation of national morality must be laid in private families."[1] That grounding of national morality was crucial for Adams, for he could not conceive of a free republic without "public virtue." As he wrote in a letter to Mercy Warren shortly before independence was declared, "public virtue is the only Foundation of Republics. *There must be a positive Passion for the public good, the public Interest, Honour, Power and Glory, established in the Minds of the People, or there can be no Republican Government, nor any real Liberty: and this public Passion must be Superiour to all private Passions.* Men must be ready, they must pride themselves, and be happy to sacrifice their private Pleasures, Passions and Interests, nay, their private Friendships and dearest Connections, when they stand in Competition with the Rights of Society."[2] The bridge from reining in "private passions" to producing a "positive passion for the public good" was the family's inculcation of public virtue.

Yet the Framers did not speak extensively about the family, except in personal letters, in which men like Washington, Adams, and Marshall spoke of the deepest gratitude for their domestic life. There is no allusion to marriage or family in the Constitution. It is barely mentioned in the Federalist Papers or elsewhere in the ratification debates. The reason why the founders "ignored" the family was that it was not an issue for them. It was not a social problem. On the contrary, the family was the accepted substratum of society. It was the basis of the economy, centered on the labor intensive farming enterprise, producing large amounts of offspring (which, along with immigration, the framers regarded as absolutely necessary for the future of the country), bonded vertically and horizontally with relations and religious communities.[3]

Today, with the family beset on all sides, hundreds of books like this one describe or defend it (while many others that attack it). But to the men and women of that generation, the family was a given: its structure, its stability, roles, and values accepted by all. The Constitution was a plan of government, not concerned with the independent government over individuals that was the family. The national government had no jurisdiction over families, and the state governments gave them legal protection.

More significantly, the founders believed the family was the source of the kinds of individuals that could be entrusted with the maintenance of a free republic. The question was not what should be done with the family, but whether the government would be able to reap the benefits of the already existing family structure in order to prosper.

The founders were a mixed lot, driven by passionate differences, mutual suspicions, and strong personalities.[4] What united them was a principled practicality. It is that which moved them to form a nation and its remarkable constitution. None of the founders romanticized the family. Few if any recognized its sacramental character. What they saw in the family, as they saw in religion, was the necessary formation of character, the inculcation of virtue without which a free republic had not the slightest chance to survive, let alone prosper.

The founders understood the symbiotic connection between family virtues and civic virtues. They knew it through their study of the classics, through their imbibing of the Scottish enlightenment, through their understanding of the providential nature of the Judeo-Christian God, through their familiarity with self-governing liberty, and through their utter respect of their own human experience of living. They looked upon the family as a model in which man's selfish impulses would be contained, where the coordination of practical tasks could be effectuated, and where sentiments of affection and mutual respect could bind a people into a nation. It was the school of the family (and its religion) that taught those virtues.

II

To trace the symbiotic connection between family virtues and civic virtue, we should touch upon those sources that the framers of the republic themselves drew upon to understand what in the family was necessary to accomplish the risky venture of a free republic. To speak of the connection between "happy" families and a healthy civic culture, we should start with the Greeks who were the first to think seriously of the connection between virtue and a healthy polity.

Being men of affairs (and the wiser for it), none of the founders wrote philosophical commentaries, though they were certainly familiar with the great thinkers. They were practical Aristotelians, and were distant from neo-Platonism that inspired the French Revolution (and, not incidentally, the French Revolution's overt war upon the family).

The founders knew, as did Aristotle, that man desires above all to be happy. According to Aristotle, happiness is not a sensation. Rather, happiness attends a being when it reaches the full actualization of its potentialities, when it reaches the final end (*telos*) of its movement through time. In other words, happiness comes to a being when it "perfects" that which was only partially realized (to which the framers of the Constitution averred, when they sought a "more perfect Union").

Aristotle taught that the "perfection" of man lies in his living well, that is, in his practice of the virtues: "But honor, pleasure, reason, and every virtue we choose indeed for themselves, but we choose them also for the sake of happiness, judging that by means of them we shall be happy."[5] Aristotle's definition of virtue can be summarized as "the habit of acting rightly."[6] The good life, the happy life, is kinetic. It is a life of reflective action.

Thus, when the framers in the Declaration of Independence spoke of the "pursuit of Happiness" as an inalienable right, they were speaking of what is required for a person to become fully human, to perfect his nature, and thereby experience a well-lived (a happy) life. It is the active practice of the virtues. George Washington said it in words that could have been Aristotle's: "[T]here is no truth more thoroughly established that there exists in the economy and course of nature, an indissoluble union between virtue and happiness."[7] It is not an etymological coincidence that "ethics" (*ethos*) in Greek means "character."

According to Aristotle, then, one cannot find one's perfection in the practice of virtue except in a healthy polity, and he directly bases a healthy polity upon healthy family life. In his *Politics* and his *Ethics*, Aristotle declares that the polity (*polis*) is the highest form of community, but that the *polis* is made up from the relationships among families. In fact, Aristotle argues that the *polis* finds its origin in the family. Aristotle sees the family as a communal enterprise made up of individuals whose relationships are grounded in nature: husband to wife, parents to children, master to slave. The life of the family was made up of relationships and tasks, and the latter is the cause of Aristotle's belief that slaves had to be a necessary element of the household.[8]

The relationship of master to slave was a form of despotism; that of parent to child was a form of monarchy; but that of husband and wife was friendship (*philia*). Although the passions of nature (*eros*) drew man and woman together for the purpose of reproduction, the virtue of friendship (*philia*) transcends the erotic. Though man and woman are unequal in nature (Aristotle presumes that only the man can hold "office," that is, possess a policy-making function for those under his authority and in his care), in the friendship of marriage and in their growth in the practice of virtue, they become free and equal in their humanity.[9]

The *philia* of husband and wife is precisely that *philia* necessary for the *polis* to exist. Aristotle declares that the reason why the barbarians do not posses a *polis* (but rather a tyranny) is that they possess imperfect families, where the wife is a slave (not the friend) of the husband. Aristotle regards the relationship between the family and political society in the same way the founders of the American republic did: the larger political community is based upon the smaller.

Christianity promised an even higher relationship between husbands and wives and parents and children. The highest form of love, *agape*, or self-sacrificing love, was brought into the Greek language through the Septuagint, and became the core of Christian belief of the relationship of God to man in Christ's redemptive sacrifice. In the Christian family, parents understood their relationship to their children as *agape*, as they understood their sacramental relationship to one another. Further, the essential equality of man and woman (transcending their familial roles and physiological differences) came through the development of marriage as a sacrament, wherein each spouse gives to the other the sacrament and the vow, and to be valid, it must be entirely and freely given.[10] Combining freely given consent with a spiritual component, marriage was, in form, the highest form of friendship. But the early Church writers disparaged the sexual aspects of marriage, thereby denying the most intimate expression and experience of marital *philia*. That error was not to be authoritatively corrected until the modern papacy. Furthermore, customs and social mores influenced (or distorted) "Christian" marriage. Commonly in Christian society, there were arranged marriages, the "sale" of the daughter by the father to the groom, the acceptability of physical chastisement, and child abandonment.

Nonetheless, by the time we arrive at the eighteenth century and the time of the founders, marriage and the family came to look very much as Aristotle had pictured it. In the previous centuries, Lutheran reforms had lodged marriage into the civil structure of society and made it more a concern of civil law,[11] but, joined by Calvin, Protestantism retained parental control over the right of children to marry. John Locke, however, saw marriage as contracted political society, and thus his image of the family as a commonwealth made up of combined individuals parallel his image of the formation of the larger political commonwealth as well.[12] Furthermore, Locke declares that parents are, "by the law of nature, under an obligation to preserve, nourish and educate" their children.[13] Since government is instituted to enforce the laws of nature, Locke states that government should make laws that enforce "the security of the marriage bed."[14]

What Americans of the late eighteenth century did was to synthesize the notion of marriage as a freely entered political institution, being an organic part of the larger political society, with a Christian notion of its interior life. This gave the institution of marriage and the family more power, authority, and inner strength than at any time in history of the West. Most marriages in the latter half of the eighteenth century were not formally arranged, but (even taking into account inevitable family pressures) were freely entered into by the spouses.[15] With the demise of slavery in most households over time (even in the South few slaves could accurately be said to be part of the "household"), the tasks of the family fell to the parents and the children, and the integration among them grew even more close than in Aristotle's time because all were involved in making sure that the joint venture of family succeeded. Indications are that nuclear families grew in loyalty and intimacy in

America during the late seventeenth and late eighteenth centuries. True, Protestantism had jettisoned the "sacramental" equality of the two spouses, but the contractual equality that was worked out in the day-to-day tasks of the family was even stronger. Nevertheless, the legal personality of the family resided in the husband alone, as the married woman became, under the law, *femme covert*, and lost control over her property. In sum, the founders' experience of the family mirrored its classical description.

III

Beyond the distant influence of the ancients, however, there were two other significant intellectual influences on how the founders perceived the family as the source of the kind of virtue that would sustain a free republic: the inheritance of the Scottish enlightenment and a Protestant notion of the role of a providential God.

Excepting Montesquieu (who praised the English), the founders had little affinity to the Enlightenment of the European continent. Their ideas and experience found more congruence in the ideas of David Hume, Francis Hutcheson, Adam Smith, and John Locke, even in the face of significant disagreements among and within that tradition. The connection between each of these thinkers and the various members of the founding generation would take more than a monograph apiece even to explicate, but I trust the reader will permit me to summarize the fundamental principles the founders drew from that philosophical tradition: utility, sentiment, and voluntary association.

Hume established utility as a fundamental standard of human action.[16] He grounded the virtue of justice, for example, in the need for a practical solution to human life in a world of scarce resources and imperfect persons. "Reverse, in any considerable circumstance, the condition of men: Produce extreme abundance or extreme necessity: Implant in the human breast perfect moderation and humanity, or perfect rapaciousness and malice: By rendering justice totally *useless*, you thereby totally destroy its essence, and suspend its obligation upon mankind."[17] Hume declared that the conventions of positive law were the only basis on which to allocate resources and resolve differences peacefully.

Hume's position was congenial to the American colonists' political and economic experiences. Through the economic, religious, and political conflicts of the seventeenth century, the American colonists had come to appreciate the practical mechanisms for adjusting (primarily through English law and local assemblies) the inevitable differences among the populations of each colony. Despite the frontier, land remained a scarce resource, engendering perpetual conflicts between creditors and debtors. Mistrust and friction among religious sects was a constant. Ultimately, Americans drew upon the principles of justice in English positive law to mediate their differences and create stable societies.

Through Hume, but more particularly though Hutcheson and Smith, Americans also understood the experience of moral coordination among persons and groups through the sentiments of sympathy and benevolence. As Adam Smith puts it in the start of his *Theory of Moral Sentiments*, "How selfish soever man may be supposed, there are evidently some principles in his nature, which interest him in the fortune of others, and render their happiness necessary to him, though he derives nothing from it, except the pleasure of seeing it."[18]

Americans lived that sentiment in the intersection of familial and religious communities that they developed in the New World. Communities created mechanisms for mutual assistance. More importantly, Americans found the sentiment of justice, that is, a shared sense of right and wrong (Smith's "impartial spectator") articulated through family mores and, outside of the family, through the legal system. The social mechanism was again the shared experience of the English common law, through which Americans resolved the conflicts between individuals, families, and groups with opposing property interests. The very litigiousness of the colonists evidenced a shared sentiment of mutual restraint under the rule of law.

Finally, to the Americans, not only did John Locke's views on the family articulate their own evolving sense of the institution, but his seminal work on politics exemplified the colonists' understanding of self-government through voluntary association as a natural right. In eighteenth century English law, "liberty" was a legal term of art. It did not mean the unhampered autonomy of the individual. On the contrary, when the King granted charters to corporations or colonies guaranteeing, among other things, their "liberties," it was a grant of self-government to the voluntary association.

A marriage, therefore, was a voluntary association of a man and woman, who contracted in liberty to create the independent legal and civic entity of the family. This resulted in an ongoing enterprise, in which all parties learned the practical arts or virtues of living together, bound together with sentiments of mutual assistance, for the purpose of survival and prosperity of the venture.

It would be remiss of me, however, having mentioned Montesquieu by the by, not to give his place among the founders due credit. Montesquieu wrote that different forms of government have underlying principles that govern how the ruled interact with the rulers. For instance, the underlying principle that governs despotism is fear. There the governed follow instructions and laws out of fear of what will happen if they do not obey their despot.[19] However, when the form of government is a republic, the underlying principle is virtue where the people live truthfulness, fidelity, frugality, and other civic virtues. More pertinent to our inquiry, Montesquieu declared that educating individuals in the public virtue necessary to maintain a republic had to come from the family.[20] Montesquieu insisted that for a republic to survive, it must foster a particular kind of republican virtue, which the Anti-Federalists insisted could only be had in small independent republics. Thus, the debate over the Constitution centered on whether the new government would, by its size and power, corrupt the body politic, or whether, as Madison argued in *The Federalist*, Number 10, the extensive republic would in fact, frustrate passions and allow public virtue to have its way. Both the Anti-Federalists and the Federalists relied upon the family as a school of virtue. Their difference was over what form of government would build upon those virtues and what form would contrive to frustrate and corrupt them.

IV

A third primary intellectual source of the founders' sense of the role of the family in a free republic lay in eighteenth-century American Protestantism. American Protestantism was in no sense univocal, but it nonetheless defined man's relationship to God and the relationship between men.

A constant theme was the notion of a providential God. This was the God who, in his great act of creation, brings order out of chaos.[21] This was the Creator who endows men with "certain inalienable rights."[22] This was, in Washington's words, "that Almighty Being who rules over the universe, who presides in the councils of nations; and whose providential aid can supply every human defect."[23] This was the God whose mercies one can only strive to be worthy of. "The propitious smiles of heaven can never be expected on a nation that disregards the eternal rules of right and order, which heaven itself has ordained." The task of ordering the handiwork of God was entrusted to man. And it was the beneficent ordering of human relationships out of the ever-imminent chaos of self-regarding passions that was the family's task.

A further insight of American Protestantism was the religiously based obligation to respect human freedom. As Madison wrote in his famous *Remonstrance,*

> Religion or the duty which we owe to our Creator and the manner of discharging it, can be directed only by reason and conviction, not by force or violence. The Religion then of every man must be left to the conviction and conscience of every man; and it is the right of every man to exercise it as these may dictate. . . . It is the duty of every man to render to the Creator such homage and such only as he believes to be acceptable to him. This duty is precedent, both in order of time and in degree of obligation, to the claims of Civil Society. Before any man can be considered as a member of Civil Society, he must be considered as a subject of the Governour of the Universe: And if member of Civil Society, who enters into any subordinate Association must always do it with a reservation

of his duty to the General Authority; much more must every man who becomes a member of any particular Civil Society, do it with a saving of his allegiance to the Universal Sovereign.[24]

That liberty is manifest in the freedom of each person to decide with whom he or she shall create a marriage and family. But much more important and directly relevant to the family was the affirmation of the limited role of government in the lives of the people.

Unlike the French notion of democracy as "the will of the people," the American standard is the "consent of the governed." Just as even accepting one's relationship to the Supreme God can only be done by free consent, the standard affirms that "the governed" had a life outside of politics, and that the government could only enter into that life with the consent of the people. The very ratification process of the Constitution affirmed the principle.

Combining with the colonists' tradition of self-government, their rights under their colonial charters, their privileges under the common law, their understanding of natural law, and the Lockean principles of the social compact, the religious sense of liberty compelled that the only legitimate government was a limited government. The family was an independent entity that did not gain its legitimacy from the government. The fundamental notion of limited government allows the most local government, the family, to govern itself, in co-ordination with other families in local communities.

Lastly, American Protestantism affirmed that man was not perfectible. Perfect men do not need to be trained in the virtues. Only imperfect men need learned character. The Protestant notion of original sin, usually translated in eighteenth-century language as the self-regarding passions, meant that without the training given by families and religion, the darker sides of our human natures would have free rein. Self-government meant not only the right to enter into voluntarily associations with others, it also meant the duty to govern oneself.

The founders were, however, practical realists. The family was a necessary but not sufficient condition for a free republic. As fine an institution as the family was for the inculcation of civic virtues, it possessed a kind of Westphalian sovereignty. The family (headed by the husband) ruled itself, and it recognized in other families the right to rule themselves. But in the experienced independence of the family, those who were not of the family were outsiders. They could be joined together in an alliance for common interests, and that alliance could be turned against other alliances as well. This was the source of the framers' dread of "factions," which Madison defined as "a number of citizens, whether amounting to a majority or minority of the whole, who are united and actuated by some common impulse of passion, or of interest, adverse to the rights of other citizens or to the permanent or aggregate interests of the community."[25]

A family might inculcate the necessary civic virtues, but each person remained free to choose his path. He may still give in, even occasionally, to the self-regarding passions. The framers understood that the nature of man was thus permanently mixed. They were no social engineers, as the French in their revolution tried to be. But the framers were political craftsmen. It was in their ken to create a political structure that gave free opportunity for the virtues to flourish and not one that would corrupt the citizens into destructive self-regarding behavior. In consequence of the hard lessons of experience, the framers crafted the entire complex and nuanced mechanisms of separation of powers, separated sovereignties, and limited government, to frustrate the self-regarding designs of men, leaving them open to practice of virtues of cooperation, honest dealings, and the sentiment of attachment to the whole, virtues that they were trained in by their families.

V

What are the civic virtues that the framers expected that the family would impart? A modern observer catalogues what virtues are necessary in men and women for a free republic to succeed: courage, loyalty, law-abidingness, fidelity, personal responsibility, self-restraint, tolerance, adaptability, leadership, duty, craft.[26] After averting to a "degree of depravity in mankind," Madison averred that "there are other qualities in human nature which justify a certain portion of esteem and confidence. Republican government presupposes the existence of these qualities in a higher degree than any other form."[27]

Perhaps the man who most incarnated these virtues was George Washington. In his prayer to the Almighty, Washington begged for those virtues for himself and his countrymen.

> And also, that we may then unite in most humbly offering our prayers and supplications to the great Lord and Ruler of Nations and beseech Him to pardon our national and other transgressions;-- to enable us all, whether in publick or private stations, to perform our several and relative duties properly and punctually; to render our National Government a blessing to all the people by constantly being a Government of wise, just, and constitutional laws, discreetly and faithfully executed and obeyed; to protect and guide all sovereigns and nations (especially such as have shewn kindness unto us); and to bless them with good governments, peace, and concord; to promote the knowledge and practice of true religion and virtue, and the increase of science among them and us; and, generally to grant unto all mankind such a degree of temporal prosperity as he alone knows to be best.[28]

It is obvious that without these virtues, a society will tip towards chaos. The reason that well-functioning families are so successful for forming persons possessing such virtues is that a family does create order out of chaos. The fact is that men and women are different, that parents and children are different, that each person has an independent personality, that each has self-regarding desires, and that they are all placed under one roof with the vow of fidelity, constancy, peace, and mutual assistance. It is an extraordinary institution that can accomplish that. As Allan Carlson describes it,

> Marriage, in turn, creates a new household. When gathered together, these form the second institutional tier in natural social life and the one on which all political life is built. The household will

normally encompass the wedded man and woman, their children, and aged or unmarried kin. Successful households are the natural reservoir of liberty. They aim at autonomy or independence, enabling their members to resist oppression, survive economic, social, and political turbulence, and renew the world after troubles have passed. Complete households have the power to shelter, feed, clothe, and protect their members in the absence of both state and corporate largesse. Such independence from outside agency is the true mark of liberty, making possible in turn the self-government of communities.[29]

The daily life of the family has strains, conflicts, and pressures. And every day, the family resolves those strains, conflicts, and pressures. The family is the most important conflict-resolution mechanism in all of society. As a phenomenological matter, the daily life of the family consists in the resolution of conflict. Within the well-functioning family, the child learns the rules of justice, the nature of authority, trust and reliance; he learns the techniques of negotiation, the constraints on sexuality, the adjustment of desires, the making of choices within scarcity, the meaning of sacrifice, and the healing that comes from forgiveness. From these accomplishments come persons of character.

The pressures and attacks on the family are well documented. The social disruptions and personal hurts to those who grow up outside of a stable marriage are equally well documented. But there are signs that character forming marriage and family is growing in strength, at least among those who do wed. Two million children are now schooled at home. There are growing numbers of educated mothers, in particular, who stay home with their children. In many parts of the country, whole neighborhoods are filled with children living with intact families. The sense of intimate friendship between husband and wife is now a central part of marriage. Among middle class and working class parents, civic culture is growing. Nearly every day or night in every suburb, parents are coaching sports, attending recitals or plays, going to church, volunteering with the Scouts, or assisting teachers at schools. While there is much to be concerned over, particularly in the short term, there is also much in the longer term to give us hope.

Marriage is not idyllic, and because it is not idyllic, some think traditional marriage and the family are a failure. But marriage and the family are successful precisely because they are not idyllic, as human existence is not idyllic. And to those who resolve conflicts and overcome differences with love, to those who nurture each other and console those who suffer, the family can produce not just character, but joy.

6

The Family and the Laws

Hadley Arkes

O NE DEPENDABLE CONSTANT IN POLITICAL LIFE is the search for that low door under the wall, the path that allows one gently to evade a pressing question of consequence, rather than facing it. In the discontents of our current political season, and the controversy over same-sex marriage, that tendency has expressed itself in the musing, more and more heard, that we might have evaded this whole problem if marriage were treated wholly as a civil affair. From what I can gather, the sense of the matter here is that the solemnity and seriousness of marriage, as a one-flesh union, pervaded with moral significance, touching on a franchise of acting with God as the co-creators of life—that this deeper sense of marriage might be preserved more readily by drawing marriage into the realm of religion and religious ceremonies. We would leave then to the civil sphere, the sphere of the law, the rather shriveled sense of marriage that is left, marriage purged of its religious and moral significance. The meaning of marriage may be diminished and disparaged, but that breakdown in the understanding and practice of marriage might be walled off and separated from another life. Sheltered behind that wall may be that other kind of life, cultivated with what remains of the moral tradition. Once again, it may be "the garden and the wilderness": In that famous line from Roger Williams, the separation of religion from politics was a demarcation meant to preserve the cultivation of the religious life from the more sordid plays of politics, even a political life directed to decent ends.[1]

I suppose we could conceive a variant here: Behind certain gentle walls, marking off boundaries, we may find a life cultivated with a persistent awareness of the moral significance that must attach to marriage, as well as every other part of our lives, including many prosaic things, like picking up one's children from their school. (As Maggie Gallagher once put it, for a married couple still in love, figuring out how to pay tuition bill in college may be an erotic experience. For a divorced husband, the tuition bills rather looks like a tax increase.) Outside those walls of traditional marriage, we may find the wreckage in a world that virtually prides itself on removing all vestiges of moral requirements and moral meanings from all roles and institutions—from the meaning of law itself, as Holmes once notoriously suggested—from the polity then, the entity marked by the presence of law; from citizenship (when citizenship loses any sense of a necessary moral commitment to a way of life regarded as rightful); from sexuality when sexuality has no natural telos, no moral end, no moral constraints; from parenthood, when procreation is detached from any necessary sense of an enduring love and commitment; and of course from the understanding of "marriage," which depends on them all. There will no doubt be the occasional flowers flourishing, as human goodness has a way of breaking through even the most desolate landscape. But the contrast between the two domains would nevertheless be clear, at once, to anyone who casts an eye upon the scene.

I may be overstating the matter with this metaphor, and so I should say that the point, stated with more sobriety, would run in this way: The laws have made provision for clergymen to "solemnize" weddings, and that is done by combining a religious ceremony with the stamp of the law. But if clergymen function in this way, as agents of the state, it may be demanded, with a short, plausible step, that they should be prepared to extend their own benedictions and preside over any marriage authorized in the law. Surely, as agents of the state, they could not engage in a discrimination, in marriage, that the state itself could not be permitted to practice when acting on its own, with its own accredited agents. In that way, the new policies on same-sex marriage will be transfused into the practice of clergymen. And, step by step, those policies will be folded into the doctrines of their churches, as the churches, in a liberal spirit, open themselves to this new teaching of the law. With this reading of the political situation—a reading, I confess, that is quite plausible—the receding of the churches from these arrangements may be the only hope of preserving, for the churches, a certain freedom to honor the integrity of their own teachings. This construction, as I say, would be quite plausible, but my own estimate is that it merely puts off the demands, the confrontation, and the eventual, predictable compliance, for another day. Once the "right" to marry a person of the same sex is installed as nothing less than a constitutional right, there will be the most formidable pressure to extend that norm to every religion that claims standing under the law as a legitimate religion.

It may but be another mark of the age that we could even conceive, for a moment, that the institution of marriage could be insulated in that way from any attachment to the laws, or to the polity marked by those laws. And yet, it may be no more illusory than the notion, still widely harbored, that a religious life could be lived with integrity even if it is undercut by the laws in its moral teaching, or removed from the minimal protections that may be afforded even in the most minimalist regime of the law. It was not for nothing that we were warned, even by the early Fathers in the Church, to respect the sword of the law. Those who speak so blithely, or speak with a certain despair, about detaching marriage from the civil law seem to forget that the problem of marriage and the laws was quite as pressing, and quite as central, in the pagan life of ancient Greece—among the most thoughtful pagans, we might say—even before the advent of Christianity. Nor is the problem likely to fade, as a problem, even if the modern project in our politics manages to make religion as peripheral in this country as it has become now in parts of Europe.

We seem to forget that the problem of marriage has been bound up with the laws from the very time that there *have been* laws. From the Mosaic laws to the laws of ancient Greece and Rome, the laws have had something emphatic to say on the subject. We may cloud over the matter these days with rather hazy talk about privacy, but the passion that has arisen over the subject in our own time may merely confirm the classic sense of the matter, running back to Jerusalem and Athens. It has become clear that, for the party of the left in our politics, *Roe v. Wade* has become the central thread. It is the mark of sexual liberation; and to switch the figure, it has been taken as the touchstone in the new liberal jurisprudence. The "right to abortion," or the rightful freedom to order up abortion, has taken the place of religious freedom as the "first freedom," among a large portion now of our political class and the constituency they have come to represent. For a certain, large portion of our people, the "right to abortion," the right to contraception, the right to new varieties of sexual orientation unencumbered by the disapproval of the law—these rights have become, far more surely, the cornerstone of that personal freedom that the Constitution was meant to protect.

We have here the central idea from which everything else radiates, and as it works out its logic there is a passion to remove, to sweep away, the legal and moral restraints from sexuality. But in a deep irony, the partisans of this new regime echo or confirm the understanding of our ancient forebears, for they too have come to see the relation of the laws to sexuality as utterly central, and even preeminent in its importance, in defining the character of the regime. In that respect, there is no radical break from the pre-modern understanding: Our forbears too thought that sexuality bore an import that touched the central concerns of the law and the kind of people who would be shaped through those laws. We may be talking, in that familiar and bantering phrase, about "private parts," but the way in which people came together in joining those parts and generating offspring could not have merely a private and trivial significance. Moral beings could place sexuality within a moral framework. If the very purpose of sexuality was the begetting of children, then the moral framework could confirm the rightful direction of sexuality to this purpose, and of course children did not emerge, directed merely by instinct and nature, to moral codes. As George Gershwin had it, fish got to swim and birds got to fly: birds will be birds and fish will act as fish without instruction. But human beings, moral beings, are in need of education and moral shaping. As Leon Kass observed, it mattered profoundly for the sons of Jacob that begetting was placed in the kind of framework that looked toward the end of shaping a Jewish people, a people cultivated with a reverence for the laws that defined the children of Israel.[2] To put it another way, the family is the first coiner of citizens, and it can never be a matter of political indifference as to the moral terms on which children are begotten and then in turn nurtured and shaped in their character.

The first recognition then of this minimal moral understanding comes with the connection between the family and the laws. We may recall that moment in Plato's *Crito* where Socrates imagines the laws of Athens embodied, standing before him, and saying, "Why would you strike at us now, Socrates?" After all, it was "through us that your father married your mother and begot you." I've often wondered whether the man on the street, in Brooklyn or Bethesda, ever felt grateful to any of our legislators, for creating those laws of marriage under which our parents were married and begot us. But Plato evidently thought it a point worth making again that the laws have ever been a part of the understanding and construction of families. Aristotle remarks, in a fascinating passage in the *Politics*, that "the polis [the polity] is prior in the order of nature to the family." Of course, Aristotle never suffered any doubt that people were quite capable of having sex even before the advent of government—and they were capable of having sex even on those occasions when governments broke down. What he meant, rather, was that the notion of what constituted a "family" was always enveloped by the moral understandings that pervade the community and find expression in the laws. What, after all, would constitute a marriage? Would it be only two people, or perhaps three or more? Could it include mothers and sons, brothers and sisters, people and their household pets? It appears that the community has never been indifferent to these questions, and indeed these matters were evidently thought to bear a serious, moral significance, a significance that warranted expression in the laws. My late friend, Allan Bloom, wrote in his last book that "sex may be 'natural,'" but "the children who are the products of nature and real love lack something that can be provided only by law and its constraints." He went on to say that "promiscuous encounters do not produce children." And by that he meant that these couplings do not produce, as he said, "the kind [of children] who are one's own and who promise immortality to the family name": "It is only within the context of the law that a man can really imagine that the offspring from his loins can people the world. . . . The law that gives names to families and tries to insure their integrity is a kind of unnatural force and endures only as long as does the regime of which it is a part."[3]

In Aristotle's time, as in ours, the presence of law marks the character of the polity, just as it marks a movement away from matters merely personal and private to matters of moral and public import. When we come to the recognition, say, that it is wrong for parents to torture their children, or to sell them as a species of property, we do not respond by saying, "therefore let us give people tax incentives in order to induce them to stop." When we come to the recognition that these acts stand in the class of "wrongs," the response, measured to the logic of the recognition, is to forbid these acts to anyone, to everyone—which is to say, we forbid them with the force of law. We may avert our eyes from many missteps on the parts of parents, and leave them officially unobserved in a domain of private lives. But when certain acts rise to a level we come to see as serious wrongs, and we have the law intervene to protect children, we are saying in effect that the larger community has a concern for these injuries inflicted even in the intimacy of the family. It is curious that, when people see these interventions as unwarranted and heavy-handed, they will insist that the "government" has no business in these private matters. But when they see serious wrongs taking place, they speak, not of the government, but of "the law"—the "law" extending its protections of the vulnerable and marking the concerns then of the *community* or the wider *public*. This kind of self-imposed haze has become quite familiar now, especially with the matter of abortion. What it curiously obscures at the same time is the remarkable fact that even the most extreme libertarians among us would not have the law recede from these matters of sexuality and marriage. And for many of the same reasons, neither would the proponents of gay and lesbian marriage. The latter have made the most dramatic demands for the receding of the law from this matter of marriage; they have argued for the most radical removal of the restrictions, and a new openness of the law to forms of marriage that lie beyond our constricted imaginations. But even these partisans of a new regime of marriage would insist on the sternest restrictions on marriage, once they have opened the institution of marriage to the couplings or the alliances they wish so devoutly to be honored.

Consider first the libertarians. They usually seek the broadest receding of the law from any inclination to interfere in personal relations, and they put the accent on the freedom to enter into contracts. It has not been entirely clear what the libertarian stance is on polygamy, or even on incest, when these engagements have the consent of the participating adults. But the libertarians are at least clear that a contract implies parties with the competence and maturity to contract, and on that basis even they would deny that their model of the free-spirited adult should have the freedom to marry a young teenager. Presumably then they would have the law forbid that kind of marriage, much as they would have the law hold to one of its minimal functions of guarding people against fraud and preserving the plausibility of contracts.

And yet the matter could not be explained away so readily with these simple formulas of libertarian life. After all, in a wide swath of our lives, we make provisions for parents to give consent for their minor children. Parents may consent to have their children leave school for the sake of working as actors in films; they consent to surgery for youngsters who may not legally order their own, and of course they may give permission for children to marry even when they have not yet attained the age of consent. Why, then, should they not be free to consent to let their teenage son marry an adult male? Several years ago, in a notable case, one of the most liberal boards of education in the country, the Board of Education in New York City, became firm in its insistence on firing a teacher at the Bronx High School of Science because he was a leader in the North American Man-Boy Love Association (NAMBLA). As a leader in that organization, Peter Melzer was quite patently committed to the principles of pedophilia. He professed to have done nothing to recruit or to proselytize for his cause among his own students. Nevertheless the Board took it as a sufficient ground of concern that Melzer was unshakeably committed to the principles that defined NAMBLA, and one of those principles involved the frankest challenge to the validity and justification of those provisions in the law for an "age of consent."[4]

It is curious that even the gay activists have not taken fully seriously the challenge that Melzer and the members of NAMBLA pose. For NAMBLA represents a "sexual orientation," and if it is wrong to draw adverse inferences, or make discriminations based on "sexual orientation," then that so-called principle should cover NAMBLA as well. The point of awkwardness here for gay activists is that, if they would seek to distance themselves from NAMBLA, they must back into the admission that it is indeed legitimate to reach judgments on sexual orientations that may be rightful or wrongful. And that recognition would have to cancel, in a sweep, all of those laws on the books that bar discriminations based on "sexual orientation." But the rejection of that premise has been one of the motor forces propelling the movement for gay rights, and if the movement holds to its own doctrines, it would bear a heavy burden if it would reject the claims of NAMBLA. The movement has sought for years to insist that sexuality need not be defined by the purpose of begetting or procreation; that it may be quite sufficiently defined by orgasmic experience combined with intimate relations (or even relations not so intimate, involving strangers). By those measures, the claims of the Man-Boy Love Association should offer a clear and even purer expression of the ethic put forth in the movement for gay liberation.

If begetting has nothing to do with the sexual relation, then why is the consent of an adult necessary? If it is a matter mainly of pleasure, of sensation and intimacy, the youngster knows as much as any adult about the things that give him pleasure. If there is a concern for safety or disease, well, youngsters are often taught about the hazards of operating lawn mowers and tractors, and they can be properly instructed. In contrast, if marriage is an enduring relation, taking its bearings from the nurturance of children, then it does become critical to gauge whether one's prospective partner has a character that is enduringly admirable, a character that promises to remain steady with the change of seasons and the passing of years. That gauging of character will indeed require a certain maturity, or a certain seasoning in the world. But if there is no such interest pointing to a commitment more enduring, the need for a matured judgment becomes in turn less urgent. Why not, then, allow the boy to marry the adult man, especially if a parent, a mature adult, sensitive to the interests and feelings of the child, is sufficiently sure that the relation threatens no harm to the child?

With the same sense of things, though, why would we need to depend on the consent of that adult who happens to be a parent? Are we "privileging," as they say these days, those relations grounded in "nature"—as though there really *is* a human nature? And would we be indulging the assumption that these relations sprung from nature inspire, in these *natural* parents, a deeper moral concern for the child? It becomes apt to remind ourselves here that we have already brought forth, in the law, some intricate maneuvers that allow minor children to avoid the barriers and tensions of seeking consent from their parents when it comes to the matter of ordering abortions. If the prospect of seeking that consent promises to foster distress and interpose some serious resistance to an abortion, the law has now contrived in many places to permit a sympathetic stranger, a judge, to step in and register consent in place of the parents. (And at times that expedient may also avert the vexing need even to inform the parents). We ought to remind ourselves also that, with abortions, we deal with serious, traumatic surgeries, which may have lasting, damaging effects for the young woman on whom that surgery is performed. In contrast, a marriage need not involve any such surgery, serious or superficial, and indeed the marriage itself may not promise to be enduring. If the arrangements for "bypassing" the parents can be regarded as plausible and legitimate in regard to abortions, then why *need* we rely, in this matter of marriage, on the consent of parents? Given the odds, parents are likely to be quite prejudiced here, anchored as they may be in the conventions of the past. Why may the consent not be given, not by a judge who is a stranger, but by a man who knows and loves the child, and whom the child, in turn, professes to love and trust, perhaps even more deeply than he loves and trusts his parents?

Many plausible things could be said, then, many precedents drawn upon, for freeing the individual from the encumbrances that the law may still cast up to restrict personal freedom. And yet, I gather that the libertarians would be quite averse to allowing teenagers to engage in this association of marriage with a person of the same sex, even if they have the consent of parents. It is reasonable to ask, though, just why they would insist on a distinction here, in regard to marriage, that they would not insist upon in many other places, where they are willing to let parents offer consent for minors. The implication, not yet explained, is that there is something different, strikingly different, about marriage; something that makes even libertarians reluctant to give way on the restrictions that are firmed up in the law.

That reluctance has become ever more visible recently among the proponents of same-sex marriage, though it is curious as to why that reluctance has been so largely unnoticed. The effect may be a trick-of-the-eye, for the arguments on behalf of gay marriage have been arguments for breaking down the traditional laws of marriage; the laws that have constricted our moral imaginations, and made us willing to bar a whole class of people as eligible spouses solely on account of their sex. The argument for gay marriage has been an argument for opening ourselves to new understandings of marriage, freed from the conventions handed down from the past. But as the argument for gay marriage has come under challenge, it has become important for the partisans of same-sex marriage to insist that marriage will not be available to ensembles of the polygamous, or even to alliances of widows or brothers and sisters, claiming no erotic or sexual relation. These new couplings, often on the part of heterosexuals, may be motivated simply by the wish to take advantage of certain benefits in taxes or social security. The proponents of gay marriage have been rather emphatic in their unwillingness to open their imaginations to all of these arrangements, arrangements made possible once the traditional cast of marriage is broken and marriage becomes open to more inventive combinations. The resistance here may spring in part from a need to be political—a concern to avoid scaring the horses and the public by admitting, at once, all of the combinatorial possibilities that would seem to be licensed once we remove the traditional framework of marriage. But the main concern may simply be a concern to preserve what may now be in reach: The activists have sought, with such artfulness and strain, to bring about same-sex marriage that they may simply not wish to see cheapened and diminished what they have sought so hard to attain.

And yet the problem is endemic and insoluble for them. The hard fact of the matter is that the parade of scary possibilities becomes virtually impossible to constrain precisely because it is brought forth by the very principles that are put in place by the argument for same-sex marriage. For some activists, the parade is not so unwelcome, for it confirms more dramatically the train of happenings they wish to bring about. The lawyer-activist Nan Hunter laid out this view of the matter with an admirable candor in an article in the early 1990s, when she wrote that "the impact of [gay and lesbian marriage] will be to dismantle the legal structure of gender in every marriage." For this arrangement, she said, has "the potential to expose and denaturalize the historical construction of gender at the heart of marriage." For Hunter, apparently, and the activists who share her convictions, there is no particular interest in shoring up marriage as an institution. For them the discrediting of marriage is indeed the end they have in view, and the disintegration of marriage is not something to be lamented. (I should point out that Ms. Hunter was the director of the AIDS Project and the Lesbian and Gay

Rights Project for the American Civil Liberties Union, before she went on to become the "deputy general counsel/legal counsel" in the Department of Health and Human Services in the Clinton Administration. Hers are not the views of people regarded then as so eccentric as to be ineligible for high office and the levers of responsibility.)

On the other hand, it is not clear that all other activists fit this description. I take Andrew Sullivan and Jonathan Rausch at their word when they insist that they are simply seeking to extend the good of marriage, that they bear no interest in injuring the traditional family. But the melancholy fact of the matter, I fear, is that there would be no stopping this erosion or disintegration in the very meaning of marriage once the notion of gay marriage is accepted, for it would make untenable any resistance, in principle, to these further challenges, or these further claims to the right to marry. And if those challenges can no longer be resisted in principle—if these new versions had to be accommodated in the understanding of marriage—marriage would lose its integrity as a concept and its durability then as an institution.

This is of course the most serious charge that the proponents of same-sex marriage have had to meet: that by extending the notion of marriage to cover couples of the same sex we will set in train the changes in principle that will undermine marriage itself. The deeper irony is that this charge becomes all the more irresistible—all the harder to rebut—when we understand the toughest argument that the activists have been able to pose against the defenders of traditional marriage. That argument is understood at its most telling level when we come to understand that it offers the most strenuous challenge *in point of principle*. The beginning of clear-headedness must come with the recognition that the challenge offered by the proponents of gay marriage is indeed a serious challenge in principle, testing propositions that run to the root. And the question must be addressed, in turn, in those same, strenuous terms.

In framing the argument against gay marriage, some of my friends have contended that the public at large is not much moved by the concern for judicial activism, that the public has a much deeper concern about children. On this point, friends such as Maggie Gallagher can cite an impressive array of findings from social science, confirming what people of ordinary wit have long understood—namely, that it makes a profound difference to have both a mother and a father. If social science can ever claim truths to reveal, no matter how tinged with contingency, the findings here are worth publishing, for it turns out that, on many measures, children fare much better when they are raised in a family with a mother and a father. They are far more likely to avert a host of social pathologies, and attain a certain stability and success in marriage, in school, in business. The findings, as they accumulate, take on an impressive weight. But as voluminous as they become, they can offer at best the generalizations that social science typically serves up, and with an argument cast in principle, mere generalizations are not enough. It has been said that most gays are not really interested in marriage, though more lesbians may be, and I suspect that is true. But even if those generalizations are true—and true with a probability of .999—they cannot supply an answer to the question of why, *in principle*, this particular gay or lesbian couple should be denied that kind of right to marry. Children may indeed do better with the presence of a mother and father, but some children will suffer the loss of a mother or father and go on to manage well the business of life. Some parents, we know, will be less than stellar, and even dysfunctional. We cannot rule out the possibility that certain gay and lesbian couples may indeed do better as parents than couplings of men and women in the traditional cast. For mere generalizations, even those that hold true most of the time, there will always be exceptions, and the hard question in principle is just why the loving, nurturing couples of the same sex should be any less fit to claim the mantle of marriage.

The findings of social science, as rich as they may be, will always be contingent propositions, always dependent on circumstances, always measured in terms of probabilities, higher and lower, and all of that is quite different from a statement in principle. When we say, for example, that it is wrong to hold people blameworthy or responsible for acts they were powerless to affect, we state a proposition that springs from the very logic of morals; a proposition that must hold true of necessity. It will be true in all places and under all conditions. The proponents of same-sex marriage fall back upon that logic as they keep skewering in courts the most popular arguments that are brought forth against gay marriage, cast merely in terms of generalizations. And the activists have drawn on that same logic as they have challenged the most important rationale brought forth to support traditional marriage—namely, that it is a framework meant to support the begetting and nurturance of children. The advocates of same-sex marriage have made the simple but apt point that not all marriages between men and women do in fact beget children. Some couples are sterile, some not interested in children. And so, as the Supreme Judicial Court of Massachusetts has declared, in postmodernist language, we may not "privilege procreation" as the ground that explains and justifies marriage. We may not even require "consummation" any longer as a necessary ingredient defining a marital relation.

Now with those moves the proponents of same-sex marriage set the bar rather high: They say that it is "not true of necessity that every traditional marriage brings forth children," and when they cast the argument in that way, they insist that laws cannot be made simply on the basis of generalizations that hold true most of the time. They insist that, behind the laws, must be propositions that hold true as a matter of necessity—propositions that can answer the question they pose when they ask, "Is it necessarily true that" . . . marriage is necessary for children?

Those are demanding terms of argument, and to my mind they are exactly the right terms in which the argument must be offered and judged. But again, the irony here is that we have a kind of political ju-jitsu at work: When the argument for same-sex marriage is put forth, in its most exacting, principled terms, it exposes its own deepest flaws and enhances the leverage of the other side, for it brings forth, in turn, the most telling counter-arguments, cast in terms of principle; and in my judgment, they are the arguments that the proponents of gay marriage, at this moment, cannot answer.

The problem was revealed most clearly by the Supreme Judicial Court of Massachusetts in the recent *Goodridge* case, the case in which the Court in effect overturned the traditional laws of marriage and installed same-sex marriage. Quite central to the argument of the majority of four judges in that case was the insistence that procreation is not a requirement of marriage, and that the laws on marriage "do not privilege procreative heterosexual intercourse between married people above every other form of adult intimacy." But the Court opened itself here to more than it realized, for by the same reasoning one may say that marriage should be open to uncles and nieces, father and daughters, who happen to be *sterile and intimate*. Or to the man willing to have a vasectomy in order to marry his mother? And yet, more than that: if people of the same sex may marry, why would the arrangement not be open to a father and son? We have seen cases of incest, as bizarre as they may seem, just as we've seen things as odd as the fellow in Maine who sought a license to marry his dog, or the fellow in Denver a few years ago, who sought to marry his horse. The impulse is there, and once again *it matters not at all in principle that these are rare cases*. Until recently it has been rare to see people of the same sex wishing to marry. The fact that there may only be a handful of cases does not relieve us of the need to explain *the grounds of principle* on which we would deny these claims of marriage—once we move out of that framework of marriage as a union between a man and a woman.

We've also learned over the ages that the law teaches: If the law becomes open to the arrangements of mothers and sons, fathers and sons, marrying, we can expect that these arrangements will not stay rare and bizarre—that we will come to see far more of them. But whether we see more or less, the people who claim rights of same-sex marriage have to deal with this critical problem of their argument: that *they have no ground in principle* to deny any longer any of these other arrangements. They cannot explain why marriage should be confined to a couple, rather than the ensemble of three or four or more who claim to be intimate and loving. Some of us made this argument eight years ago during the hearings over the Defense of Marriage Act.[5] And sure enough, as though sprung from the argument itself, we have now seen the advent of the "polyamorous," the people who claim a right to be joined in marriage to the fuller range of people they are capable of loving. But if the notion of marriage comes to encompass the polyamorous or the polygamous, or the father and son, or the two brothers, the notion of marriage will have lost its coherence. And along with that coherence, it will have lost the most compelling ground of its explanation and defense, as something desirable, something we are justified in preserving.

We might get at that problem from a different angle by opening ourselves to the fuller implications of that argument by the Supreme Judicial Court, when the judges insisted that marriage cannot privilege procreative relations, that it must be open to adults who are *attached* to one another. The argument cast in that form not only opens itself to the father and son, but to an exploding variety of marriages, which may have *no erotic claim at all*: For example, why should there not be a tennis marriage for couples or foursomes seeking commitment, or for that matter a marriage for bridge? ("Tennis is just not the same for me if I can't play with Ted, or bridge with Louise." Why may we not commit ourselves, promise to meet every week—with faults assigned, and perhaps fines assessed, if those expectations are not met and those promises are not kept?)

And indeed there *are* situations in which relatives and unmarried people bear responsibilities together, and they could benefit by having some of the privileges associated with marriage. Two sisters taking care of an orphaned nephew or an aging uncle could indeed benefit from special provisions in insurance for a family or joint tax returns. In fact, one proposal here is to make these benefits available to all couples on a *non-discriminatory* basis, without implying any erotic relation, or any sexual relationship at all. Indeed the point has recently been made by a lawyer in Worcester, David Wojcik, that this new form of marriage could be quite attractive to *heterosexuals*, as arrangements of convenience, perhaps for widowed friends, who could enter these arrangements in order to "share Social Security benefits, health insurance, or to defer estate taxes or to protect real estate from Medicaid liens incurred for long term nursing home care." But once marriage is stretched in this way, he argues, it will indeed lose its coherence—and it will lose also its special standing as something to be esteemed and sought.

My experience has been that people on the other side insist that marriage be reserved for loves expressing themselves in an erotic, sexual way. And after all, the Supreme Judicial Court in Massachusetts had said "intimate" relations. The activists would wish to insist that these sexual relations, among couples of the same sex, be marked off for a special standing and recognition, apart, say, from the two sisters taking care of a nephew. But how would that special standing be marked or even noticed any longer in the law? For the Court has also said, as part of its argument, that the law cannot require "consummation" any longer, or any sexual congress at all as a defining feature of a marriage. And that insistence has been a critical part of the argument against the institution of marriage as we have known it. Now the judges have not been overly strenuous in their logic, but even the four judges in the majority in Massachusetts are not likely to insist that sexual consummation is quite unnecessary as a defining ingredient of traditional marriage—and then turn around and insist that it is an absolutely necessary feature of any other coupling that would claim the name of "marriage" for two people of the same sex.

From my own conversations, I gather that the proponents of same-sex marriage are not really willing to have the notion of marriage encompass relations among sisters or relatives, relationships without an erotic or sexual dimension. And yet, if that is the case, it must be even more plausible to insist that marriage is *inescapably sexual* in its meaning, and in the strictest definition that applies to sexuality even now, the sexuality that marks us as men and women: the sexuality that President Clinton understood when he remarked, in one of the truest lines he ever spoke, that "I did not have *sex* [real sex] with that woman."

There is no getting away then, from the N-word: nature, or for that matter, from the s-word: sex; or the L-word: law. To collect again some of the strands in this argument, even the people who urge us to enlarge our notion of marriage fall back on the notion that marriage can find its coherence, not as an arrangement of friendship or even love, but of sex, and sex in the strictest sense, the sex that is marked in our gender—in the fact that we are made men and women. And of course there is the telos, the very purpose, imprinted in that nature: the begetting of children. As the Congregation for the Doctrine of Faith once pointed out, nations may come and go—there has not always been an Italy; and Czechoslovakia has now disappeared. But as long as there are human beings, there will be men and women.[6] We know also that marriage cannot be broadened to take in, with the most generous sweep, the relations of love that fill in the world. No one can deny the genuine love that subsists between grandparents and grandchildren, parents and children, brothers and sisters. And in the nature of things—the nature of things—nothing in those loves can possibly be diminished as loves—they cannot be reckoned in any way as "lesser loves"—because they are not attended by penetration or expressed in marriage. Nor are parents and children diminished in their "civil rights" when they are barred from marrying one another.

At the same time, it is a point worth noting that these restrictions of the law are not regarded as intrusions, and they are not rejected in principle, by the people who are posing now the most radical challenge to the laws of marriage. They may be the partisans of same-sex marriage, or libertarians simply raising again the flag of liberty unencumbered (or mostly unencumbered); but they are still not willing to have the law recede even from matters as intimate as sexuality and marriage. In insisting on the essential presence of the law, they concede perhaps more than they quite realize, for they concede that sexuality and marriage cannot be regarded as wholly private matters, depending on the subjective feelings of the participants. When even the libertarians and the partisans of same-sex marriage insist on having a law of marriage to preserve the integrity of marriage, they back into the recognition that there is something of moral and public significance about marriage—something that runs beyond matters of private taste and reaches matters of right and wrong. And reaches them in a way that calls out for the recognition of their seriousness—the recognition that comes precisely by invoking the laws.

Chesterton once imagined a story about a group of intrepid explorers who ventured out to sea, eventually spotted land after several weeks afloat, and when they came on shore discovered that they had landed at Brighton. In the version I've described, we might say that a band of revolutionaries, determined to pose the most serious challenge to the laws of marriage, found themselves backing into the very terms and requirements that have ever defined the meaning of marriage. They insist that friendship and love are not enough; that the relation must involve sex; that there are rightful and wrongful forms of sex; that the laws must come into play to mark those differences and preserve the integrity of the kind of marriage they would seek. These adventurers in the law, out to remodel the laws on marriage, have found their way back to home ground. Or they had never left it in the first place.

Still, they could earnestly turn to us and say: "What about you? You throw in our faces the test of principle, and that is fair enough. But are you accepting that discipline fully yourself? When you ask us how we could reject polygamy, we argue that a relation confined to two has the sense of something more exclusive and intense—something more special, in a word—rather than a relation diffused among three, four or more people. You tell us, in response, that this is all contingent, for we may indeed encounter people who seem capable of loving, in an intense, exclusive way, two or three other people rather than one. Fair enough, but what of the argument on your own side? You have expended your wit mainly in showing us that the opening to same-sex marriage would make it harder to deny polygamy and preserve the character of marriage as relation confined to one man and one woman. But have you told us what is so good in principle about that arrangement, and so bad in principle about polygamy, for polygamy too may be directed to the end of begetting, and directed with effects even more bountiful.

"This is a question also that most of your allies step around, for the argument they still respect more than others is the argument drawn from social science. For them the concern is with the pathologies and the harms done to children when they are deprived of that chemistry that comes from the presence of fathers and mothers. Your friends argue that there is a compelling need for opposites—for the temperaments and sensibilities that come into play in the merging of men and women. We of course would challenge the arguments based on those generalizations served up by social science. And so do you, but what principle do you bring forth finally as the ground of your own position?"

Once again, I think the challenge, properly posed, would push us to consider whether we could not in fact frame an argument measured more strenuously to the question before us; an argument that may rise above the more contingent findings of social science. Could we state a case more strenuously in principle; a case at least as compelling as the case that ordinary people can understand as we register our concern for children? Whether I'm the best person to offer or complete that argument is another matter; but I think I've put in place the ingredients that furnish the right and necessary starting point. Even the most radical participants in the debate find themselves backing into the right frame of the problem, as they touch again on the inescapable grounds of nature, sexuality, and the laws. But they are all of course connected, as Aristotle understood. The polity, he taught us, was a *natural* association, as natural as the family, because it sprung from something distinct in human nature. The defining mark of the polity was the presence of laws, and laws could spring only from the nature of a being with a moral sense. Animals could emit sounds to indicate pleasure or pain, but human beings could give reasons about the things that were good or bad, right or wrong. Only humans had the capacity to reason over moral things, and it was that very awareness of moral things, of the things that were right and wrong, that found its logical expression in laws, the laws that would forbid, say, to everyone, to anyone, the torture of infants. The recognition of a "wrong" would not express itself coherently in a contract: When we recognize that it is wrong, for example, to torture infants, we do not offer DVD players or tax incentives if people would agree to cease that torture. Chesterton once remarked that animals did not have a religious sense: that no one had ever heard, say, of cows giving up grass on Fridays. What he meant of course is that there are the "ways" of cows and horses, but the nature of cows and horses does not contain the capacity to respect a law that commands our obedience, beyond our own inclinations and appetites.

We begin in a distinctly different way, and begin in the right way, when we begin with the awareness that, with the question of marriage, we are dealing of course with the special meanings that envelop sexuality and love in beings who are "moral agents." It is not that beings of this kind are incapable of having casual sex, and even meaningless sex. As the line went in that classic by Cole Porter, "We're merely mammals/let's misbehave." The point rather is that beings constituted with a capacity for moral judgment can invest relations of love with a meaning that is never available for animals. They may have reasons, good reasons, to consider their prospective partners as persons who truly deserve their admiration and their enduring attachment. To speak of a love that endures even as age withers, and custom stales, the marks of beauty, is to speak of a love that is tendered for reasons that endure; the reasons that make a spouse enduringly worthy of affection and respect. Animals may persist, but they do not really persist with the understanding of a "commitment." But whether a commitment is truly necessary or relevant depends on "what marriage is for." As I've noted, it is not strictly necessary for love, but it happens to be a matchless framework for the begetting and nurturance of children. For it conveys to the children the sense that the parents are as committed to them as they are to one another, for with the presence of the law the parents have foregone the freedom to quit this association as it meets their convenience. Even when it is not made explicit, that sense of things might be read in the "performative acts," by which I mean those daily acts of being together, with the lives embodied and enacted, in full sight of the children.

The same sense of things used to inform our sense of what was meant by the "natural teleology" of the body—from the hard fact that it took two people, not three, that it required a man and a woman, to beget a child. The sense of a one-flesh union seemed clear then, especially to people who had been brought up to recognize "sacraments"—that is, to recognize that principles may reveal themselves more fully when they are embodied in persons and practices. Even rather prosaic things—a wafer, a sip of wine—may be understood to bear a larger significance. With that sense of things there seemed to be a fact so evident that people after a while could stop noticing. And that was: that there was the clearest correspondence between the coupling of bodies of a man and a woman, and the generation of that new life that would embody the features of both partners, or make into one flesh the partners who form the "wedding." I don't think this is merely poetic or metaphorical. There is indeed the signifying of things with the body, and with acts of the body. But the things signified do not arise merely from local conventions—it's not like the fact that the word "opportunist," in some settings, may be a compliment. It is not a matter of the way we happen to use words, or the way in which an upraised arm is understood in certain places as a salute or a menacing gesture. It is more like a natural language—like the difference we can read, in faces, between love and hatred, between the approving smile and the ominous frown. Here it is a matter of recognizing the meaning that attaches in the same way to the manner in which a body and its parts are engaged. I would suggest, then, that the meaning of coupling of bodies is confirmed for us in the recognition that a rape is no less a rape, no less an assault quite different from other kinds of assaults, even when the victim happens to be sterile and incapable of becoming pregnant through the rape. The rape would not only be an assault, but an assault at another level of presumption: The assailant enters the victim with force, he enters where he would never be bidden in. He makes an entry that is invited only for the man who is accepted by the woman as the potential father of her child, as the enduring partner in the shaping and raising of that child.

We can imagine, in another scene, a solution in a Petri dish in the process of *in vitro* fertilization—and imagine a researcher with irreverence, or a bantering nonchalance, pouring the liquid solution as a dressing on his salad. For all we can see, it is merely liquid. But we know what that liquid really is, and the simplest, most direct way of explaining our natural recoil is that we know what that liquid or solution "is made for." We know its proper end, and to see it employed in this way is to see something so flippant and disparaging as to be debased. In the same way, we know what the coupling of sexual organs *is for.* We know the most important purpose for which those organs are made, and to which they are directed. We know, then, the difference between a flippant use and a serious use, between a masturbatory use and the engagement of those parts in an act of love—an act enveloped, that is, by the love of the partners, and open, in the understanding of the partners, to the welcoming of new life.

With that venerable, and rudimentary, sense of the matter, we might consider a problem posed to us in what could be called—if you will pardon the expression—an "original position." Let us suppose that we were faced with this question and this choice: If human beings are to be generated, are there arrangements that are *in principle* better or worse, morally preferable or undesirable? The query makes sense of course only for beings capable of affecting the problem, in the first place, with a moral question. And so we might put the problem quite as aptly in another way by asking whether an answer to this question springs from the very nature of this moral being, or from the logic of a moral judgment itself. With that sense of things we might ask then, Is it better to have offspring spawned in random or evanescent matings among strangers, or better that the generation of new life take place within a framework of lawfulness—a framework, that is, of *commitment*, in which people acknowledge these offspring as their own, accept responsibility for their nurturance and upbringing, and forego their freedom to quit these responsibilities at the first signs of strain?

In point of principle, the answer, I think, should be plain. One side in the problem dismisses altogether the notion that there is anything of moral significance that would justify or require any sense of a framework of commitment that envelops the acts of sex or seeks to convert them into acts of love. The question may be pressed of course as to why the same sense of commitment could not characterize the same man, locked in the same intense relation with two different women, bearing children. My hunch is that the presence of the children thickens the problem: To say that one is committed with one's wife to the nurturing of these children cannot possibly mean the same thing if one happens to be equally "committed" to another woman with another set of children. Three friends may be committed to one another, but the "commitments" springing from a one-flesh union, in contemplation of children, cannot claim the same kind of elasticity. As Roger Scruton has argued, sexual relations cannot be fungible: we cannot casually replace one partner with another, as though we were replacing a partner in tennis. Something in these relations, as he argues, commands exclusivity, and I would suggest that the same sense of things spills over to the understanding that a commitment in marriage would have to be exclusive in the same way, or it would strain coherence to refer to it any longer as a "commitment."[7]

In filling out the argument I would point out that nothing in this understanding in principle implies anything about the outcomes. In point of principle we can tenably claim that it is better for people to come together, in sexuality, within a framework of love and commitment, especially with the prospect of children. But we are dealing with sublunary creatures, with all the imperfections of fallen creatures, and it cannot surprise us that not all of these people turn out to be fit partners in a true marriage of souls. There will be no doubt people affected with self-love, given to disloyalty and exploitation, and even to passions that are lethal. Even people otherwise artful in the world may turn out to be dysfunctional as parents. And along with everything else, we are dealing with a world of contingency, in which failures and sickness may depress the spirits and damage the marriage. All of that is quite to be expected, and yet none of it may impair the notion that one way of life, or one understanding of marriage, may be deeply better in principle than another.

This should not strike us as in any way novel or especially jarring. We commit ourselves, for example, to certain principles about the need to assess evidence in trials. We understand in principle why there should be an obligation to hear the evidence or the witnesses so that the accused has the chance to rebut the evidence and vindicate his innocence. We commit ourselves to those procedures in principle because we understand that we are committed to the most rational process for testing evidence. For we are committed foremost, not to punishing, but in making the most strenuous discriminations between innocence and guilt before we visit punishment on people. And yet we fully understand that the same procedures could work with dramatically different results in different places at different times. In one place we find judges and juries making mistakes, throwing out valid evidence for trivial reasons, or failing to grasp the evidence put before them. It is entirely possible that in one city, the procedures work to set free many vicious characters, ready to prey on others; while in another place the rules work fairly well to confine the guilty and to protect the innocent. But my point again—a point, I think, well understood among us—is that nothing in these contingent happenings would impair in any way our sense that these are the procedures that spring fittingly from the very *logic of rendering justice*. Their claim to our respect is not diminished in any way by the evidence, amply to be found, that the people who apply these procedures in different places often turn in records that are less than stellar.

The reasoning, as I say, is hardly novel. The only novelty may come in pulling together the strands and bringing them to bear on this problem that has been vexing us of late in our politics. But the redeeming part of the issues that truly vex us is that they may force the question upon us in the most strenuous and searching way. That has indeed been done in the challenge posed by the proponents of same-sex marriage. As they have insisted on engaging the problem as a matter of principle, they compel us to follow the same course, and to understand with a certain sobriety the properties that attach to an argument in principle. I've sought to argue here that the argument, engaged in that way, brings us back to the surer ground of the argument for marriage; the argument that does not depend on the shifting and contingent findings of social science, no matter how powerful they are in the domain of probabilities.

As we trace matters back to the root of principle, I've suggested that we make our way back to home ground. And as we survey the ingredients that are decisive, in the meaning of nature, sex, and the laws, we find that everything has its source finally in the nature of that being, grounded in the world of animals, but touched with the divine gift of reason. As we face the question in a serious way, we may find ourselves tracking back to the anthropology of John Paul II. For we are simply led back once again, as John Paul II would say, to the deeper truth about the human person. At the end of the *Republic* Plato has Socrates say of the republic that he and his interlocutors had sketched, that whether it existed in fact anywhere or not, the principles that defined this polity, or marked its character, described the only polity in which the thoughtful man would wish to take part.[8] We might say, in our own day, that marriage may undergo a serious remodeling, a remodeling that alters or even dissolves marriage as we have come to know it. But the principles that define the rightful idea of marriage will remain. And whether that kind of marriage is sustained or even offered any longer in this country, after the reshaping of our laws, it is the only kind of marriage in which the thoughtful man or woman would wish to be joined.

7

What's Sex Got to Do with It?
Marriage, Morality, and Rationality

Robert P. George*

THE EMINENT POLITICAL SCIENTIST James Q. Wilson has examined the institution of marriage over time and across cultures in developing an analysis and explanation of the distressing state of current marital and sexual practices. He has done so, thoroughly and convincingly, in his book, *The Marriage Problem*,[1] and in an earlier lecture titled "Marriage, Evolution, and the Enlightenment."[2] Professor Wilson observed that, as a plain matter of social fact, marriage is culturally universal, and monogamous marriage is by far the dominant form. Nevertheless, he remarked, "what is hard to understand is why marriage occurs at all."[3] Professor Wilson's exploration of the question of marriage proceeded from a social scientific point of view and deployed, in an astute and sophisticated way, the methods and resources of contemporary social science. I propose to explore the question from a different viewpoint, a practical philosophical one.

---

* The author would like to thank the Earhart Foundation for its generous support and Leah Silver for excellent research assistance. Parts of this article are drawn from an article by the author originally published under the title "Marriage and the Illusion of Moral Neutrality," in T. William Boxx and Gary Quinlivan (eds.), *Political Order and Culture* (Grand Rapids, Mich.: Wm. B. Eerdmans Publishing Co., 1998), pp. 114-27, and reprinted elsewhere.

After exploring some of the difficulties of explaining marriage and its universality in evolutionary biological terms, Wilson concluded that "the reason [marriage] endures is not that it is about sex but that it is about children and property."[4] What ultimately explains marriage, according to Wilson, is that it is "a reproductive alliance."[5] Individual men and women enter into marriages, and the larger social groups of which they are members promote and protect marriage as a valued and, indeed, privileged institution, because experience teaches that the marriage relationship is indispensable to the rearing of the young. "If the human infant were born able to move about and feed itself, as is true of sharks," Wilson noted, "marriage would not exist."[6]

At the same time, Wilson argued that "[f]or most of history, marriage has not simply been about sex or reproduction, it has been about property."[7] There are significant, albeit limited, variations through history and across cultures in the definitional terms of marriage, and these terms—for example, whether marriages are by and large arranged—are shaped in large part by prevailing economic patterns, practices, and institutions—for example, the group, as opposed to the individual, control of land. (Reciprocally, the terms of marriage influence patterns of economic relations and help to shape the system of exchange. So, for example, Wilson concurs[8] in Alan MacFarlane's argument that the marriage system made possible by the emergence of individual land ownership in turn helped to make England "the natural place for the emergence of capitalism."[9])

Addressing the condition of marriage in contemporary America and in other western cultures, Wilson argued that the preservation of the integrity of marriage as an institution is indispensable to the well-being of society. Family, he observed, "is the foundation of public life."[10] Yet, as is plain to Wilson and even to the casual observer, the institution of marriage is in trouble. Wilson offered this diagnosis:

> [T]he family now rests almost entirely on affection and child care. These are powerful forces, but the history of the family suggests that almost every culture has found them to be inadequate to producing child support. If we ask why the family is, for many

people, a weaker institution today than it once was, it is point-less to look for the answer in recent events. Our desire for sexual unions and romantic attachments is as old as humankind, and they will continue forever. But our ability to fashion a marriage that will make the union last even longer than the romance that inspired it depends on cultural, religious, and legal doctrines that have slowly changed. Today people may be facing a challenge for which they are utterly unprepared: a vast, urban world of personal freedom, bureaucratized services, cheap sex, and easy divorce.

Marriage is a socially arranged solution for the problem of getting people to stay together and care for children that the mere desire for children, and the sex that makes children possible, does not solve. The problem of marriage today is that we imagine that its benefits have been offset by social arrangements, such as welfare payments, community tolerance, and professional help for children, that make marriage unnecessary.[11]

To understand the roots of the decline of marriage, Wilson sketched an historical account, a key moment in which was the development of a marriage market in Britain and other western European cultures. The defining feature of this development, originating in the emergence of a system of individual land ownership, was individual, as opposed to familial, choice of marriage partners.[12] This "expansion of choice," Wilson said, was "given a powerful boost by the Enlightenment,"[13] particularly its tradition-trumping rationalist impulse. Of course, as Wilson pointed out, Scottish Enlightenment thinkers, such as Adam Smith and David Hume, were anything but enemies of traditional matrimonial norms. They explicitly defended the institution of marriage and opposed whatever was likely to harm it, such as easy divorce. And they understood marriage—indeed, permanent, monogamous marriage—as a rational institution because of its value in providing a reliably sound—indeed, the only reliably sound—context for the rearing (and particularly the moral education) of children.[14]

So far forth, as Wilson tells the story, Enlightenment rationalism posed no threat to marriage. But there was another, and more revolu-tionary, Enlightenment—the French one. "In Scotland," Wilson said, "a constrained, cautious, and sober view of human nature was the basis for a prudent judgment about the reach of human reason."[15] However, "in France, an unconstrained, boundless, and wildly optimistic view of human nature supplied the grounds for recklessness about what reason could achieve."[16] And the French Enlightenment, according to Wilson, eventually "triumphed over the Scottish one."[17] Ideas have consequences. The consequences of French Enlightenment ideas regarding marriage, sex, and childrearing were catastrophic. Wilson remarked: "Divorce, once illegal, has become commonplace, and bastardy, once only an upsetting prelude to a later marriage, has become not only more customary but also a lifestyle rather than an embarrassment. The reason is that the total emancipation of reason from custom and tradition, whatever its origin, will embolden some people to think that any arrangement that does not impart an immediate and palpable harm to another person is legitimate, provided only that it has been freely chosen."[18]

For these baleful consequences, Professor Wilson—despite his manifest admiration of, and debt to, Smith, Hume, and other Scottish Enlightenment thinkers—refused to exonerate them: "Whatever the difference, the Scottish Enlightenment led the way to the French version. Once reason has been separated from experience, and thought has been freed from tradition, people will increasingly challenge any arrangement that seems to be grounded in experience and tradition as opposed to cognition and ideals. It took a century or more for this to happen, but it happened."[19]

Despite the overwhelming evidence that a culture of divorce in fact weakens the institution of marriage and harms children, people in the grip of Enlightenment ideology—and I daresay that we are all influenced by it to some extent—tend toward an understanding of marriage as a mere contract, and even less than a contract since, unlike a contract, a marriage can today be broken by either party at will.[20] Moreover, illegitimacy and absent fathers are viewed by many people less as moral problems than as pragmatic ones, where they are viewed as problems at all. And sex outside the bond of marriage—once perceived as something not only wrong in itself but dangerously undermining the virtues and self-understandings necessary for marriage to flourish in a culture—is today understood by a significant segment of the elite opinion-forming class (and not only those on the cultural left fringe) not as a moral wrong, but—despite the absence of any textual or historical support for it—some sort of constitutional right.[21] People who persist in thinking otherwise are condemned for the sin of being "judgmental."

Still, Wilson expressly and resolutely declined to conclude his lecture on a note of pessimism. Indeed, he stated that, despite deplorably high rates of divorce and single-parent families, we are not quite in a state of crisis. Our hope, he insisted, is in the fact that "human nature makes people responsive to an overriding concern—child care."[22] Despite the fact that "this great and natural force for good has suffered mighty blows delivered by people who do not understand how that good is produced," he counseled, "we can take a deep breath and consult the experiences of millennia: Men and women differ, and a strong culture must be designed and maintained that will keep them together in achieving what most want and what most, when they get it, cherish. Their own child."[23]

I. UNDERSTANDING OF MARRIAGE

As stated above, while Wilson employed the tools of social science, I intend to explore the topic of marriage from a different viewpoint, a practical philosophical one. Practical philosophy aims at a reflective critical understanding of people's reasons for choice and action. My purpose in adopting this viewpoint is by no means to contradict Professor Wilson's analysis, which, in fact, I find altogether illuminating. It is rather to complement it. As with the study of social phenomena of any description—phenomena, that is to say, that are constituted at least in part by human choices and actions—social scientific accounts of marriage can tell important parts of the story, but not all of it. Individual men and women, in choosing to marry, and polities, religious communities, and other social groups in choosing to foster and protect the institution of marriage, choose and act in light of *intelligible goods* that provide *basic reasons* for choice and action. Therefore, philosophical reflection is necessary to bring these goods and reasons into focus, clarify their relations to one another, and evaluate social practices by reference to their integral directiveness.

In the prosecution of this task, social science cannot serve as a substitute for philosophy. In fact, even within the limits of its own purely descriptive ambitions, social science needs philosophy. Any sound descriptive account of behaviorally constituted phenomena will depend, in part, (as in the matter of concept formation, and especially in the identification of focal or paradigmatic cases) on practical philosophy's contribution of a critical understanding of the intelligible reasons for people's choices and actions.[24] Apart from such an understanding, social scientific "explanations" inevitably will treat human behavior as *caused*, rather than, in a robust sense of the term, *chosen*. And the truly damnable vice of this sort of reductionism is not the alleged amorality for which it stands so often condemned by moralists, but rather, its inability to produce explanations of social phenomena that, in the words of British legal philosopher Herbert Hart, "fit the facts."[25]

As Hart observed, the accurate and refined description of behaviorally constituted phenomena presupposes the adoption by historians, sociologists, political scientists, and other descriptive scholars of the "the internal point of view," that is, the viewpoint, not of a purely external observer who sees what he takes to be causes and effects (e.g., cars stop at red lights; therefore, the red lights cause drivers to stop their cars), but, rather, that of participants in social practices who do what they do (such as conforming their behavior to traffic laws) for *intelligible practical reasons*.[26]

The thesis I set before you is that a key source of the pathologies afflicting marriage in contemporary societies is not, strictly speaking, the substitution of reason for tradition. Rather, it is the significant erosion, and in certain circles nearly the complete loss, of a sound understanding of marriage, especially in its sexual dimension, as an intrinsic, rather than merely instrumental, human good. The problem, in other words, is that many people have lost their grip on the nature of the marital good, or goods, and on the *reasons* for marrying and supporting marriage that these goods supply. The failure is precisely a failure of practical understanding—of *reason*. At the same time, I do not wish to be misunderstood to suggest that tradition is unimportant to the health of marriage or to deny that the success of the Enlightenment rationalist (but hardly rational) assault on tradition is, in important respects, tragic. As Alasdair MacIntyre has shown, traditions supply background understandings in the absence of which important achievements of practical intelligence—practical insights—are scarcely possible.[27] In other words, traditions can be, and sound traditions always are, bearers or carriers of the resources of practical rationality—that is, of reasonableness in the moral sphere.

Consider the particular manifestations of weakness of the institution of marriage today. There is a great deal of divorce and much of it is the result of infidelity. Even where infidelity is not an issue, men often abandon their wives, and sometimes wives their husbands, or spouses mutually agree to dissolve marriages, because they are not getting what they wanted or expected out of the "relationship." Middle-aged men, at the peak of their careers and earning capacities, frequently trade in the wives of their youth, whose contributions to their success were, more often than not, considerable, for younger and sleeker models—so-called "trophy wives."[28] Indeed, young women entering marriages can no longer count on legal or social pressure to reduce the likelihood that they will be cast off by their husbands in middle age. People of both sexes do not seem to take the vows and responsibilities of marriage seriously anymore. And many people do not bother to respect even the form of marriage. Cohabitation and illegitimacy are common, and as Professor Wilson remarked, hardly raise eyebrows.[29] Law and public policy, instead of placing obstacles in the way of these trends, have largely accommodated themselves to them.[30] Even many people who *publicly* express conservative beliefs about sex and marriage *privately* behave incompatibly with those beliefs—*privately*, that is, until their private lives become public and they are exposed as hypocrites.[31]

We know that the facts of human sexual psychology have not changed. Social circumstances have, of course, changed in myriad significant ways, putting strains of various sorts on marriages and making infidelity easier and less risky than it used to be. But these are only partial explanations. A candid and complete explanation will attend to the fact that a great many people lack a robust understanding and appreciation of the goods that are honored and protected by the principles of permanence and exclusivity in marriage. People casually violate their vows to "forsake all others" and "cleave to each other for better or worse, for richer or poorer, in sickness and in health, till death do us part," because they no longer hold securely a conception of marriage in light of which the content of these vows makes sense. Only if marriage is understood to be an end-in-itself, and not merely a means to other ends, do people have intelligible reasons for respecting its norms of permanence and exclusivity even in the absence of the satisfactions that marriage can indeed, when all goes well, be counted on to produce.

If marriage is understood (or, in my view, misunderstood) as a purely instrumental good, then it is worth having and preserving precisely and only to the extent that it produces the satisfactions (or other concrete ends—companionship, safe and reliable sexual satisfaction, social standing, heirs, or any number of other benefits) to which it is a means. Permanence and fidelity make perfect sense as intrinsic features of marriage when it is viewed as an end in itself. By contrast, and despite anyone's merely emotional and sentimental attachments to these marital ideals, it is a struggle to make sense of permanence and fidelity when marriage is viewed as a means.

II. THE INTRINSIC GOOD OF MARRIAGE

A central division in moral philosophy since the Enlightenment has to do with the question whether there are *any* intrinsic human goods. On the one side are those who follow David Hume in denying the very possibility of more-than-merely-instrumental practical reasons and reasoning. In Hume's famous formulation, "reason is, and ought only to be, the slave of the passions and may never pretend to any office other than to serve and obey them."[32] For them, reason does not and cannot ultimately tell us *what* to desire—it has no power to identify what is intelligibly *desirable*. It can only tell us how to obtain what we *happen to desire*, how to satisfy our *given desires*. Our ultimate motives are not, indeed, cannot be, *rational*—even in part. Rather, the ends of human action are necessarily supplied by subrational motivating factors—by feeling, emotion, what Hume called "the passions."

On the other side of the philosophical divide are contemporary followers of Aristotle and St. Thomas Aquinas who hold that practical reason is not merely instrumental. Rather, human persons, as rational animals, not only experience desires (as do brute animals) and identify efficient means to their satisfaction, but are capable of grasping the intelligible point of certain options that present themselves to the practical intellect not, or not merely, as a means to other ends, but also as ends-in-themselves.[33] On the Aristotelian-Thomistic understanding, practical reasoning begins precisely from our understanding of those ends or purposes which, insofar as we grasp the point of pursuing or participating in them not merely as a means to other ends but for their own sake, are intrinsic, and not merely instrumental, goods—what I and other contemporary natural law theorists call "basic human goods."

Elsewhere I have stated my reasons for rejecting the Humean "non-cognitivist," "subjectivist," and "instrumentalist" view of practical reason and affirming the Aristotelian-Thomistic alternative.[34] The Humean view fails both normatively and descriptively. It is unsound normatively inasmuch as it necessarily denies true practical principles—principles that proponents of the view themselves rely on and appeal to every day, not least when making the case for their viewpoint and defending it against its critics—such as the principle that there is an intelligible point to (and not simply an emotional or other subrational motive) for pursuing, say, intellectual knowledge for its own sake (as in philosophy and the other humanities or in pure science or mathematics).

As a putative description, the Humean view radically oversimplifies and fails to account for ordinary human motivation and moral experience. I mention the issue here because one's basic understanding of practical reason has profound implications for such issues as the nature of marriage, the reasons for individuals to marry and for social groups to foster and protect the institution of marriage, and the role of sex in marriage. If one adopts the Humean view, one's understanding of sex and marriage and their human significance will be along the lines of the purely instrumentalist, and, it must be said, reductionist, account offered by Richard Posner in his lengthy and (let me cheerfully concede) in many ways highly informative treatment of the subject in his book *Sex and Reason*.[35] If one adopts, instead, the Aristotelian-Thomistic view, one's understanding will be along the following lines.

Marriage, considered not as a mere legal convention or cultural artifact, but, rather, as a one-flesh communion of persons that is consummated and actualized by acts that are reproductive in type, whether or not they are reproductive in effect, or are motivated, even in part, by a desire to conceive a child, is an intrinsic human good and, precisely as such, provides a more than merely instrumental reason for choice and action. The bodily union of spouses in marital acts is the biological matrix of their marriage as a comprehensive, multilevel sharing of life: that is, a relationship that unites the spouses at the bodily (biological), emotional, dispositional, and even spiritual levels of their being. Marriage, precisely as such a relationship, is naturally ordered to the good of procreation (and is, indeed, uniquely apt for the nurturing and education of children) as well as to the good of spousal unity.

Further, the procreative and unitive goods of marriage are tightly bound together. The one-flesh unity of spouses is possible *because* human (like other mammalian) males and females, by mating, unite organically—they form a single reproductive principle. Although reproduction is a single act, in humans (and other mammals) the reproductive act is performed not by individual members of the species, but by a mated pair as an organic unit. The point has been carefully explained by Professor Germain Grisez: "Though a male and a female are complete individuals with respect to other functions—for example, nutrition, sensation, and locomotion—with respect to reproduction they are only potential parts of a mated pair, which is the complete organism capable of reproducing sexually. Even if the mated pair is sterile, intercourse, provided it is the reproductive behavior characteristic of the species, makes the copulating male and female one organism."[36]

Although not all reproductive-type acts are marital—adulterous acts, for example, may be reproductive in type (and even in effect), but are intrinsically nonmarital—there can be no marital act that is not reproductive in type. Masturbatory, sodomitical, and other sexual acts that are not reproductive in type cannot unite persons organically: that is, as a single reproductive principle. Therefore, such acts cannot be engaged in for the sake of marital (that is, one-flesh, bodily) unity as such. They cannot be marital acts. Rather, persons who perform such acts must be doing so for the sake of ends or goals that are extrinsic to themselves as bodily persons: sexual satisfaction, or (perhaps) mutual sexual satisfaction, is sought as a means of releasing tension, or obtaining (and sometimes sharing) pleasure, considered either as an end-in-itself or as a means to some other end, such as expressing affection, esteem, friendship, and so forth. In any case, where one-flesh union cannot (or cannot rightly) be sought, sexual activity necessarily involves the instrumentalization of the bodies of those participating in such activity to extrinsic ends.

Securely grasping this point, and noticing its moral significance, Hadley Arkes has remarked that "'sexuality' refers to that part of our nature that has as its end the purpose of begetting. In comparison, the other forms of 'sexuality' may be taken as minor burlesques or even mockeries of the true thing."[37] Now, Professor Arkes is not here suggesting that sexual acts, in what he calls the "strict sense of 'sexuality,'"[38] must be motivated by a desire to beget a child; rather, his point is that such acts, even where no such motivation is present, must be reproductive in type if they are to consummate or actualize marriage as a one-flesh union. This, I think, is what makes sense of what liberal critics of Arkes's writings on sex and marriage find to be the puzzling statement that "every act of genital stimulation simply cannot count as a sexual act."[39]

In marital acts, however, the bodies of persons who unite biologically are not reduced to the status of extrinsic instruments of sexual satisfaction or expression. Rather, the end, goal, and intelligible point of sexual intercourse is the intelligible good of marriage itself as a one-flesh union. On this understanding, the body is not a mere instrument of the conscious and desiring aspect of the self whose interests in satisfactions are the putative ends to which sexual acts are means.

Nor is sex itself instrumentalized. The one-flesh unity of marriage is not a merely *instrumental good*, that is, a reason for acting whose intelligibility as a reason depends on other ends to which it is a means. This unity is an *intrinsic good*, that is, a reason for acting whose intelligibility as a reason depends on no ulterior end. The central and justifying point of sex is not pleasure (or even the sharing of pleasure) per se, however much sexual pleasure is sought—rightly sought—as an aspect of the perfection of marital union; the point of sex, rather, is marriage itself, considered as an essentially and irreducibly (though not merely) bodily union of persons—a union effectuated and renewed by acts of sexual congress—conjugal acts. Because in marital acts, sex is not instrumentalized, such acts are free of the self-alienating and dis-integrating qualities that have made wise and thoughtful people from Plato to Augustine and from the Biblical writers to Kant, treat sexual immorality as a matter of the utmost seriousness.

III. MARRIAGE AS ONE-FLESH UNITY

Let me here address some possible misunderstandings. Nothing in the view of marriage and sexual morality that I am sketching excludes various forms playful and affectionate foreplay to marital intercourse; nor does the traditional view have any implications whatsoever for who, if anybody, should be on top of whom in the marital embrace. It carries no brief for the "missionary position." Still less does it hold that sex should not be fun, and even "for fun." Furthermore, it is important to see that by "marital act," I do not mean just any sexual act between a married couple. Any two people, whether married to each other or not, are capable of performing sodomitical and other non-reproductive-type sexual acts, and these are intrinsically nonmarital. Indeed, the marital quality even of sexual acts of spouses that are reproductive in type can be vitiated by, for example, manipulation, deceit, abuse, coercion, and other unloving and unjust behaviors that are, as such, incompatible with a will to marital unity—a will to regard one's spouse as a person equal in worth and dignity to oneself and as one's unique and beloved partner in the mutually self-giving relationship of marriage.

In truly marital acts, the desire for pleasure and even for offspring (where conception is possible and desired), are integrated with and, in an important sense, subordinated to the central and defining good of one-flesh unity. The integration of subordinate goals with the marital good ensures that such acts effect no practical dualism which volitionally and, thus, existentially (though not, of course, metaphysically, since the person is in that respect a dynamic unity of body, mind, and spirit and cannot be otherwise without ceasing to be) separates the body from the conscious and desiring aspect of the self and treats the body as a mere instrument for the production of pleasure, the generation of offspring, or any other extrinsic goal. As John Finnis has observed, marital acts are truly unitive, and in no way self-alienating, because the bodily or biological aspect of human beings is "part of, and not merely an instrument of, their personal reality."[40]

But one may ask, what about procreation? On the traditional view of marriage, is not the sexual union of spouses instrumentalized to the goal of having children? It is true that St. Augustine was an influential proponent of something like this view.[41] The strict Augustinian conception of marriage as an instrumental good was rejected, however, by the mainstream of philosophical and theological reflection from the late Middle Ages forward, and the understanding of sex and marriage that came to be embodied in both the canon law of the Church and the civil law of matrimony does not treat marriage as merely instrumental to having children.[42] Western matrimonial law has traditionally and universally understood marriage as consummated by the reproductive-type acts of spouses; by contrast, the sterility of spouses—so long as they are capable of consummating their marriage by a reproductive-type act (and, thus, of achieving true bodily, organic unity)—has never been treated as an impediment to marriage, even where sterility is certain and even certain to be permanent (as in the case of a woman who has been through menopause or has undergone a hysterectomy).[43]

According to the traditional understanding of marriage, then, it is the nature of marital acts as reproductive in type that makes it possible for such acts to be unitive in the distinctively marital way. And this type of unity has intrinsic, and not merely instrumental, value.

Thus, the unitive good of marriage provides a noninstrumental (and sufficient) reason for spouses to perform sexual acts which by uniting them as bodily persons (that is, as one flesh) consummate and actualize their marriage. At the same time, where the central defining good of marriage is understood to be one-flesh unity, children who may be conceived in marital acts are understood not as ends extrinsic to marriage (either in the strict Augustinian sense or in a modern liberal one), but rather, and uniquely, as gifts that supervene on acts whose central defining and justifying point is precisely the marital unity of spouses.

On this point, Leon Kass, in his moral critique of human cloning[44] and in other writings, has explored with great insight the way in which our very humanity is implicated in decisions about the terms, conditions, and understandings on which we choose to bring new human persons into existence. Of course, neither Professor Kass nor I deny that it is legitimate for people to desire or want children. Our concern is merely to explicate the sense in which children may be "desired" or "wanted" under a description that does not reduce them in principle— all sentimentality aside—to the status of "products" to be brought into existence by their parents' wills and for their ends. Desired under a proper description, that is, with a proper understanding and disposition, and sought by means that are in line with such an understanding and disposition, children are treated by their parents, even in their conception, not as means to their parents' ends, but as ends-in-themselves; not as objects of the desire or will of their parents, but as *subjects* whose fundamental interests as human beings are protected by principles of justice and human rights: not as *property*, but as *persons*.[45]

It goes without saying that not all cultures have fully grasped these truths about the moral status of children. What is less frequently noticed is that our own culture's grasp of these truths is connected to a basic understanding of sex and marriage that is not only fast eroding, but is now under severe assault by people who have no conscious desire to reduce children to the status of means, objects, or property.

People who reject the traditional understanding of sex and marriage that I have been sketching commonly assume that defenders of this understanding deny something whose possibility its critics affirm. "Love," these critics say, "makes a family." And it does not matter whether the love is between two people of opposite sexes or the same sex (though we may ask, why only two?); nor does the mode of "sexual expression" of that love make any difference. In fact, however, at the bottom of the contemporary debate over marriage is a possibility that defenders of traditional marriage affirm and its critics deny, namely, the very possibility of marriage as a one-flesh communion of persons. The denial of this possibility is central to any argument designed to establish that the moral judgment at the heart of the traditional understanding of marriage as inherently heterosexual and monogamous is unreasonable, unsound, or untrue. If reproductive-type acts are, in fact, capable of uniting spouses interpersonally, thus providing the biological matrix of the multilevel union and sharing of life that marriage is according to the traditional understanding, then truly marital acts differ fundamentally in meaning, value, and significance from sodomitical or other intrinsically non-marital sex acts.

Revisionist sexual morality, in denying that true marriage is inherently heterosexual and monogamous, necessarily supposes that the value of sex must be instrumental either to procreation or to pleasure, considered, in turn, as an end-in-itself or as a means of expressing affection, tender feelings, etc. Thus, according to proponents of the revisionist view, homosexual sex acts, for example, are indistinguishable from heterosexual acts whenever the motivation for such acts is something other than procreation.[46] That is to say, the sexual acts of homosexual partners are indistinguishable in motivation, meaning, value, and significance from the marital acts of spouses who know that at least one spouse is temporarily or permanently infertile. Thus, the revisionist argument goes, the traditional understanding of marriage is guilty of unfairness in treating sterile persons of opposite sexes as capable of marrying while treating same-sex partners as ineligible to marry.

Stephen Macedo has accused the traditional view and its defenders of precisely this "double standard." He asks: "What is the point of sex in an infertile marriage? Not procreation: the partners (let us assume) know that they are infertile. If they have sex, it is for pleasure and to express their love, or friendship, or some other good. It will be for precisely the same reason that committed, loving gay couples have sex."[47] People today who are inclined to a liberal view of sexual morality tend to find this sort of criticism impressive, and more than a few conservatives seem to find themselves stumped by it. Once the core of the traditional view is brought into focus, however, it is clear that the criticism straightforwardly fails because it presupposes as true precisely what the traditional view denies, namely, that the value (and, thus, the point) of sex in marriage can only be instrumental. It is a central tenet of the traditional view that the value (and justifying point) of sex is the good of marriage itself, consummated and actualized in and by sexual acts that unite spouses as one-flesh and, thus, interpersonally.

The traditional view rejects the instrumentalization of sex (and, thus, of the bodies of sexual partners) to extrinsic ends *of any sort*. Of course, as I have already pointed out, this does not mean that procreation and pleasure are not rightly sought when they are integrated with the basic good and justifying point of marital intercourse, namely, the one-flesh union of marriage itself.

IV. BIOLOGICAL UNITY

It is necessary, therefore, for critics of the traditional understanding of marriage to argue that the apparent one-flesh unity that distinguishes marital intercourse from sodomitical and other nonmarital sex acts is illusory, and thus, that the apparent bodily communion of spouses in reproductive-type acts, which, according to the traditional view, forms the biological basis of their comprehensive marital relationship, is not really possible.

And so Richard Posner declares that John Finnis's claim that "the union of reproductive organs of husband and wife unites them biologically and, thus, interpersonally," is unclear in its meaning and moral relevance, and cannot "distinguish sterile marriage, at least when the couple *knows* that it is incapable of reproducing, from homosexual coupling."[48] Turning to the claim that "intercourse, so long as it is the reproductive behavior characteristic of the species, unites the copulating male and female as a single organism," Posner asserts that "intercourse known by the participants to be sterile is not 'reproductive behavior,' and even reproductive intercourse does not unite the participants 'as a single organism.'"[49]

Now, on this question of "reproductive behavior" or, better, the idea of "reproductive-type" acts, it is worth adverting to the fact that identical behavior can cause conception depending entirely on whether the nonbehavioral conditions of procreation obtain. And the intrinsic, and not merely instrumental, good of marital communion gives spouses reason to fulfill the behavioral conditions of procreation even in circumstances in which they know the nonbehavioral conditions do not obtain. This is true just in case the fulfillment of the behavioral conditions of reproduction is, in truth, unitive of the spouses as persons—in other words, just in case there is a truly unitive (as well as procreative) good of marriage that, as the traditional philosophy of sex and marriage has long held, is capable of being realized in and by the sexual intercourse of spouses. So, the question is whether Posner is right to deny what the traditional view affirms: namely, that reproductive-type acts unite a male and female as a single reproductive principle, that is, make them truly (and not merely metaphorically) "two-in-one flesh."

It is a plain matter of biological fact that, as Grisez says, reproduction is a single function, yet it is carried out not by an individual male or female human being, but by a male and female as a mated pair.[50] So, in respect of reproduction, albeit not in respect of other activities (such as locomotion or digestion), the mated pair is a single organism; the partners form a single reproductive principle: they become "one-flesh." In response to Posner, Grisez proposes a thought experiment. Imagine a type of bodily, rational being that reproduces, not by mating, but by some individual performance. Imagine that for these beings, however, locomotion or digestion is performed not by individuals, but only by biologically complementary pairs that unite for this purpose. Would anybody have difficulty understanding that in respect of reproduction the organism performing the function is the individual, while in respect of locomotion or digestion the organism performing the function is the united pair? Would anybody deny that the unity effectuated for purposes of locomotion or digestion is an organic unity?[51]

Of course, the question remains, is there any particular *value* to the biological (organic) unity of a male and female human being committed to each other and their possible future offspring in a comprehensive sharing of life that is permanent and monogamous? One will judge the matter one way or the other depending, for example, on whether one understands the biological reality of human beings, as Finnis says, as an intrinsic part of, rather than merely an instrument of, their personal reality.[52] But as to the fact of biological unity, there is no room for doubt. As to its moral implications, I suspect that Posner's difficulty is a specific instance of his general skepticism regarding the possibility of noninstrumental practical reasons and reasoning. If pressed to deal with the question, Posner would no doubt deny that the biological reality of human beings is anything more than an instrument of ends which are themselves given by feelings, emotions, desire, or other subrational motivating factors. As I observed earlier, and as I argued in detail in a review of Posner's book *Sex and Reason* in the 1993 Columbia Law Review,[53] the implicit operating premise of Posner's treatment of sex, and other moral questions, is the Humean instrumentalist and non-cognitivist understanding of practical reason as "the slave of the passions." Marital communion cannot be a noninstrumental reason so far as Posner is concerned, because, on his account of human motivation and action, there are no noninstrumental reasons.

Professor Macedo, by contrast, is no Humean. He rejects Posner's instrumentalist understanding of practical reason. Still, Macedo claims that "the 'one-flesh communion' of sterile couples would appear . . . to be more a matter of appearance than reality."[54] Because of their sterility, such couples cannot really unite biologically: "their bodies . . . can form no 'single reproductive principle,' no real unity."[55] Indeed, Macedo argues that even fertile couples who conceive children in acts of sexual intercourse do not truly unite biologically, because, he says, "penises and vaginas do not unite biologically, sperm and eggs do."[56]

Finnis has aptly replied that "In this reductivist, word-legislating mood, one might declare that sperm and egg unite only physically and only their pronuclei are biologically united. But it would be more realistic to acknowledge that the whole process of copulation, involving as it does the brains of the man and woman, their nerves, blood . . . secretions, and coordinated activity is biological through and through."[57] Moreover, as Finnis points out, "The organic unity which is instantiated in an act of the reproductive kind is not, as Macedo . . . reductively imagine[s], the unity of penis and vagina. It is the unity of the persons in the intentional, consensual act of [sexual intercourse]."[58]

The unity to which Finnis here refers—unity of body, sense, emotion, reason, and will—is, in my view, central to our understanding of humanness itself. Yet, it is a unity of which Macedo and others who deny the possibility of true bodily communion in marriage can give no account. For this denial presupposes a dualism of *person* (as conscious and desiring self), on the one hand, and *body* (as instrument of the conscious and desiring self), on the other hand, which is flatly incompatible with this unity. This dualism of person and body is implicit in the idea, central to Macedo's denial of the possibility of one-flesh marital union, that sodomitical acts differ from what I have described as acts of the reproductive type only as a matter of the arrangement of the "plumbing." According to this idea, the genital organs of an infertile woman or man are not really "reproductive organs"—any more than, say, mouths, rectums, tongues, or fingers are reproductive organs. Thus, the intercourse of a man and a woman, where at least one partner is infertile, cannot really be an act of the reproductive type.

But the plain fact is that the genitals of men and women are reproductive organs all of the time—even during periods of sterility. Acts that fulfill the behavioral conditions of procreation are reproductive in type even where the nonbehavioral conditions of procreation do not happen to obtain.[59] Insofar as the point or object of sexual intercourse is marital union, the partners achieve the desired unity (become "two–in-one-flesh") precisely insofar as they mate, or if you will, perform the type of act—the only type of act—upon which the gift of a child may supervene—what traditional law and philosophy have always referred to interchangeably as "the act of generation" and "the conjugal act."

The dualistic presuppositions of the revisionist position are fully on display in the frequent references by Macedo and others to sexual organs as "equipment."[60] Neither sperm nor eggs, neither penises nor vaginas, are properly discussed in ethical discourse in such terms. Nor are reproductive and other bodily organs "used" by persons considered as somehow standing over and apart from these and other aspects of their personal reality. In fact, where a person treats his body as mere equipment, a mere means to extrinsic ends, the existential sundering of the bodily and conscious dimensions of the self that he effects by his choices and actions brings with it a certain self-alienation, a damaging of the good of personal self-integration.

In *The Gay Rights Question in Contemporary American Law*, Andrew Koppelman develops more fully, and in important ways radicalizes, some of the lines of argument advanced by Macedo.[61] Koppelman asserts that the classification of all heterosexual penile-vaginal sexual acts (with the right intentions) as reproductive in kind is arbitrary. In defending this position, he makes two claims: (a) that marital acts performed by sterile or elderly couples are *not* reproductive in kind, but also (b) if they *are* considered reproductive in kind, then *any* seminal ejaculation can be classified as reproductive in kind. The key assumption in Koppelman's argument for (a) is the following: "No act which cannot succeed (in a suitable environment under certain circumstances) in producing x can be of the kind that is oriented toward x." Or, put more specifically: "No act in which the agents (or parts of the agents) lack the full internal resources (in a suitable environment, under certain circumstances) to produce x can be internally oriented toward x." Because the sterile man does not have all of the internal resources to fulfill the male role in procreation, then, according to Koppelman, his sexual acts cannot be oriented toward procreation. In fact, says Koppelman, his sexual organs in that case are not genuinely reproductive organs at all: they are reproductive, he says, only in some "taxonomic" sense,[62] which seems to mean they merely can be classified that way, but without any substantive basis for that classification.

But these claims do not hold up under scrutiny. A composite entity may have several constituents internally arranged so as to cooperate to produce x, but also have a defect that prevents it from producing x. For example, a hand is oriented toward grasping objects, and remains oriented toward that, even though a defect—a broken bone, for example—prevents it from actually doing so. Thus, a reproductive organ remains a reproductive organ in fact and not just in name (merely "taxonomically"), even if some condition or defect in the agent makes actual reproduction impossible.

A similar point applies to a reproductive-type *act*. In the generative act the male and the female perform an act (intercourse) in which the sperm is deposited in the vaginal tract of the female. This act, performed by the male and the female together, is the first part of the process of reproduction. In performing this first part of the reproductive process together, the male and the female act as a single unit, even where in many cases the second part of the process cannot (for any of a variety of causes) be completed. (Of course, if the process continues, they continue to act as a unit (though at a distance, by means of their gametes). A condition, or even a defect, which prevents the second part of the process cannot change the fact that the male and the female did actually unite—became organically one—in the first part of that process. If conception *does* occur, it won't be until several hours later (at the earliest); and whether they *now* become one cannot depend on events that occur only later. So one cannot say that a male and female become a single organism for reproductive purposes only in those coital acts that actually result in conception. In coitus itself—whatever may happen *after* coition—the male and the female become one flesh.

Moreover, just as marriage is more complex than most other forms of friendship or community, so genuine sexual intercourse is more complex than other acts. The orientation of the first part of the process (coition itself) is not related to the rest of the process (fertilization) in the same way that a simple means is related to a single end. Rather, the orientation of the sexual acts of a couple toward procreation belongs to the *set* of sexual acts, not directly to each act. Also, the only behavior which the partners have direct control over is coition itself, performed in such a way as to fulfill the behavioral conditions of reproduction. This is the only act, the only behavior, which they directly perform, and it disposes them to procreation (rather being the direct act of procreating). Thus, the other conditions (an adequate sperm count, time of ovulation, etc.) are not part of the couple's behavior, not part of *what they do*. So, when Koppelman says that only acts which have the power to reproduce are genuinely reproductive in kind, he is mistaken. Many acts that are fully reproductive in kind—uniting the male and female organically as a reproductive unit—will not actually result in conception, and, in many cases, this will be known to the persons performing the acts.

But what about Koppelman's claim that if the sexual intercourse of heterosexual sterile couples is considered reproductive in kind, then it is equally plausible to say that *all* acts of seminal ejaculation are reproductive in kind? (Recall that Koppelman wants to say that heterosexual acts of sterile or elderly couples are not reproductive in kind—but *if* they were, then so would homosexual acts be.) Do not the agents in homosexual acts also exercise part of their reproductive capacities and organs?

The answer is that of course same-sex partners (or opposite-sex partners who perform sodomitical acts) make use of their reproductive capacities and organs, but, unlike elderly or other infertile heterosexual couples who unite in sexual intercourse, they do not perform an act which constitutes the first part of the reproductive process. It is true that acts of sodomy may be *abstractly* described simply as "seminal ejaculation," but sodomy plainly does not fulfill the behavioral conditions of procreation; sodomitical acts do not result in procreation even if the nonbehavioral conditions of reproduction happen to obtain for the agents performing the acts. That is, *what the sodomitical act is*, as opposed to *an extrinsic condition* of that act, makes it impossible to reproduce; and, as a consequence, sodomy is simply not an act in which the agents become one organism. (Of course, neither nocturnal emissions nor instances of solitary masturbation are reproductive-type acts either, and for the same reason.)

Koppelman is likely to object that the infertility of the heterosexual couple is not an extrinsic condition (as I say it is) but should be considered as modifying what the partners do—and so they are, after all, in the same boat as same-sex partners. (In effect, his claim is that being reproductive in kind is not morally significant.) But there are two reasons why this objection fails. First, as I've already noted, every aspect of the behavior the heterosexual couple (in a marital act) chooses to perform may be the same on two different occasions, and yet one act may result in procreation and the other not. This fully establishes that the difference is a difference extrinsic to *what they do*. Of course, if they know that procreation is impossible, then they cannot intend or hope for procreation. This is all that Koppelman's well-known analogy of the unloaded gun shows: "A sterile person's genitals are no more suitable for generation than an unloaded gun is suitable for shooting . . . . Dependencies of deception and fright aside, all objects that are not *loaded* guns are morally equivalent in this context . . . . But the only aspect of reproductiveness that is relevant to the natural lawyers' argument, namely the reproductive *power* of the organ, does not inhere in *this* organ."[63] Just as one cannot intend to kill with a gun one knows is unloaded so one cannot intend or hope to procreate by an act one knows cannot in these circumstances result in procreation. But my proposition is not that in a marital act one must intend to procreate, hope to procreate, or even think that procreation is in these circumstances possible. It is that a marital act is an act in which a man and woman, as complementary bodily persons, unite organically (and thus interpersonally) by jointly performing a single act—single in that it is an act that is oriented to procreation, though some other condition in the agents may prevent procreation from occurring.

A second reason why the marital acts of infertile spouses are reproductive in kind is that they bespeak and bear witness to the intrinsic goodness of marriage, the kind of community that is naturally fulfilled by the bearing and rearing of children. Hence the marital acts of all spouses, including infertile ones, by actualizing, renewing, and fostering their conjugal love, contribute to the good of marriage in the whole community (as well as to the strengthening of their own marriage). Even the marital acts of spouses who cannot (or cannot any longer) conceive, nested into a relationship of exclusivity and fidelity whose intelligibility is itself grounded in the idea of marriage as a one-flesh union—indirectly but importantly contribute to the aspect of the good of marriage which their own marriage does not directly realize, namely, the good of procreation, or the bearing and raising of children, something that cannot be said of sodomitical or other non-marital sex acts.

Now, in universities and other elite sectors of our culture, the revisionism proposed by Professor Macedo and others is hardly considered radical. On the contrary, his views about sex and marriage are considered by many to be conservative, even old-fashioned. Like Gabriel Rotello, Bruce Bawer, and Andrew Sullivan, Macedo has come in for criticism from sexual liberationists for affirming the value of marriage as an institution, despite his proposals for the revision of its definition. He and the others I have mentioned have been taken to task for affirming the principle of sexual fidelity and criticizing, if usually only implicitly, promiscuity.[64] At the same time, their conservative critics have suspected that their talk about commitment and fidelity is a clever effort to subvert the institution of marriage from within, as it were, and even some liberationists were willing to cut them some slack on the assumption that this is exactly what they were doing.[65] I do not share this suspicion. I think that they honestly believe in marriage as a permanent and exclusive sharing of life integrated around (but certainly not reducible to) sexual activity. But they think that the nature of the sexual activity just does not matter. Sex is sex. It cannot really unite people as one-flesh, but it can enable them to express their affection in a special way. Its significance is emotional, not bodily. The question is, having abandoned the concept of marriage as a one-flesh union, are they left with any basis in moral principle to insist on commitment and fidelity? I do not see how they are. The moderate liberalism they affirm has nothing more than a Maginot line of sentiment to protect it against an assault from, and collapse into, sexual liberationism.[66]

V. INSTRUMENTAL GOODS

Once marriage and marital intercourse are reduced to the status of instrumental goods, the intelligibility of marriage as providing a reason for people to enter it derives from its status as a means to other ends. What ends? Well, for contemporary liberals, the end of procreation, if that is what the spouses happen to want and, indeed, if they, for whatever subjective reasons, prefer sexual reproduction to other means now available or soon to be. But, if they would prefer not to have children, then contraception and, if need be, abortion can provide for that. Whether a particular marriage is a "reproductive alliance," or an alliance for purposes entirely unrelated to reproduction, is purely a matter of the *subjective preferences* of the parties entering into the alliance. In no way is marriage considered to be naturally ordered to the coming to be and nurturing of children. Nor are the contours of the marital state, or the terms of the marital relationship, understood to be established or shaped by its child-rearing function.

Marriage, on the liberal understanding, is marked by a plasticity or malleability that sharply distinguishes it from the traditional view. Marriage is also unnecessary—even for childrearing. If two (or perhaps more) people find, or suppose, that the state of being married works for them, then they have a reason to marry. An instrumental reason, you will note. If not, then marriage is not as a matter of principle understood to be a uniquely, or even especially, apt context for them to structure their lives together.

What about sex? What is the point of that in the liberal conception? What is sometimes referred to as lifestyle liberalism (to distinguish it from the old-fashioned political liberalism of say Franklin Roosevelt or Hubert Humphrey) rejects the view that sex is to be restricted to the marital relationship. It certainly has no ground of principle to object to sexual cohabitation outside of marriage. And even with regard to sex apart from stable relationships, lifestyle liberalism is "nonjudgmental." Its main principle of rectitude in sexual matters is the principle of consent, not, as in the traditional view, the principle of marriage. So long as there is no coercion or deceit in the procurement of sex, sexual choices, as Frederick Elliston, for example, insists, do not raise moral questions.[67]

Even adultery is unproblematic under the lifestyle liberal conception of marriage if, as in so-called open marriages—a concept that makes sense only under a lifestyle liberal conception—there is no deception of a spouse involved. Indeed, under the lifestyle liberal conception it is impossible to identify any reason—there are only subjective preferences—for spouses to demand fidelity of each other. Why should they "forsake all others"? What is the point? There is no reason, strictly speaking, not to have an "open marriage," only emotions that some people happen to have and others happen not to have.

As a matter of subjective preference, people can commit themselves to fidelity and enter into loving, long-term, monogamous relationships that mimic what, on the traditional understanding of marriage, they have strict moral reasons to do. But the key thing to see is that on the lifestyle liberal conception, there are no such strict moral reasons. Even the choice of fidelity is an emotionally motivated subjective preference. And that, I submit, explains why people who reject the traditional terms of marriage—even for putatively conservative reasons, for instance, to make the good of marriage available to people who prefer sex with partners of their own sex, find it impossible, in the end, to condemn promiscuity and the like, except, occasionally, on pragmatic grounds. Thus, even Andrew Sullivan, who has long framed his case for altering the traditional understanding of marriage in conservative terms, finds himself reassuring his friends on the left of his belief in the "beauty" and even "spirituality" of anonymous sex"[68]—that is, I assume, sex with strangers in which the participants do not even tell each other their names.

But you will have noticed that I did not answer the question I put a moment ago: What is the point of sex in the lifestyle liberal conception? Even if sex is permissible outside of marriage, is it nevertheless an intrinsic part of marriage? The answer has to be "no." Under the lifestyle liberal conception, the point and value of sex, even in marriage, is instrumental. Marriage is not, in principle, a sexual relationship. Rather, at its core, marriage is a form of domestic partnership. It is the sharing of a *household*. If the partners happen to want to have sex with each other, fine—their goals might be to conceive children, to have or share pleasure or intimacy, or to express tender or affectionate feelings toward each other. But not only is it the case that all these goals can be legitimately pursued outside the marital context, it is also the case that there is no reason to pursue them within the marriage—or at all—if the people involved happen not to desire having sex with each other, or at all. There is no sense in which sex consummates or actualizes marriage as such. Just as you can have sex without marriage, you can have marriage without sex. The relationship of sex to marriage is extrinsic rather than intrinsic, in this view. Thus, the whole idea of the sexual consummation of marriage loses its intelligibility.

We can contrast this view of marriage with the traditional view. Reproduction, or procreation, is not an action directly under our control. Its conditions are non-behavioral as well as behavioral. What we perform is an act which in some instances may result in procreation. Moreover—and here reproduction is distinct from other acts—by performing that act the male and the female become one organism, two-in-one-flesh. When that one-flesh unity is an aspect of a total marital communion, it is a rational and sufficient motive and justification for that act. But humans (and other mammals) become one flesh (one organism) only if they perform the type of act which in some instances (that is, when the non-behavioral conditions of reproduction obtain) results in procreation—only if they perform a reproductive-type act.

Koppleman's argument has two parts, one about marriage and the other about sexual acts. In the previous section I replied to his objections to my understanding of reproductive-type acts. Here, let us examine the part about marriage. Contrary to Koppelman's claim, marriage is not simply an historical accident which can now be modified as our culture—or a small fraction of our culture—might choose. The complexity of marriage stems from the fact that one of its distinctive purposes—bearing and raising children—requires a stable and loving environment formed by the children's parents. In order to form a stable and loving environment this union cannot be a mere contractual and instrumental agreement entered solely for the sake of children—this would depersonalize both the children and the parental union. Hence the parents—and any couple who might become parents—should form a stable union of love *for each other*, an interpersonal union *that is valued for its own sake but that would be naturally fulfilled by bearing and raising children*. But since this type of interpersonal union (that is to say, *marriage*) is in itself good (that is, *intrinsically* valuable) even if this natural fulfillment is not reached, it follows that sterile couples must be included within the extension of this kind of community—otherwise, marriage would be reduced to a mere means—an extrinsic end—and would cease having value once that end was realized or if it was found to be impossible of realizing.

Moreover, man and woman are complementary—physically, of course, but also in certain other respects. They are capable of complementing and supporting each other, especially (though far from exclusively) in the parental roles of mother and father. So the union of a man and a woman in a healthy marriage provides a uniquely valuable environment for children. It provides them with male and female parents and parental role models and supports. Unless one embraces a strict (and implausible) belief in androgyny, it is clear that such a community is scarcely an arbitrarily drawn class.

The *normativity* of this class stems from its being a basic and irreducible good perfective of human persons. Marriage, so defined, that is, defined as it has been for centuries in our civilization, is a fundamental and irreducible aspect of human flourishing—a basic human good—and precisely as such is worthy of pursuit, promotion, protection, and respect.

VI. MARRIAGE, LAW, AND CULTURE

Let us conclude by briefly considering the intersection of these principles with law and public policy. A standard liberal response to the defense of traditional marriage is the claim that even if the traditional position is, from the moral viewpoint, true, it is nevertheless unfair for the law to embody it. Macedo, for example, argues that if disagreements about the nature of marriage "lie in . . . difficult philosophical quarrels, about which reasonable people have long disagreed, then our differences lie in precisely the territory that John Rawls rightly marks off as inappropriate to the fashioning of our basic rights and liberties."[69] So Macedo and others claim that law and policy must be neutral with regard to competing understandings of marriage and sexual morality.

This claim, I believe, is deeply unsound. Because the true meaning, value, and significance of marriage are fairly easily grasped (even if people sometimes have difficulty living up to its moral demands) where a culture—including, critically, a legal culture—promotes and supports a sound understanding of marriage, and because ideologies and practices that are hostile to a sound understanding and practice of marriage in a culture tend to undermine the institution of marriage in that culture, it is extremely important that governments eschew attempts to be neutral with regard to marriage and embody in their laws and policy the soundest, most nearly correct, understanding.

The law is a teacher. It will teach either that marriage is a reality in which people can choose to participate, but whose contours people cannot make and remake at will (for instance, a one-flesh communion of persons united in a form of life uniquely suitable to the generation, education, and nurturing of children), or the law will teach that marriage is a mere convention, which is malleable in such a way that individuals, couples, or, indeed, groups, can choose to make of it whatever suits their desires, interests, or subjective goals, etc. The result, given the biases of human sexual psychology, will be the development of practices and ideologies that truly tend to undermine the sound understanding and practice of marriage, together with the development of pathologies that tend to reinforce the very practices and ideologies that cause them.

Joseph Raz, himself a liberal who does not share my views regarding sexual morality, is rightly critical of forms of liberalism, including Rawlsianism, which suppose that law and government can and should be neutral with respect to competing conceptions of moral goodness. In this regard, he has noted that: "Monogamy, assuming that it is the only valuable form of marriage, cannot be practised by an individual. It requires a culture which recognizes it, and which supports it through the public's attitude and through its formal institutions."[70]

Of course, Raz does not suppose that, in a culture whose law and public policy do not support monogamy, a man who happens to believe in it somehow will be unable to restrict himself to having one wife or will be required or pressured into taking additional wives. His point, rather, is that even if monogamy is a key element in a sound understanding of marriage, large numbers of people will fail to understand that or why that is the case—and therefore will fail to grasp the value of monogamy and the intelligible point of practicing it—unless they are assisted by a culture that supports, formally by law and policy, as well as by informal means, monogamous marriage. What is true of monogamy is equally true of the other elements of a sound understanding of marriage.

In short, marriage is the kind of good that can be chosen and meaningfully participated in only by people who have a sound basic understanding of it and choose it with that understanding in mind; yet people's ability to understand it, and thus to choose it, depends crucially on institutions and cultural understandings that both transcend individual choice and are constituted by a vast number of individual choices.

8

Soft Despotism and
Same-Sex Marriage

Seana Sugrue

A RADICAL REDEFINITION OF MARRIAGE from the union of one man and one woman, to the union of two consenting adults, is taking root in American public life.[1] Proponents of same-sex marriage justify this redefinition on the basis of two foundational American values: liberty and equality. Echoing Mill, it is often said that what is done in the sanctity of one's home, between consenting adults, is not the business of the state. People should be free to fulfill their sexual and emotional needs without fear of punishment. Moreover, if heterosexuals are free to couple as they see fit, and some choose to have their union formally recognized by the state through the institution of marriage, so too should same-sex couples. After all, to exclude same-sex couples is to deprive them of the benefits and responsibilities made available through marriage to heterosexual couples, and to assign to their unions second-class status.[2]

The judicial branch of government is at the forefront of legitimating this redefinition of marriage through its jurisprudence pertaining to privacy rights. Privacy rights have been defined to include sex, procreation, marriage, and the rearing and education of children.[3] This jurisprudence is now at a critical juncture in American history as it appears that the United States Supreme Court, together with the highest courts of various states, are poised to push the boundaries of this jurisprudence still further.[4] The logic of their jurisprudence leads to a redefinition of marriage from the union of a man and a woman to the union of any consenting adults who believe their emotional needs would be better met through a ceremony legitimizing their sexual relations. Same-sex unions and polygamous and incestuous couplings are the obvious taboos on the cusp of being shattered.

The thesis of this paper is not primarily that same-sex marriage leads to the further demise of marriage, although this is true. My thesis is that the establishment of same-sex marriage will contribute to the demise of political liberty. One of the unintended consequences of the jurisprudence of privacy rights is that it serves to diminish liberty as it leaves us, and especially our children, increasingly susceptible to statist regulation in those domains where the state is utterly unfit to rule. By promoting "liberty," the Supreme Court is making us less free. By promoting equality, it is compromising our children. Not only are we, and our children, being invited to be Humean slaves to our passions, we are subordinating ourselves to the very power that we have the most reason to fear: coercive state power.

To understand why this is so, one must understand the respective roles of the market, the family, and religion in supporting our liberties, and especially our abilities to be self-governing. These institutions, and others, will hereinafter be called "institutions of civil society" or "civil institutions" to evoke the Enlightenment's appreciation of forms of social order separate from the state. Institutions of civil society are typically understood to be supportive of political liberty. As the family, the market, and religion are society's most foundational institutions for securing freedom and self-governance—as they limit state power and sustain robust republican governance—it would be remiss to exclude these from the rubric of institutions of civil society.[5]

Institutions of civil society are too often ignored by judges and political theorists alike who tend to focus almost exclusively on the state and its relation to individuals, as though the state were the only desirable form of social order for the advancement of human goods.[6] Institutions of civil society, and especially the market, the family and religion, serve to socialize and to coordinate people within their distinctive yet overlapping spheres. None of these institutions is perfect (no institution is) but they are better than any of the alternatives in fulfilling the specific human needs that account for their existence. To function effectively, each of these institutions requires the state to maintain a measure of respectful distance and to uphold their core norms. There is no guarantee, however, that the state will do so, and when it does not, the governance that results in these spheres tends to range from the inept to the despotic.

Seen from this perspective, the sexual revolution is to the family what communism is to the market. Both entail statist assaults on core institutions of civil society, leading to human misery that the state is not equipped to put right. In both cases, what results from the erosion of a core institution is a citizenry ill-equipped to be self-governing; accordingly, state power inevitably grows. In both cases, citizens lose the buffer of an intermediate form of social order between the citizen and the state, resulting in their further atomization and defenselessness in the face of state power. In both cases, the state justifies its assaults in the name of a treasured principle that it flouts. In the case of communism, that principle is equality, but equality is achieved through an extremely powerful state that can equalize all else, while it looms supreme; in the case of the sexual revolution, that principle is liberty, but liberty is achieved through the empowerment of a state with the strength to destroy sexual norms, and hence the institution of marriage as the foundation of the family wherein children are primarily socialized and learn to be self-governing.

The movement to permit same-sex marriage is not the first or the final blow to marriage, which has traditionally been understood as the union of a man and a woman who, if they procreate, rear their biological children. It is, however, a relatively novel assault in that it attacks a norm that has not previously been seriously questioned in the United States. An institution is nothing if it is not a set of conventions, or norms, that serve a coordinative function.[7] As marriage is a normative institution, the move to redefine it by erasing one of its constitutive norms is a potent attack, one that can be expected to have long-term and far-reaching consequences. By taking upon itself the power to change the definition of marriage, the state, through judicial action, is effectively dismantling the connection between marriage and family. The state gains power through this move, while the family, and its most defenseless members, our children, lose their bearings.

Complicit in this assault upon the family are advocates of the market who mistakenly assume that the principles of the market are equally applicable to the domain of marriage and family.[8] Seen through the normative lens of the market, sex is simply another good or service around which people can contract to bind themselves. Accordingly, one's freedom of choice ought to include the liberty to opt into public goods like marriage, where this serves the desires of those who would like to choose this option. Alternatively, it may be argued that marriage ought to be abolished, at least as far as state entitlements are concerned. Consenting adults simply ought to be free to define the terms of their relationship by themselves.[9]

It should suffice to dispel the notion that market principles trump in family life to point out that children, who arise from heterosexual relations, can never recompense their parents for giving them life and for rearing them. Children soil the tidy contractual relationships of the adults under whose custody they are placed.[10] It is around this simple truth that the institution of marriage arises. Moreover, those who support unbridled freedom of choice in the domain of the market may be reminded that John Locke, that great defender of property rights who continues to inspire modern-day libertarians,[11] appreciated that a different logic applies to the domain of marriage and family, which he called "conjugal society." The nature and purposes of conjugal society are very different from those of the market, and must be approached as such.

Locke also recognized that the market and conjugal society require a measure of autonomy from overly zealous state regulation to function effectively. In their respective spheres, the state ought to uphold the core norms of conjugal society and market relations but otherwise it ought not interfere, unless patent injustices or irregularities occur within them. The state should not seek to usurp the market or the family; it should limit itself to correcting specific abuses and deficiencies.

Locke's account of conjugal society also deserves attention because he is widely regarded as the philosopher of the American founding.[12] His political philosophy, which was put into practice through the Declaration of Independence, merits consideration in constitutional interpretation. This is particularly true of the due process clauses of the Fifth and Fourteenth Amendments, which enshrine the Lockean ideals of "life, liberty, or property." The due process clause is at the heart of the Supreme Court's privacy rights jurisprudence. While recognizing that Locke's political philosophy is not always consistent or desirable,[13] it does have the merit of being of historical importance and of stipulating clearly that rights and responsibilities, including those pertaining to conjugal society, are not created by the state. Normative institutions, such as conjugal society, exist because they are compelling forms of social order that advance basic human goods, and no substitute arrangement could be nearly as compelling and sensible.

THE MARKET VS. THE FAMILY

That there are forms of social order the existence of which are independent of the state was well-known to John Locke. In his *Second Treatise on Government*, Locke meditated upon the normative underpinnings of two distinct spheres of pre-political social order, which he identified as the realm of property and the realm of conjugal society. For Locke, property and conjugal society have different purposes or ends; accordingly, the principles that guide them are different in many important respects. Property primarily promotes one's life and liberty, while the family promotes the life and liberty of a unit that includes husband, wife, and most importantly, their children. From this, Locke concluded that the core norm in the realm of property is self-preservation; the guiding principle in the realm of conjugal society is duty, especially where children are concerned.

In a classic statement defining what has, without controversy, been understood for generations to be the definition of marriage, Locke wrote: "Conjugal society is made by a voluntary compact between man and woman; and tho' it consist chiefly in such a communion and right in one another's bodies as is necessary to its chief end, procreation; yet it draws with it mutual support and assistance, and a communion of interests too, as necessary not only to unite their care and affection, but also necessary to their common off-spring, who have a right to be nourished, and maintained by them, till they are able to provide for themselves."[14]

Locke identified two sets of relationships that coexist within conjugal society. These are the relationship between husband and wife, on the one hand, and the relationship between parent and child, on the other. Demonstrating an understanding of the dignity and equality of women that was ahead of his time, Locke stipulated that the wife maintains rights as against her husband, and may leave him where he fails to adhere to the core terms of their relationship. According to Locke, "the wife has in many cases a liberty to separate from him, where natural right, or their contract allows it, whether that contract be made by themselves in the state of nature, or by the customs or laws of the country they live in."[15] Moreover, where her authority over her children is concerned, the wife is the equal of the husband, "if we consult reason or revelation, we shall find, she hath an equal title [over her children]."[16]

The contractual obligation between husband and wife is ancillary, however, to the relationship that may arise through marriage between parent and child. Locke argued that it is the potential for children that gives marriage its distinctive *raison d'etre*, and which makes it more than a mere contract. The potential for children elevates marriage to the status of a sacred obligation. In Locke's words, through marriage, a man and woman may be bestowed with "the privilege of children, and the duty of parents." Where this occurs, "the nourishment and education of their children is a charge so incumbent on parents for their children's good, that nothing can absolve them from taking care of it."[17]

The reality of sex differences between men and women, leading to the potential for offspring, is essential to the pre-political foundation of marriage. From this emerges the sense of obligation for most, but not all, parents. As Locke notes, "God hath woven into the principles of human nature such a tenderness for their off-spring, that there is little fear that parents should use their power with too much rigor."[18] Where parents fail to live up to this natural obligation, however, it may be assumed by step-parents.[19] Yet the foundation of conjugal society remains natural love and duty by biological parents as husbands and wives for their biological children.

Property, on the other hand, is the tangible form that one's liberty takes and is necessary for the sustenance of one's life. By property, Locke meant not merely tangible goods or estates, but also, and most importantly, life and liberty.[20] Locke believed that, in its origins, property, like conjugal society, is pre-political. He proposed that it is initially acquired by mixing one's labor with the bounties of nature, and through the act of exertion, one extends one's dominion from oneself to those things within one's possession.[21] Property is acquired for self-preservation, which is a right common to all.

Given the basic equality of all mankind, Locke viewed the preservation of property to be in everyone's interests. Moreover, property rights are contingent upon not depriving others of what they could acquire through their own labor, and upon not spoiling the bounty of nature that could be used by others.[22] Furthermore, property rights often led to the betterment of others. Labor results in excess, or more than one can use, and which can be used by others.[23] From the production of excess, rooted in property rights, arises the market.

Locke understood that the market, rooted in property rights, is premised upon the basic *equality* of all. Ownership in property is just, because each is capable of acquiring it through effort. In using one's property, each retains an obligation to not interfere with the efforts of others who seek to acquire their own property, or otherwise to injure them. However, each cares for the self.[24] The domain of the marriage and family, on the other hand, finds its core justification in the basic *inequality* of some members of humanity, especially the basic inequality of children.[25] Unlike adults, children do not reason according to moral principles, and hence cannot be self-governing. They need to be taught how to exercise liberty responsibly. As Locke stated so aptly: "The freedom then of man, and liberty of acting according to his own will, is grounded on his having reason, which is able to instruct him in that law he is to govern himself by, and make him know how far he is left to the freedom of his own will. To turn him loose to an unrestrained liberty, before he has reason to guide him, is not . . . [to] allow . . . him the privilege of his nature to be free; but to thrust him out amongst brutes, and abandon him to a state as much beneath that of a man, as their's.[26] Hence the crucial difference between the market and conjugal society lies in this: the former is premised upon the equality of all competent adults, the latter accepts the reality of human inequality. Equality begets the liberty of the market that flourishes through property rights; inequality begets the duty of family that flourishes through marriage.

The market presupposes the equal capacities of adults to exercise their liberty responsibly and their common need for self preservation. Conjugal society arises from the fact that not everyone has the capacities to act responsibly. For this reason, the application of market principles to the domain of marriage and family is inappropriate. The family, rooted in marriage, is an institution for the protection of our most vulnerable members of humanity, and includes not just children, but also those who by reason of age or infirmity, are incapable of providing for themselves.[27] The market, rooted in property, is an institution in which each takes care of herself as each is presumed to possess relatively equal capacities.

Although their normative underpinnings are very different, the market and the family are alike in one crucial respect. They are alike in that they both operate best when political power can be put to use to enforce their core norms and to curb abuses where these occur. However, the invocation of political power in the domains of the market and the family begets a significant risk: state interference that extends beyond what is essential to preserve the integrity of these institutions of civil society.

This conclusion is consistent with Locke's understanding of the purpose of political society. According to Locke, the chief end of government is the protection of property, which includes one's life and liberty.[28] Although property rights exist independently of political power, without government, everyone would be responsible for protecting their own life, liberty, and property. Everyone would be judge in their own case yet partial to their own interests. Such a condition inevitably leads to over-reaching and abuse as each attempts to enforce rights as against others.[29] Political society exists to protect the life, liberty and property of all, and to ensure that an impartial arbiter judges the interests of equals. A society that does not protect life, liberty, and property exercises powers beyond right. It acts tyrannically.[30]

In the realm of conjugal society, Locke understood parental governance over children to be natural and hence not dependent upon political society. In this respect, it is unlike political society, which is formed by the consent of the governed.[31] However, within the domain of the family, parents do not have absolute or arbitrary authority over their children, nor do husbands hold such dominion over wives.

Moreover, the state does not create the responsibilities that parents owe to their children, nor can it take away these obligations. "[T]he power that a father hath naturally over his children, is the same, wherever they be born, and the ties of natural obligations, are not bounded by the positive limits of kingdoms and commonwealths."[32] Like the market, conjugal society, consisting of marriage and family, is not the creation of the state. It is a pre-political institution, rooted in sex difference and procreation.

Given the pre-political nature of conjugal society, the state regulates it rightly by recognizing it as a natural fact with its own norms and purposes. The state ought not treat conjugal society as its own creation. Where there is evidence that parents are failing in their duties to each other or to their children, the state may intervene. Absent this, however, the state ought to leave conjugal society, rooted in the union of one man and one woman, alone.[33]

SAME-SEX MARRIAGE VS. CONJUGAL SOCIETY

Conjugal society, being a pre-political form of social order, the existence of which is independent of the state, is precisely what advocates of same-sex marriage seek to change. Marriage rooted in procreation and sexual difference is to be replaced by marriage for the gratification of two consenting adults. If this change is to take hold fully, it will depend upon widespread acceptance of two justifications for same-sex marriage.

The first of these is that there is merely a contingent relationship between marriage and procreation. For this reason, marriage is not primarily an institution for the rearing of children, but one that advances the comforts and needs of adults who choose it. Pointing to infertile heterosexual couples, advocates of same-sex marriage argue that if infertile heterosexuals may be permitted to marry, so too must same-sex couples. As infertility is a biological reality, yet infertile men and women marry, it is concluded that the goods of companionship and mutual support that adults provide to one another through marriage must be the decisive criteria for determining who may marry. Far from being the foundation from which springs a sacred duty rooted in the inherently unequal status of children, marriage is a contract, binding two adults for so long as they may choose.[34]

The analogy between infertile heterosexuals and same-sex couples misses the point. The extension of marriage to infertile heterosexual couples serves not to deprecate same-sex couples, but to preserve the equal status of women in marriage. A test for fertility would be unfair to women because *all* women spend most of their adult lives in a state of infertility. Fertile women are infertile most days of a month, and post-menopausal women are always infertile. A fertility requirement would also render women susceptible to enormous abuse by men, providing a ready excuse for men who would trade in older women for nubile brides. The status of women in marriage would be intolerably diminished through this practice. Infertility is less common among men, as they can sire children into old age. Moreover, men, like women, typically do not discover that they are infertile until they attempt to sire children, at which time they ought already to be married.

A measure that serves primarily to protect women and to preserve their equal status within the institution of marriage is not a measure that is an appropriate basis by which to judge that the same should go for same-sex couples. One of the great challenges men and women face in marriage is in coming to terms with their differences while respecting the status of the other as an equal. Acceptance of infertility is a measure promoting this end. A measure to accommodate the reality of sex-based difference in marriage is no reason to extend marriage to same-sex couples. Moreover, accommodation for infertility in no way diminishes the reality that the inequality of the parent-child relationship is what differentiates marriage from other contractual relationships. It is the parent-child relation, as it emerges from sexual difference and procreation, which elevates marriage above a mere contract, and renders it a sacred duty.

Moreover, the attempt by advocates of same-sex marriage to sever marriage from procreation is more chimerical than real.[35] One would be hard-pressed to find an advocate of same-sex marriage who would accept the proposition that same-sex couples should be given the right to marry but that right does *not* entail a right to procreate and rear children. Were marriage and family truly severable, as the contractual view suggests, the one would not entail the other. However, advocates of same-sex marriage want it both ways. They want the contractual view of marriage *plus* the option of raising children.

This, then, leads to the second major justification for same-sex marriage. It is noted that same-sex couples do rear children and they are effective at childrearing. Given this reality, it is argued that same-sex couples should be permitted to marry for the sake of their children. Same-sex marriage will protect the children under their care so that these children will not be stigmatized, or otherwise disadvantaged, by having two parents of the same sex.[36]

To this, it is countered that the same-sex conception of marriage and family is, and must be, parasitic upon the demise of conjugal society, wherein biological parents are *not* taking responsibility for the rearing and education of their own children. Having no natural justification, the dominion of two adults of the same sex over children in their custody is crucially dependent upon the state to enforce their claim to these children as against the claims of the biological parent(s). Same-sex marriage is necessarily a political form of social order, invoking the power of the state to make it so.

For same-sex marriage to be regarded as a serious option by serious people, marriage must be failing. Indeed, all justifications for same-sex marriage for the sake of children arise out of social tragedy accepted as the status quo. Same-sex marriage for the sake of children requires the existence of men and women who are not forming stable unions conducive to the rearing of their biological children. It requires biological parents who are not willing or able to raise their children. It accommodates husbands or wives who would like to divorce to join lovers of the same sex. It envisions men and women offering their sexual organs, or sperm and eggs, to others without intending to accept the responsibilities of being parents to the children they bring into the world. In short, same-sex marriage for the sake of children can only exist in a world in which a sufficiently critical mass of parents are willing to walk away from their biological children and the mother (or father) by whom they sired (or conceived) these children.[37]

Marriage does not serve primarily to accommodate or to mitigate social tragedy of this sort. Its principal function is to prevent or limit the occurrence of such tragedies in the first place. Nevertheless, it is readily conceded that where social tragedy occurs, adoption may be laudable. At the same time, caution is in order where same-sex couple adoptions are concerned. Although there is evidence to substantiate the claim that adopted children fare satisfactorily with an adoptive mother and father, and in some cases, even with a single parent,[38] there is insufficient evidence to make judgments about how children fare with same-sex couples. In such cases, children in need participate in a social experiment.

Yet in the rare case where no other placement is possible, adoption by same-sex couples would be permissible, although a legislature may rationally decide not to engage in this social experiment.[39] In cases where an adoptive mother and father cannot be found, other responsible adults may be permitted to adopt children in need and thereby make these children their own. Adults who voluntarily take upon themselves the responsibility of parenthood for children in need provide an enormous social service. Such adults deserve praise; the full range of tax benefits and parental rights should be accorded to them. However, the existence of adopted children in the care of same-sex couples is not sufficient to justify same-sex marriage.

Proponents who advance the needs of children to justify same-sex marriage do not distinguish between cases in which same-sex couples adopt needy children from cases in which a parent leaves a husband or wife for a same-sex lover. Nor do they distinguish between adoption of a needy child and the production of children using surrogate sperm or eggs or wombs. In cases apart from the adoption of children in need, same-sex couples who take children into their custody do not ameliorate social evils but share in them. In many instances, they exacerbate them.

The principal reason for the tendency of same-sex marriage to make the plight of children worse is straightforward. Once same-sex couples are given a right to marry, they will claim from this a right to procreate. The fact that they cannot do so naturally will not stop them from achieving procreation through artificial means. Same-sex marriage will increase demand among gays and lesbians for reproductive technologies to produce children. The cloning of children will become an area deemed worthy of further exploration by those who cannot mate but who can marry. It does, after all, clean up the aesthetically unpleasing reality that one of the partners in the same-sex marriage might otherwise forever be tied through a child to someone of the opposite sex. In short, where the logic of the market is applied to marriage, the result is the commodification of children.[40]

In all cases apart from adoption, same-sex marriage fosters the vulnerability of children to advance the desires of adults. Children are rendered vulnerable not because same-sex couples make bad parents; the evidence of their competency as parents remains too scanty to make such a determination.[41] Rather, children are made vulnerable because they do not naturally belong to same-sex couples. They belong to them to the extent that their biological parents renounce responsibility for them and to the extent that the state will grant same-sex couples parental rights. In a very real sense, same-sex marriage normalizes the practice of entrusting the care of children to strangers. It is a socially constructed family that can survive only as long as favorable social conditions exist.

None of this is intended to refute the right of adults to enter into contracts for their mutual support and sustenance. One should presume that adults are capable of taking care of themselves and that they will do so. It would be wrong, however, to equate these arrangements with marriage. Unlike same-sex marriage, marriage is a distinctive, pre-political form of social order that is first and foremost about *duty*, especially to offspring, while it also promotes the mutual support and sustenance of the husbands and wives. Its justification does not rest on the equality of all adults, regardless of sexual orientation, but upon the inequality and vulnerability of some members of our species, particularly children. Marriage demands that men and women curb their sexual appetites, that they commit to a member of the opposite sex, and that they accept the burdens of parenthood if and when children result from their union.

Neither do these arguments against same-sex marriage deprecate adoption by same-sex couples or other adults. Adoption is a humane and laudable measure to mitigate the tragedy of children without parents willing or able to raise them. Adoption is not, however, a justification for same-sex marriage. Far from benefiting children, same-sex marriage encourages the severance of children from their biological parents. Children are thereby made vulnerable as it becomes unclear to whom these children belong as they are produced, or commodified, to fulfill the desires of adults.

SAME-SEX MARRIAGE AND SOFT DESPOTISM

According to Tocqueville, one of the peculiar evils to which democratic nations are prone is soft despotism. Soft despotism arises from the desires of democratic people to have their wants gratified, and to be left alone to indulge in their private lives. To this end, they cede their political freedom to the state, which cares for their wants. Tocqueville describes this state of soft despotism, emerging from the love of democratic peoples for equality and comfort, as follows: "Over this kind of men stands an immense, protective power which is alone responsible for securing their enjoyment and watching over their fate. That power is absolute, thoughtful of detail, orderly, provident, and gentle. It would resemble parental authority, if, fatherlike, it tried to prepare its charges for a man's life, but on the contrary, it only tries to keep them in perpetual childhood. It likes to see the citizens enjoy themselves, provided that they think of nothing but enjoyment. It gladly works for their happiness but wants to be sole agent and judge of it."[42]

Tocqueville observed that the primary means by which Americans resist this peculiarly democratic impulse toward puerility in citizens, and concomitantly, toward soft despotism, is through their tradition of political self governance.[43] Their habit of political engagement then spills over into a habit of organizing civic associations.[44] Through such associations, Americans regulate themselves without the need for state intervention and oversight. Liberty, understood in the sense of taking responsibility for one's self governance, tempers the tendency toward soft despotism, which arises from the desires of all to be equally comfortable and left alone. Tocqueville appreciated that this tradition of self governance is one of America's principal strengths, as it fosters a political order that is dynamic and energizing, yet orderly.[45] In short, it is a political order that is sustainable over time as its people can respond to the unexpected and the threatening.

Like Locke, Tocqueville could not have imagined an age in which self-indulgence would become tolerated to such an extent that it would be commonplace for parents to put their desires for sexual gratification above their duties to rear their biological children with the partner by whom these children are conceived. This is a tragedy of our times, and same-sex couples reflect it but are not primarily responsible for it. Sexual licentiousness is more dangerous to social order among heterosexuals than among gays and lesbians, as it is heterosexual unions that beget children.

Unlike conjugal society, however, same-sex marriage requires a condition of soft despotism to exist. In this political condition, gays and lesbians are liberated with their heterosexual counterparts to gratify themselves as they see fit. Self-indulgence in the realm of sexuality demands exactly the kind of gentle despotism that Tocqueville understood democracies have good reason to fear. It requires that the state increasingly step into the role of *parens patriae* to pave the way for the pursuit of self-gratification. Self-indulgence is what the United States Supreme Court encourages through its doctrine of privacy rights, which it decrees to be fundamental to the American constitution. Privacy rights include the right to use contraceptives, to abort children, and to have sexual relations with the partner(s) of one's choice so long as there is consent.[46] It is a doctrine that allows individuals to believe that they can enjoy sex without consequences; indeed, that they have a right to do so.[47] This is the state to which liberty has been degraded in our times. Rather than to be equally free and autonomous, we are to be equally indulged and infantilized to pursue our sexual desires.

Few doctrines are more disingenuous or dangerous than the Court's doctrine of privacy rights. The name of the right speaks volumes. It is a right to turn inward, to have regard only for one's self, to do what one wants to do without interference from the government. It is precisely the disposition that Tocqueville warned against, for it is the disposition that turns us from being men and women, capable of self-governance, into children who confuse liberty with license. As critically, the centralization of power that results has the potential to result in social and political stagnation.[48] Those who demand privileges from the state do not govern themselves; they do not exercise rights that exist independently of the state. They accept their "rights" as gifts of the state, which are accepted as entitlements. In the case of privacy rights, these degrade humanity while they clothe slavish passion with sacred right. Moreover, if Tocqueville is right, these rights come at a high price for they risk weakening the long-term viability of the political system. Like communism in the Soviet Union, excessively centralized political power runs the risk of collapsing from its own weight and inertia. For this reason, a reform that substantially weakens critical institutions of civil society ought to be regarded as threatening to political freedom.

Without the power of the state, privacy rights, like same-sex marriage, would not exist. The right to do whatever one wants to do can only exist in a society that removes all impediments and tidies up the social dislocations and inconveniences created by the sexual indulgence of its members. What results is soft despotism incarnate; adults are free to gratify themselves so long as they don't seek to rule themselves in common with others. This turn inward, for the sake of self-gratification, is politically enervating and potentially oppressive.

It may be countered, however, that same-sex marriage will have just the opposite effect. It is contended that by broadening marriage, our society encourages gays and lesbians to channel their passions into a solemn, stable, monogamous union. Responsibility and restraint ought to ensue. To the extent that marriage teaches heterosexuals responsibility, it ought to do the same for homosexuals.[49] As gays and lesbians accept greater responsibility with social approval, they will in fact contribute greatly to the common good, they will strengthen marriage and family, and they will energize political life.

Such a conclusion misunderstands the nature of marriage, and hence the ways in which the state usurps it to turn it into another means of self-gratification. Same-sex marriage is necessarily a *political* institution, whereas marriage is *pre-political*. Marriage has an existence independent of state power; same-sex marriage does not. The reality of children, and the duty of care imposed upon mothers and fathers to rear their offspring, would exist absent a political order. The duty of same-sex couples to rear children would not exist absent a political order which decrees that specific children belong to them. It is the nature of the former to bind a man and woman together in the solemn duty of caring for their children and each other. No such pre-political obligation exists for same-sex couples; they are bound together only for as long as they both shall want.

Same-sex couples can only marry insofar as the state decrees that they can. In claiming for homosexuals the right to marry, the state also claims for itself the ability to declare what constitutes marriage. It endows itself with the prerogative of defining its terms. It transforms marriage from a pre-political obligation into its own creation. At the same time, it replaces marriage as an obligation within conjugal society to marriage as a choice and a means of self-gratification. In this way, it changes the character of marriage not just for same-sex couples, but for everyone. By allowing same-sex marriage, the state decrees that, henceforth, marriage is what the state says it is. Marriage then loses its status as a fundamental institution of civil society, and becomes a right, granted by the state, for the desiring self.

As marriage loses its independence, rooted in biology and moral obligation, it also loses its ability to order society without state inter-ference. Where marriage is a pre-political institution, husbands and wives know that they are bound to each other, especially through their children. They don't need the state to create parenthood or to define who belongs to whom. The proper role of the state in regulating par-ent-child relations is simply to recognize the reality that this man and this woman are the parents of this child.

With same-sex marriage, this changes. The ability of same-sex couples to be parents depends crucially upon the state declaring that they possess such rights, and by extinguishing or redefining the rights of biological parents. With the rise of same-sex marriage, the obli-gations parents owe to their biological children are reduced to mere convention. This is true for everyone. Parents come to owe obligations to their children not because they are parents, but because they choose to be parents.

The obligations of parenthood are onerous and are felt to be especially so by a people who demand self-gratification. Furthermore, lacking roots in biology, in tradition, in a sense of duty, same-sex marriage is not sufficiently resilient to fend off the vicissitudes which the ordinary and extraordinary demands of life place upon all of us. Being entirely a creation of the state, it is an institution that needs to be coddled, and which demands cocooning to protect it. Its very fragility demands a culture in which it is protected. It is desperately in need of state intervention to support it. For these reasons, once marriage becomes a statist institution for the sake of consenting adults, the state will increasingly be called upon to create the social conditions to protect these unions.[50] The need of same-sex unions to be culturally coddled also increases the likelihood that the state will use public education for this end.[51] In this way, same-sex marriage affects not just those who participate in it; it affects everyone, and especially our children.

With the demise of marriage, children are being raised to fit better the lifestyle demands of their parents. Children are to understand their parents' needs; the importance of being accepting of sexual orientation and alternative lifestyles; the contingencies of all attachments; the need for each of us to create our own meaning of the universe. Such children are also taught a worldview that is intended to make them accepting of difference and adaptable in a world in which there are no permanent moral obligations. These dispositions are useful in resigning children who have no choice but to adapt as they are shuffled from household to household. These lessons are reinforced in their homes as children learn from the adults in their lives that self-gratification is good, that a sense of entitlement is normative, and that acts or omissions need not have consequences. The experience with the demise of sexual norms in Scandinavia indicates that such children do not flourish; they respond with a sense of despondency. [52]

It is a sad feature of our current political thought and jurisprudence that the importance of conjugal society to republican governance has been all but lost in the rhetoric of liberty and equality. Through force of law, a movement is afoot to transform marriage from a pre-political organization rooted in duty to offspring, to a political institution rooted in self-gratification. Same-sex marriage will likely not affect the material well-being of children, but it cannot but affect the character of the rising generation. Same-sex marriage will further erode political liberty by undermining the cultural milieu in which children learn to be self-governing and to care for themselves and their families. This is damaging both to the wellbeing of children and to the long-term sustainability of America's political order.

SAME-SEX MARRIAGE VS. RELIGION

The demand for a culture to nurture same-sex marriage has profound effects not just for traditional marriage, and the rights of parents to raise their children as they see fit. It affects *all* intermediary institutions of civil society standing between the individual and the state, but particularly those which threaten same-sex marriage. Foremost among these are religious organizations that do not support same-sex marriage. The Catholic Church, by virtue of its strength in American society, tops the list, but it is not alone. Many Christian, Jewish, and Muslim communities are morally, culturally, and intellectually opposed to same-sex marriage. To the extent that they exert cultural influence, they pose a threat to the sustainability of this fragile political institution.

Religious institutions opposing same-sex marriage are faced with a formidable adversary once same-sex marriage is recognized. That adversary is the state itself, or at least that branch of it that decrees same-sex marriage to be a right. The state necessarily stands in opposition to religious institutions who refuse to recognize same-sex marriage, and this opposition is heightened by the fact that same-sex marriage is in need of a protective culture to be sustainable. When a state creates same-sex marriage by political means, religious organizations are placed in the undesirable position of being in a contest for the hearts and minds of the people. In this contest, religious institutions are at a marked disadvantage, given that the tenets of religious faiths are primarily transmitted through conjugal society. As the state undermines conjugal society, it also undermines religions that support it.

Marriage and religion have a long and mutually supportive history.[53] Religion has traditionally served to recognize and regulate marriage either independently or concurrently with the state; husbands and wives, in turn, educate their children in the tenets of the faith in which their marriage is recognized and regulated. Moreover, in democratic societies, religion, more often than not, serves civic purposes. It teaches children and adults about their responsibilities to their fellow men and to society at large. As Tocqueville rightly observed, religion tends to serve as a bulwark against soft despotism in that it encourages citizens to look beyond their immediate self-interest and material comforts.[54] Religion is a principal means by which people become actively involved in tending for the well-being of others.[55] Children nurtured in faith are prone to learn dispositions that make them more capable of self-governance, and less in need of the state to care for them.[56]

State efforts to institutionalize same-sex marriage undermine religious authority in a number of ways. First, as the state claims for itself the right to redefine marriage, it limits the traditional regulatory powers of religious organizations in the realm of matrimony. It forces upon religious institutions the need to come to terms with a political institution regarded by them as contrary to reason and at odds with the tenets of their faiths. In so doing, it also indicts as intolerant religious institutions that stand in opposition to same-sex marriage. Through this charge, the moral authority of religious institutions is undermined in the eyes of the public who are encouraged to view uncompromising faiths as unreasonable and unsupportive of marriage (as it is now defined).

Secondly, in its effort to create a culture in which same-sex marriage can be sustained, the state, through education, inculcates within children beliefs at odds with the tenets of traditional faith. In the United States, the state has the additional advantage that it can call upon the establishment clause to keep religious points of view out of public schools.[57] By this means, the children are indoctrinated into narrow secular ideology. Exposure to prayer led by teachers is prohibited, while acceptance of sexual behavior at odds with traditional faiths is encouraged. Traditional beliefs are thereby stigmatized.

Thirdly, and most importantly, the state drives a wedge between religion and children by taking away the desires of their parents to be guided by religion. Parents, raising children in a society in which religion is widely regarded as inconsistent with official public policy, are less apt to expose their children to it. Parents thereby choose to deprive themselves of a fundamental support for their own marriages, as well as a source of civic education and spiritual inspiration for themselves and their children. As families shy away from religion, religious organizations tend to wither, for they cannot exist if people do not believe in the tenets of their faith or accept the moral authority of their religious institutions.

Same-sex marriage, then, is not simply a statist assault upon the independence of marriage as a pre-political institution. It is also statist assault upon religion, and especially those religions which oppose it. Unlike marriage, however, the state cannot usurp religion by claiming for itself the power to define it. Instead, it relegates it to the private realm, where it is treated as a matter of individual conscience. Rather than being an institution of civil society, religion is reduced to a matter of individual belief.[58] In this way, the state overcomes religious opposition by refusing to recognize the ability of any given religion to speak with one voice. It also limits effective political action among those who might otherwise be united by an authority independent of the state.

What results from the wedge that is driven between marriage and religion through the creation of same-sex marriage is cause for great concern for anyone who values political freedom. By creating same-sex marriage, the state does a great deal of harm to two principal civil institutions: conjugal society and religion. It also limits the effectiveness of these institutions in their capacity to serve as buffers between the state and individuals. As Tocqueville well understood, individuals in a democracy are weak. The principal means by which they preserve their freedom against centralized political power is by means of associations.[59] Crucial to this effort to protect political freedom are marriage and religion, both of which stand as pre-political forms of social order. Both of these institutions serve to inculcate within people, and especially within children, the dispositions needed to be self-governing. These include a concern for the welfare of others, a sense of duty that permits one to be self-sacrificing, a sense of justice tempered by mercy, a belief in the fundamental equality of all men, a love of liberty but not license and the sense to know the difference.[60]

Much as proponents of same-sex marriage may profess that these values are sustained by same-sex marriage, their professions are in vain. By virtue of being a political institution to satisfy personal needs, same-sex marriage promotes a sense of entitlement, not obligation; a love for tolerance that erodes moral standards of judgment; a desire for uncritical approbation; a love of license over liberty; a slavish equality of all beneath the rule of a gentle despot. It is an institution that is antithetical to political freedom. Its very existence depends upon an exercise of state power, and its sustenance equally depends upon frequent state intervention to shape a public culture in which same-sex marriage can be coddled. Moreover, same-sex marriage stands opposed to religions that regard it as an illegitimate usurpation by the state, and in this contest, religions stand to lose as the choices of same-sex couples become the object of state protection. As the state undermines authentic marriage, it concurrently undermines religious authority in the domain of family life.

The society resulting from same-sex marriage is deeply disordered, as far from enabling people to govern themselves to the extent possible, it creates dependence on the state to define and order marriage and family life. It is contrary to the principle of subsidiarity, which stipulates that individuals ought to be encouraged to regulate themselves within simple and proximate associations wherever possible to foster their own wellbeing.[61] In practice, subsidiarity is a call to work to establish good governance within our families, religious communities, workplaces, neighborhoods. It also carries with it the expectation that state regulation should not be sought unless it is needed to solve problems for the common good. The principle of subsidiarity calls upon each of us to become fully engaged in, and responsible for, social order and justice. Each person has an immediate and pressing responsibility for the promotion of the common good, but this responsibility starts at an immediate and proximate level.

Same-sex marriage is antithetical to this principle. A creature of the state, dependent upon the state for its existence and sustenance, it invites state intrusions into the lives of children, as it transforms society from the top down. It undermines conjugal society, rooted in responsibility, and the religious institutions that nurture it. It leaves persons without robust institutions of civil society through which to govern themselves effectively and without state intervention. It promotes bad choices, while also making individuals both unfit and without the full array of institutional resources through which they can govern themselves without recourse to the state.

CONCLUSION

A just regime is one that makes its peace with the market, the family, and religious authority, allowing each to govern in their proper domains. A just regime is one that is content with the decentralization of power and legitimate governance that results. An unjust regime is one that folds one or all of these civic institutions into the state, or which undermines them. Such a regime regulates ineffectively at best, and despotically at worst when it usurps or undermines our society's core civic institutions.

As a pre-political form of social order, the *raison d'etre* of marriage does not stem from the purposes of the state, even if those purposes include the seemingly laudable principles of promoting equality and liberty. It also does not stem from the desires of adults. Marriage arises from the peculiar vulnerabilities of children and the biological reality that it is the sexual coupling of men and women that begets children. Marriage serves to place upon these two, as full and equal human beings, the sacred responsibility of raising and educating the children begotten by their sexual union. It thereby elevates one man and one woman above the realm of contract, imposing upon them, and upon them only, the sacred duty of rearing and educating their children.

Same-sex marriage is a radical denial of marriage. By importing market principles into the domain of marriage, same-sex marriage denies that marriage is necessarily connected to procreation, while it also seeks to advance the rights of same-sex couples to procreate and rear children. Same-sex marriage is a political institution. It is entirely dependent upon the power of the state for its very existence. It is also dependent upon the power of the state to create the cultural conditions in which it can survive.

Finally, same-sex marriage undermines not simply marriage, but religious authority as well. Here, the state is called upon to limit the influence of religions that pose a threat to its creation. This end is effectively achieved by severing the mutually supportive relationship of marriage and religious authority.

Same-sex marriage undermines core civil institutions so as better to gratify consenting adults. This is not liberty. One's masters become state power and sexual desire. The cost of same-sex marriage, and the privacy rights upon which it is based, is soft despotism, not simply for oneself, but also for one's children.

9

(How) Does Marriage
Protect Child Well-Being?

Maggie Gallagher

ARRIAGE IS A UNIVERSAL HUMAN INSTITUTION. Virtually every known human society has some form of marriage.[1] While the norms of marriage in different cultures vary considerably, marriage always has something to do with creating a public (not private) sexual union between a man and woman so that socially-valued children have both a mother and a father, and so that society has the next generation it needs.

As Margo Wilson and Martin Daly put it recently: "Marriage is a universal social institution, albeit with myriad variations in social and cultural details. A review of the cross-cultural diversity in marital arrangements reveals certain common themes: some degree of mutual obligation between husband and wife, a right of sexual access (often but not necessarily exclusive), and expectation that the relationships will persist (although not necessarily for a lifetime), some cooperative investment in offspring, and some sort of recognition of the status of the couples' children. *The marital alliance is fundamentally a reproductive alliance.*"[2]

Why does the marriage idea arise again and again in widely varying societies? Here is the most likely reason: because sexual relationships between men and women create children. Every society must find some way to regulate these relationships, to channel some portion of the erotic energies of men and women attracted to the opposite sex into the kind of sexual union where (a) childbearing is acceptable because (b) children and society's interests are protected. Does marriage continue to play an important role in protecting children in the modern context and if so how?

This paper does not attempt to explain whether and how same-sex marriage will reduce child well-being or injure marriage.[3] My goal is more modest: it is to (1) review the social science evidence on whether married mothers and fathers are important to child well-being; (2) review the claim that the social science literature on gay parenting contradicts the claim that children do best when raised by their own married mother and fathers; and (3) draw some inferences from this evidence about how and when marriage protects child well-being, based on current social science evidence.

I. DOES MARRIAGE PROTECT CHILD WELL-BEING?

Do mothers and fathers matter for kids or in the contemporary context are all kinds of family forms equally protective of child well-being?

In the last thirty years, thousands of studies evaluating the consequences of marriage for children and society have been conducted in various disciplines (psychology, sociology, economics, and medicine). In virtually every way that social scientists know how to measure, children do better, on average, when their parents get and stay married (provided those marriages are not high-conflict or violent). By contrast, every major social pathology that can trouble an American child happens more often when his or her parents are not joined by marriage: more poverty, dependency, child abuse, domestic violence, substance abuse, suicide, depression, mental illness, infant mortality, physical illness, education failure, high school dropouts, sexually transmitted diseases, and early unwed childbearing, and later on, divorce.[4]

Twelve leading family scholars recently summarized the vast research literature this way: "Marriage is an important social good associated with an impressively broad array of positive outcomes for children and adults alike."[5] Among their conclusions:

- Marriage increases the likelihood that children enjoy warm, close relationships with parents.
- Cohabitation is not the functional equivalent of marriage.
- Children raised outside of intact married homes are more likely to divorce or become unwed parents themselves.
- Marriage reduces child poverty.
- Divorce increases the risk of school failure for children, and reduces the likelihood that they will graduate from college and achieve high status jobs.
- Children in intact married homes are healthier, on average, than children in other family forms.
- Babies born to married parents have sharply lower rates of infant mortality.
- Children from intact married homes have lower rates of substance abuse.
- Divorce increases rates of mental illness and distress in children, including the risk of suicide.
- Boys and young men from intact married homes are less likely to commit crimes.
- Married women are less likely to experience domestic violence than cohabiting and dating women.
- Children raised outside of intact marriages are more likely to be victims of both sexual and physical child abuse.

They conclude, "Marriage is more than a private emotional relationship. It is also a social good. Not every person can or should marry. And not every child raised outside of marriage is damaged as a result. But communities where good-enough marriages are common have better outcomes for children, women, and men than do communities suffering from high rates of divorce, unmarried childbearing, and high-conflict or violent marriages."[6]

Recent analyses by mainstream child research organizations confirm this emerging scholarly consensus that family structure matters. For example:

- A *Child Trends* research brief summed up the scholarly consensus thus: "Research clearly demonstrates that family structure matters for children, and the family structure that helps the most is a family headed by two biological parents in a low-conflict marriage. Children in single-parent families, children born to unmarried mothers, and children in stepfamilies or cohabiting relationships face higher risks of poor outcomes. . . . There is thus value for children in promoting strong, stable marriages between biological parents."[7]

- A Center for Law and Social Policy Brief concludes, "Research indicates that, on average, children who grow up in families with both their biological parents in a low-conflict marriage are better off in a number of ways than children who grow up in single-, step-, or cohabiting-parent households."[8]

While scholars continue to disagree about the size of the marital advantage and the mechanisms by which it is conferred,[9] the weight of social science evidence strongly supports the idea that family structure matters and that the family structure that is most protective of child well-being is the intact, biological, married family.

II. THE SOCIAL SCIENCE OF GAY PARENTING

Most of the preceding research on family structure, however, does not directly compare children in intact married homes with children raised from birth by same-sex couples. Thus the powerful new social science consensus on family structure is on a collision course with a separate emerging consensus from a related field: the social science literature on sexual orientation and parenting.

Judith Stacey summed up this new challenge to the social science consensus on family structure in testimony before the U.S. Senate:

"The research shows that what places children at risk is not fatherless-ness, but the absence of economic and social resources that a qualified second parent can provide, whether male or female. . . . Moreover, the research on children raised by lesbian and gay parents demonstrates that these children do as well if not better than children raised by het-erosexual parents. Specifically, the research demonstrates that children of same-sex couples are as emotionally healthy and socially adjusted and at least as educationally and socially successful as children raised by heterosexual parents."[10]

Other researchers, including at least two prominent professional associations, have made similar claims.[11] Advocates for same-sex mar-riage often rely on these studies to assert that scientific evidence shows that married mothers and fathers hold no advantages for children. As Mary Bonauto, counsel for the plaintiffs in the Massachusetts mar-riage litigation, wrote in the Summer 2003 edition of *Human Rights*, "[C]hild-rearing experts in the American Academy of Pediatrics, the American Psychiatric Association, and the American Psychological Association insist that the love and commitment of two parents is most critical for children—not the parents' sex or sexual orientation."[12]

Similarly Evan Wolfson, head of Freedom to Marry, asserted re-cently, "[T]here is no evidence to support the offensive proposition that only one size of family must fit all. Most studies—including the ones that [Maggie] Gallagher relies on—reflect the common sense that what counts is not the family structure, but the quality of dedication, commitment, self-sacrifice, and love in the household."[13]

For many people the question of how children fare when raised by same-sex couples is at the heart of the gay marriage debate. My own views on how same-sex marriage will hurt marriage as a social institu-tion have been developed elsewhere.[14] I take up here the social science evidence on gay parenting for a different (if related) purpose.

Several decades of public and scholarly debate has established a broad consensus on the importance of married mothers and fathers for child well-being. There is only one outstanding scholarly body of evidence challenging this hard-won consensus that the intact, married family consisting of a mother and father is the "ideal" family form for children: the separate scientific literature on sexual orientation and child well-being. The family structure debate and the gay parenting debate have developed largely in isolation from each other, and few efforts have been made to weigh their claims as competing bodies of social science evidence.

How should legal thinkers and decision-makers evaluate such competing claims about family structure and child well-being when both are allegedly grounded in social science evidence?

Numerous reviews of the literature on sexual orientation and parenting have been conducted.[15] At least three such reviews have pointed to the serious scientific limitations of the social science literature on gay parenting.[16]

One of the most thorough reviews was prepared by Steven Nock, a sociologist at the University of Virginia who was asked to review several hundred studies as an expert witness for the Attorney General of Canada. Nock concluded: "Through this analysis I draw my conclusions that 1) all of the articles I reviewed contained at least one fatal flaw of design or execution; and 2) not a single one of those studies was conducted according to general accepted standards of scientific research."[17] Design flaws researchers have found in these studies include very basic limitations:

- *No nationally representative samples.* Even scholars enthusiastic about unisex parenting, such as Stacey and Biblarz, acknowledge that "there are no studies of child development based on random, representative samples of [same-sex couple headed] families."[18]

- *Limited outcome measures.* Many of the outcomes measured by the research are unrelated to standard measures of child well-being used by family sociologists (perhaps because most of the researchers are developmental psychologists, not sociologists). Studies of gay parenting typically focus on measures such as the development of sexual identity, self-esteem, and sexual orientation. The family structure literature in general, by contrast, includes a wide array of outcome measures.

- *Few long-term studies.* Most of the studies conducted to date focus on static or short-term measures of child development. Few or none follow children of unisex parents to adulthood.

But perhaps the most serious methodological critique of these studies, at least with reference to the family structure debate, is this:

- *The vast majority of these studies compare single lesbian mothers to single heterosexual mothers.* As sociologist Charlotte Patterson, a leading researcher on gay and lesbian parenting, summed up as of 2000, "[M]ost studies have compared children in divorced lesbian mother-headed families with children in divorced heterosexual mother-headed families."[19]

Moreover, even within this literature, some research finds that although sexual orientation "per se" is not associated with negative outcomes, father absence is. For example, Golombok, Tasker, and Murray (1997)[20] compared a snowball sample of thirty children with lesbian moms to forty-one children living with opposite-sex couples and forty-two single heterosexual single mother families. Families experiencing economic hardship were excluded. Lesbian families had significantly higher social class: 28 percent of heterosexual families were in manual labor compared to 3 percent of lesbian families. Nonetheless, "Children in father-absent families perceived themselves to be less cognitively competent and less physically competent than children in father-present families, with no differences between children in lesbian and single heterosexual families."[21]

Most of the gay parenting literature thus compares children in some fatherless families to children in other fatherless family forms. The results may be relevant for some legal policy debates (such as custody disputes) but are not designed to shed light on family structure per se, and cannot credibly be used to contradict the current weight of social science: family structure matters, and the family structure that is most protective of child well-being is the intact, married biological family.

III. (HOW) DOES MARRIAGE PROTECT CHILDREN?

What is it about marriage as a legal and social institution that protects children? Is it the mere presence of two adults in the home? Is it the special social validation that marital status enjoys? Do children benefit because the law provides special legal incentives to married people that are denied single mothers or cohabiting parents?

This is an important question, particularly in the light of claims that extending marriage to same-sex couples will provide important protections for the children in these unions.[22] Understanding the mechanisms through which marriage protects children is essential to crafting effective strategies for strengthening marriage as a social institution.

With the advent of the gay marriage debate, the most prominent theory of the way marriage law protects children is that marriage carries important legal benefits which directly or indirectly benefit children living with married parents. As Mary Bonauto, citing from the *Goodridge* decision, wrote in the *Maine Bar Journal* earlier this year, "All that is certain is that denying marriage to gay and lesbian families penalizes the children in those families 'by depriving them of state benefits because the state disapproves of their parents' sexual orientation.'"[23]

This view is consistent with the *Goodridge* court's bald declaration that "government creates . . . marriage."[24] In this view, marriage is primarily a legal construct and its importance for children and society consists of the legal benefits and responsibilities the law dispenses along with a marriage license.[25] However, this view is not particularly consistent with the social science evidence we have on the effects of family structure on child well-being.[26] If the legal benefits or social status of marriage played the critical role in protecting child well-being, we would expect children who live with remarried parents to do better than children who remain with an unmarried parent. In fact, children in remarried families do no better (or worse) on average than children raised by single mothers. As the *Child Trends* research brief quoted above carefully suggests, it is not any marriage that protects child well-being, but the intact, married, reasonably harmonious union of the child's own biological mother and father.[27]

For the most part, the legal duties and obligations of parents have been severed from marital status (in part by the Supreme Court decisions abolishing "legitimacy" as a legal category).[28] In theory, unmarried fathers have exactly the same legal support obligations to their children as married fathers, as well as the same rights to care and custody of their children. Moreover, marriage as a legal institution is more likely to give rise to financial penalties for spouses than financial benefits, primarily through tax and welfare policies.[29]

So a realistic appraisal of how marriage matters to children's welfare divides into two key questions: (1) How does the existence of marriage as a legal and social institution increase the likelihood a child will be raised by his own mother and father? (2) How and why are children better off if their biological parents marry rather than cohabit?

Let me suggest two main mechanisms: First, marriage as a legal and social institution substantially reduces the likelihood that children will be conceived in a home without a committed father. Marriage produces important "selection" effects in terms of who becomes a parent, at what time of life, and with what partner. Second, marriage may increase the likelihood that a particular child's parents will stay together in one family unit rather than separate.

Increasing the likelihood of committed fathers

Almost every child conceived and born to a married couple will begin life with both her mother and her father already committed to caring for her and raising her together. The majority of children born outside of marriage do not begin life with this advantage.[30] Moreover, as time passes, the majority of children raised outside of intact marriages do not have a close, warm relationship with their father.[31]

Moreover, for young men and women attracted to the opposite sex, avoiding an out of wedlock pregnancy or birth is difficult. Regardless of what we think of the options morally speaking, the logical possibilities single men and women face are: sterilization, surgical abortion, ruthlessly contraception,[32] confining sexual relationships to engaged partnerships or other romantic partners who will probably marry in the event of pregnancy, or sexual abstinence until marriage (as well as sexual fidelity thereafter).

What all these strategies have in common is they require effort. What gives single men and women who do avoid unmarried childbearing the strong motivation necessary to do any of the difficult things they must do prevent unmarried pregnancy and unwed births? Part of the answer is the existence of the public and legal category called "marriage" that signals the conditions under which children are normative, expected, and welcomed. The existence of the legal category allows other, more important players than the law (such as families, friends, and faith communities) to raise children to become young men and women willing to do some of the hard things necessary to postpone pregnancy until marriage.

The existence of marriage as a public and legal category thus regulates even the behavior of people who are *not* married. Even in poor communities, young unwed mothers and fathers often make dramatic changes in their lives and behaviors under the influence of norms surrounding marriage. Kathy Edin, for example, documents that while poor Americans do not consider a baby a good reason for marriage, they do consider it a good reason for staying together. Staying together demands living together. And a couple who is living together and raising a child should at least be aiming for marriage, which in their minds involves working towards a harmonious relationship and financial stability.[33] The existence of marriage as a distinct legal category and of social ideals associated with marriage, cast a long shadow over relationships between men and women, whether married or single.

For men and women attracted to the opposite sex, the default (or passive) option is many pregnancies and births in fatherless households. If the goal is children raised by their own mothers and fathers united in one loving family, an enormous amount of social energy is needed on the part of young people and on the part of families, educators, friends, meaningful adults, faith communities and other institutions of civil society to channel the sexual energies of the young in order to produce this result.

Marriage as a legal, shared, public norm helps reduce the likelihood that children are born to fathers who are not committed to them or to their mother. The pledge of sexual fidelity in marriage has an important side benefit for children. It reduces the likelihood that the emotional, psychological, spiritual, and financial resources of fathers will be subdivided across many mothers and households, making effective fatherhood difficult if not impossible.

Conscientious social scientists invest considerable effort in trying to control for "selection effects" in evaluating the consequences of marriage. This is necessary and appropriate to answer the question: Would the children of this particular couple be better off if we could persuade that couple to marry? But as important as that question may be, focusing on it exclusively may obscure rather than reveal the prime mechanism through which a marriage culture protects children.

For marriage, as a social institution, is designed to create huge selection effects in who has children with whom. A marriage culture asks young people to consider with what kind of person they wish to have children. The kind of qualities that make for an enduring mate, someone that you are likely to want to keep around for the rest of your life, are likely to be quite different from the kind of qualities that are sufficiently attractive for less enduring relationships. The kind of man who is "good enough" for a Saturday night date, or even for a cohabiting relationship, is often very different from the kind of man one envisions as a life-long mate.

The long-term horizons of marriage help focus attention of young people on the kind of qualities that make for a good mother or father: dependable, responsible, reliable, committed; marriage as a social and legal institution allows men and women to signal to one another when that person has arrived on the scene.[34]

Keeping parents together

Marriage reduces the likelihood that parents will part. Even biological cohabiting parents are more likely to separate than married parents.[35]

In part this is because parents who are married have already declared an intention to stay together for life. Marriage as a public vow and legal promise allows partners who seek a permanent commitment to signal clearly their intention to one another.

Marriage is also supported by stronger community, religious, and familial norms than are most informal partnerships. Most Americans continue to believe that marriage is a lifelong commitment, and that extramarital sexual relationships are wrong. There is thus greater community support for staying together when parents are married rather than when parents are single or cohabiting. Greater community disapprobation of "cheating" in marriage reduces the risk of developing competing sexual and intimate relationships that threaten long-term marital happiness and stability.[36] Married people are more faithful than either cohabiting or dating couples and also more likely on average to report high levels of sexual satisfaction than unmarried people.[37] Marriage appears to be associated with reduced domestic violence and conflict compared to cohabiting relationships, and thus indirectly encourages stability in the relationships between married mothers and fathers.[38]

The long-term perspective encouraged by marriage also helps improve relationship satisfaction, encouraging the delayed gratification, investments, and sacrifices of short-term gratification that help create a loving, enduring bond.

Finally, marriages can be dissolved only by taking legal action. The legal requirement of divorce acts as a barrier to relationship dissolution, as well as signaling the special importance the community places on keeping marriage together.

IV. HOW DO MOTHERS AND FATHERS MATTER?

Marriage provides children not just with any two adults, but with their own two parents: the mother and father who made them biologically are expected to maintain that parenting union socially, economically, sexually, and psychologically as well. The social science evidence we have establishes fairly powerfully that this family structure is best for children (at least of all the family structures that have been well-studied), but it does not tell us as clearly why or how.

Many of the features that make marriage better for children might be expected to apply to remarried families or cohabiting and same-sex families as well. Two adults in the home means twice the manpower available for parenting tasks: two potential breadwinners, and two potential nurturers, educators and discipliners as well. Economies of scale mean that two adults providing for children can live more cheaply (and thus have more money available to the family) than two parents or partners who maintain separate households. The decline in commitment to sex roles and sex role ideology suggests to many Americans that two fathers or two mothers can do all the things that a mother and father might do in raising children together.

What then is it about married mothers and fathers raising children together that matters? From the social science evidence on this question, two great possibilities suggest themselves: gender and genes.

Marriage brings together the two sexes, male and female, in the only kind of sexual union that can give children their own mother and father in a single family. In general, outside of intact marriages, relatively few children have committed and dependable fathers.

How does gender matter?

One theory of how and why marriage matters, is that fathers and mothers parent differently, in ways that complement one another and boost child well-being. There is evidence that mothers' and fathers' parenting styles differ in reasonably systematic ways, although the evidence of the causal relationship of such differences to child well-being is not as well-established.[39]

But a "task-oriented" vision of how fathers matter to their children may be missing a deeper point. Men and women do differ and tend at least to parent somewhat differently; when men and women are parents together, these differences may become even more apparent as each person "specializes" in the aspects of parenting most congenial.

But parents are more than caretakers. A child's need for a father may not be captured by breaking parenting down into a set of tasks performed, whether they are performed the same or differently by men and women.

What do I mean? Gender is a human universal, although particular gender roles may not be. Every human society notices that human beings consist of two different sexes, and strives to assign social meaning of some kind to this biological distinction. A distinguished group of thirty-three neuroscientists, pediatricians, and social scientists recently reviewed the evidence on gender as a basic reality: "In recent years dozens of studies of the behavior of young children show that boys and girls differ significantly in a number of areas, including who they want to play with, the toys they prefer, fantasy play, tough-and-tumble play, activity level, and aggression. Some portion of these differences is likely attributable to . . . environmental factors. . . . But a number of basic differences in gender role behavior are also biologically primed and even established prenatally."[40] Moreover, "In the area of gender identity (typically at about 18-24 months of age) [as the child] begins to show a deep need to understand and make sense of her or his sexual embodiment, the child's relationships with mother and father become centrally important. For the child searching for the meaning of his embodiment, both the same-sex-as-me parent and the opposite-sex-from-me-parent play vital roles."[41]

At puberty, all societies typically mobilize to "define and enforce the social meaning of sexual embodiment. . . . *[T]he need to attach social significance and meaning to gender appears to be a human universal.*"[42]

Much of gender meaning is socially constructed. But as these scientists point out, "Gender also runs deeper, near to the core of human identity and social meaning—in part because it is biologically primed and connected to differences in brain structure and function, in part because it is so deeply implicated in the transition to adulthood."[43]

What a boy gets from experiencing the dependable love of a father is a deep personal experience of masculinity that is pro-social, pro-woman, pro-child, and not at odds with love. Without this personal experience of maleness, a boy (who like all human beings is deeply driven to seek some meaning for masculinity) is vulnerable to a variety of peer and market-driven alternative definitions of masculinity, often grounded in real gender differences in aggression, physical strength, and sexual proclivities.

The importance of a father in giving a boy a deeply pro-social sense of his own masculinity may be one reason why one large national study found that boys raised outside of intact marriages were two to three times more likely to commit a crime leading to imprisonment.[44] Similarly, a girl raised without a father does not come to adolescence with the same deep experience of what male love feels like when it is truly protective, not driven primarily by a desire for sexual gratification. At the same time, fatherless girls may experience a hunger for masculine love and attention that leaves her particularly vulnerable to use and abuse by young adult males. (Girls raised without fathers are at high risk for unwed motherhood.)[45]

Gendered differences in response to father absence are themselves affirmation that gender is a deeply important human category. Indeed sexual orientation as a concept presumes that gender exists and is an important category for human relationships. It would be odd to presume (as the gay parenting debate often does) that gender is all-important to adult romantic relationships, but has no significance at all in the hungry love a child feels for his or her parents.

Genes and Parenting

Marriage ordinarily provides not just a generic male adult for a child, but the child's own biological father. Evolutionary psychology now suggests that genetic relationships do make a difference in human affairs, and that men are particularly likely to be affected by the existence or absence of a biological relationship with a child.

The data are perhaps most clear for child abuse, where children who live with unrelated males are at extremely elevated risks of sexual and physical abuse. Martin Daly and Margo Wilson report that living with a stepparent has turned out to be the most powerful predictor of severe child abuse yet.[46] Both stepfathers and boyfriends have been found to commit disproportionate levels of child abuse. One study found that a preschool child living with a stepfather was forty times more likely to be sexually abused than one living with both of his or her biological parents."[47]

Many people are capable of loving and caring for a child who is not biologically related to them. Nonetheless, the phenomenon of "kin altruism" suggests that creating social connections between children and their biological parents has value, over the broad sweep of history, for children.

V. THE BENEFITS OF MARRIAGE

Marriage has powerful benefits for children and communities. When parents get and stay married, children do better in every way that social scientists know how to measure, provided those marriages are not high-conflict or violent. Communities benefit from more productive, law-abiding citizens, more orderly schools and neighborhoods, and fewer troubling and expensive social problems.

These benefits, however, are not a direct product of law. They are not the result of special financial benefits distributed by government to married couples, and married couples alone.

The benefits of marriage that have been documented by social science for children flow from (1) the "selection effects" created by marriage as a legal and social institution, in shaping who becomes a parent, with whom, and at what point in their lives, as well as (2) the unique capacity of marriage to offer to the child the natural benefits that flow from being raised by his or her own mother and father united in one loving family.

10

The Current Crisis in Marriage Law, Its Origins, and Its Impact

Katherine Shaw Spaht

> *Words strain,*
> *Crack and sometimes break, under the burden,*
> *Under the tension, slip, slide, perish,*
> *Decay with imprecision, will not stay in place,*
> *Will not stay still. Shrieking voices*
> *Scolding, mocking, or merely chattering,*
> *Always assail them.*
>
> T. S. Eliot, *Burnt Norton,*
> *Four Quartets*

MARRIAGE? A word assailed by the "shrieking voices" of various activists who urge legal recognition of a variety of adult sexual arrangements under the increasingly broad umbrella of marriage. They use the megaphone offered by the intellectual and influential opinion-shapers. "Gay" activists insist that marriage merely reflects an intimate *personal* commitment and thus should include them. Feminists insist marriage is anachronistic, essentially patriarchal, and in the end irrelevant; and polygamists and polyamorists insist that the legal regulation of such intimate, personal commitments should extend beyond two persons. The "shrieking voices," which began as the equivalent of a stage whisper in the early 1970s, have had their effect on the cultural landscape as well as in legal arenas; for, admittedly, culture and law interact in a complex way which is difficult both to unravel and to understand. The cultural wars of the late twentieth and early twenty-first centuries find a focus "in the intensifying struggle over how to define the word 'marriage' as a *legal* term of art."[1] Remarkably, the word marriage has lost much of its cultural meaning, not to mention an understanding of the role of the law in privileging and protecting marriage.

With the secularization of the broader American culture,[2] the modern meaning of marriage began to evolve away from its religiously grounded definition. Once begun in the early 1800s, the evolution of the meaning of marriage and the increasingly *laissez-faire* attitude towards its protection and promotion proceeded incrementally and fitfully in state legislatures and state courts. By the end of the 1940s marriage no longer enjoyed the same legal protection it had at the beginning of the twentieth century, leaving it naked and vulnerable. During the 1960s, with the arrival of the birth control "pill" effectively separating the consequences of sexual union between a man and a woman from the act itself, the process accelerated. In 1969 California enacted its radically new "no-fault" divorce law, and in 1972 the first reported appellate case of a same-sex couple asserting the "right to marry" appeared.[3] At virtually the same time the United States Supreme Court, hitherto relatively deferential to state law regulating marriage, began more "actively to reshape the law of the family to accord with their own secularized ideals."[4] Those secularized ideals have continued to evolve in opinions examining the constitutionality of state marriage legislation, in tandem with opinions concerning abortion and homosexual rights which continue to expand the notion of an individual's "liberty" interest under the Fourteenth Amendment to the United States Constitution.

Strong cultural trends and attitudes about marriage and divorce, having developed over decades, took hold and flourished during the sixties, reinforcing a "new" understanding of marriage. Those legal and social forces included the long tradition of legal non-intervention in the family, affirming its "privacy"; the changing societal mores, particularly those related to sexual morality; the rise of psychological man and the therapeutic society; and a highly individualized notion of personal autonomy.[5] Often emanating from an intellectual elite within Western industrialized countries,[6] these damaging cultural trends still permeate the thinking and attitudes of average citizens. Any reversal of these attitudes will require enormous effort and a fundamental shift in perspective—from an adult-ordered and centered world, intent upon satisfying virtually *any* desire of an adult regardless of how harmful to others, to a child- and community-focused world, intent upon protecting our most vulnerable citizens and providing them with an environment that promotes human flourishing.

THE RETREAT OF LAW

Examining the history of the law of marriage and divorce from the beginning of the nineteenth century until the beginning of the twenty-first, approximately two hundred years, provides a thumbnail sketch of the progressive rejection of the traditional understanding of marriage.[7] First, the traditional model of marriage includes permanency along with sexual complementarity and mutual fidelity (its three characteristics), and permanency was the first element to be rejected by the law. The other two elements—mutual fidelity and sexual complementarity—survived the nineteenth century. Yet the survival of both of these elements in the law by the end of the twentieth century can best be described as imperiled. The legal permissibility of divorce contributed to the dismantling of laws that protected marriage from both internal and external threats. Marriage by the end of the twentieth century had evolved legally from an institution once heavily guarded from actual and perceived threats to a naked, fragile, and unenforceable agreement of the parties themselves.[8]

Rejection by the law of the element of permanency in marriage developed differently in Catholic and Protestant countries after the

Reformation: "Until the Reformation, and after it in countries remaining in the Catholic faith, divorce was not permitted."[9] Ecclesiastical and canonical courts which once had exclusive jurisdiction over matters of marriage developed a conservative jurisprudence that continued to have some influence even after jurisdiction was wrested from those courts by the state, a process that began during the sixteenth century and culminated in the middle of the nineteenth century. Although religious courts denied parties a divorce, a separation from bed and board or divorce *a mensa et thoro*, authorizing the parties to live separate and apart, was available.[10] Although the American colonies "never had ecclesiastical courts, they did receive the English ecclesiastical rules concerning marriage"[11]: "Fortunately, however, the Catholic and Anglican doctrine that marriage is of divine origin and indissoluble did not prevail in those colonies settled by Protestants. The Protestants in Europe, Luther and Calvin, for example, did countenance divorce as a legal matter, and colonies like Massachusetts Bay had general divorce statutes from earliest times. On the other hand, the colonies strongly influenced by Anglicanism, those in the middle Atlantic and southern parts of the country, generally followed the English example."[12]

From the end of the eighteenth century to the middle of the twentieth, divorce once unobtainable under the governing law in Western European countries became available in America.[13] However, to obtain a divorce in most states required proof of *fault* in the nature of adultery, desertion or abandonment, various impediments (ordinarily considered grounds for annulment), and cruelty (in the more liberal New England states).[14] In most states a spouse could obtain a legal separation for additional reasons in the nature of serious misconduct by the other spouse. Requiring proof of grounds in the nature of serious misconduct protected marriage from internal threats to its stability posed by a dissatisfied spouse. To further discourage serious misconduct of a spouse and to reinforce the barrier around marriage, the law punished the offender by conditioning certain claims at divorce upon the lack of wrongdoing, or fault. For example, a spouse at fault was not entitled to custody of the children of the marriage or alimony. As a protection against external threats to marriage, state laws recognized the tort of alienation of affection[15] and, in Louisiana, an action for nullity of the marriage of an adulterer and his accomplice.[16]

Not only did grounds for divorce and legal separation in the nature of fault constitute a barrier to easy exit from marriage but they also served to prescribe inferentially a standard of conduct for spouses during the marriage. Fault grounds articulated the public's expectation as to how spouses should act towards each other. For example, a spouse should act (1) faithfully, by not sharing his or her sexual potential with another person (adultery was a breach of the element of marriage requiring fidelity); (2) not cruelly, either physically or mentally, and not intemperately by abusing alcohol or drugs; and (3) willingly living together so as to fulfill the cooperative tasks of this unique form of partnership.[17] Society spoke eloquently in a collective voice through the law: "Certain conduct was so egregious and such a serious violation of one's marital obligation that the law permitted the aggrieved spouse to seek [a legal separation], which did not have the effect of terminating the marriage, or, if the conduct was especially egregious, a divorce."[18]

During the second half of the nineteenth century, the settlement of the western United States and the women's suffrage movement had a further impact upon the law of marriage and divorce. "In general, the western states administered their divorce law with greater liberality than the older states, although Connecticut's 1849 act was very broad, authorizing divorce for conduct which would defeat the purpose of the marriage."[19] In the late 1800s, women began to work outside the home and resented the legal disabilities imposed upon them in favor of their husbands, who were by law designated as the heads of the household. Although the women's suffrage movement concentrated upon obtaining the right to vote for women, "[a] liberalized divorce law was one of the reforms advocated by the women's suffrage movement."[20] Accounts of this period in American history "saw nearly as much popular discussion of marriage and divorce as has our own time."[21] The divorce rate rose gradually in many states, which had the effect of activating church organizations. The desire for greater specificity in the law as to the grounds for separation and divorce sparked demands for uniformity[22], culminating in an unsuccessful attempt to amend the United States Constitution "to give Congress authority to enact a federal law of divorce."[23] Sound familiar?

The first half of the twentieth century saw "increasingly lax judicial treatment of grounds for divorce, the development of large scale divorce mills in a few jurisdictions, and some legislative tinkering with marriage and divorce statutes."[24] The United States Supreme Court weighed in to assure that the state with the most liberal divorce law would prevail in a contest with a state having a more conservative divorce law [25]—essentially, defining divorce down to the lowest common denominator. Judicial tinkering occurred in the form of expansion of the definition of cruelty as a ground for divorce: "By 1950 in many states proof of cruelty had come to be a formality, involving a bit of exaggeration, a little perjury at times, and a judicial atmosphere tolerant of both in the interest of processing the maximum number of divorces per hour."[26] Some of the legislative tinkering, moreover, introduced for the first time a "no-fault" ground for divorce: living separate and apart for a statutory period of time. Nonetheless, "[t]here were no dramatic changes in marriage and divorce statutes until 1969," despite constant criticism of traditional grounds for divorce from sociologists and psychologists "who thought that such activities as adultery, cruelty, or desertion were merely symptoms, not causes, of marital failure."[27]

Over the same two hundred years, while rejecting the element of permanency of marriage and incrementally relaxing the rules of exit from marriage, legislatures and judges also relaxed the legal rules of entry into marriage. Historically, entry into marriage was highly regulated by the law. There were, and in Louisiana still are, legal consequences for a breach of the promise to marry in the form of an action for damages.[28] Reflective of a different moral universe and heavily "gendered" social culture, the law permitted a defendant in a breach of promise action to prove lack of chastity of the plaintiff as an affirmative defense, at least if the plaintiff was the bride. Seduction by the defendant, the prospective groom, who subsequently breached the contract by breaking the engagement, served to aggravate the amount of damages awarded; the injury was deemed greater than in an ordinary case because the plaintiff was no longer a virgin. Such legal consequences communicated in a most direct fashion "the public's view about the seriousness of the decision to marry . . . [and] society's view of sexual relations before marriage."[29] By the 1950s most states had abrogated their breach of promise action.[30]

A myriad of lesser legal regulations necessitated some delay in marrying by requiring a lapse of time to complete formalities and often "provided information about the other party that could prove decisive [in some cases], such as a medical certificate attesting to a fiancé's freedom from venereal disease."[31] By the end of the twentieth century most of the laws regulating entry into marriage had been repealed or judicially declared to be merely directory,[32] thus not affecting the validity of the marriage. Legal regulation intended to encourage careful deliberation and choice of a marital partner, to protect the vulnerable from exploitation by a fiancé and an unwitting innocent from a dangerous choice, and to discourage impulsive decisions to marry had been gradually dismantled. Thus, the law left prospective spouses unprotected from their own folly and communicated society's increasing lack of interest in what had historically been considered the most important decision of a person's life. Easy entrance and easy exit. [33]

At the beginning of the nineteenth century, "how one entered marriage and with whom, as well as the conduct of spouses during the marriage, were matters of utmost concern to the community in which the married couple lived, including most importantly their own children."[34] Spouses were to behave toward each other civilly and compassionately so that the marriage might serve the public interests of channeling the two adults' sexual passions into marriage[35] and of assuring that the acculturation of any children born of the union be done in a cooperative and caring manner.[36] Law communicated society's deep concern and involvement with a couple's marriage, including the expectations about a married person's conduct. If those expectations were not met, "although deeply interested in preserving the stability of marriages, society was willing to yield to the individual desires of the aggrieved spouse."[37]

Whether by repealing enacted legislation or by changing the law in judicial opinions, the law of marriage over the last two hundred years has found significantly less to prohibit, less to protect and less to regulate. Trends identified as early as the mid-nineteenth century and reflected in the heretofore described legal changes intensified and accelerated in the 1960s. The convergence of a series of events in the mid-1960s propelled enormous change in the law of divorce: (1). A committee appointed by the Archbishop of Canterbury issued a report entitled *Putting Asunder* in 1966 which "advocated 'marriage breakdown' as the sole ground for divorce."[38] (2). A commission appointed by the Governor of California recommended eliminating all grounds for divorce except "irreparable breakdown of the marriage."[39] (3) A special committee formed by the influential National Conference of Commissioners on Uniform State Laws released a monograph in 1969, the date of enactment of the California "no-fault" divorce legislation, and a proposed Uniform Marriage and Divorce Act in 1971 adopting irretrievable breakdown as the sole ground for divorce.[40] These disparate events did not represent a "grassroots" movement to radically change divorce law. Instead, each event in the United States and the resulting recommendations were driven by an elite cadre of legal academicians, judges and lawyers.

The arrival of "no-fault" divorce in the late 1960s and its interpretation by the judiciary had the effect of transferring to *one* of the two married persons whom the law had previously regulated, the moral decision to terminate the marriage.[41] The enactment of the formulated grounds for "no-fault" divorce, especially if such grounds were exclusive, also meant that moral discourse in the law about the proper conduct of spouses during marriage was purged.[42] Both consequences confirmed the growing understanding that marriage is a personal, hence private matter.[43] The discourse of psychology and particularly, that discourse in its popular cultural form, replaced the discourse of morality. Buoyed by increasingly radical notions of individual autonomy that *unilateral* divorce endorsed, Americans concluded that legal "no-fault" divorce was "societal" recognition of the proposition that guilt is dysfunctional and harmful to a person. "No-fault" divorce endorsed the notion that an individual inherently possesses the freedom to pursue the purpose of life, which is personal self-fulfillment, and in most cases should not be constrained from doing so. By the mid 1980s every state had adopted a "no-fault" ground for divorce, either in combination with other fault grounds[44] or as the exclusive ground for divorce.[45]

As the law of marriage has evolved, marriage understood legally bears little, if any, resemblance to the definition of an institution that anchors a decent society and constitutes the bedrock of democracy.[46] The history of marriage law serves as a cogent reminder that "[e]ven by its absence, law can shape culture in destructive ways"[47]: "Culture does not exist in a legal vacuum. . . . For law is necessary to civilization. Even the absence of law—the choice to omit or remove legal regulation in some area of cultural life—shapes culture, for better or for worse. . . . Alone, it cannot cure moral defects in a people. It can, however, change people's sense of their hierarchy of values and of what finally falls out of the realm of acceptable behavior. Law teaches more than it prevents."[48]

THE DECISIONS OF THE UNITED STATES SUPREME COURT

Even though in the United States individual states, rather than Congress, have the general power to regulate marriage,[49] state statutes nonetheless must not infringe upon constitutional guarantees of individual freedom and equal treatment.[50] In a series of United States Supreme Court cases beginning in the mid-1960s, state statutes regulating intimate marital conduct and marriage itself, according to the Court, failed to afford to the particular individuals involved sufficient "privacy" and equal treatment under the law. Just as the retreat of state law from the regulation of marriage accelerated and a radical form of "no-fault" divorce was introduced, decisions of the Supreme Court began to reflect the influence of some of the same legal trends and powerful cultural forces already discussed. By the end of the 1980s, the language in these decisions had transformed marriage from a public institution as described in *Maynard v. Hill* at the end of the nineteenth century[51], to a public intimate commitment described in *Turner v. Safley* in 1986, almost one hundred years later. In parallel jurisprudence involving abortion and homosexual rights, the United States Supreme Court continued to expand the individual's "liberty" interest to be free from unnecessary governmental interference, a "liberty" interest which by the late 1960s included "the right to marry." Law at the state level and in federal cases, reinforced by cultural forces, was moving in logical tandem towards rejecting the most defensible and least unique of the three elements of the traditional view of marriage—sexual complementarity and with it probably mutual fidelity.

In 1965, in *Griswold v. Connecticut*[52] the Supreme Court declared unconstitutional a Connecticut criminal statute prohibiting the use of contraceptives and the distribution of information about them.[53] Connecticut had prosecuted and convicted two employees of Planned Parenthood of Connecticut for providing birth control information to married couples. They appealed their conviction upon the ground that the statute creating the offense was unconstitutional. Despite declaring that the Supreme Court does "not sit as a super-legislature to determine the wisdom, need and propriety of laws that touch . . . social conditions,"[54] Justice William Douglas concluded that the due process clause was implicated because "[t]his law . . . operates directly on an intimate relation of husband and wife and their physician's role in one aspect of that relation."[55] Included within the "penumbra" of rights protected under the rubric of "liberty" is a "right of privacy older than the Bill of Rights—older than our political parties, older than our school system"[56]: "Marriage is a coming together for better or for worse, hopefully enduring and intimate to the degree of being sacred. It is an association that promotes a way of life, not causes; a harmony in living, not political faiths; a bilateral loyalty, not commercial or social projects. Yet it is an association for as noble a purpose as any involved in our prior decisions."[57]

In the opinion in *Griswold* there is ample support for later descriptions of the right protected under the due process clause as a right to privacy with emphasis on "the marriage relation and the protected space of the marital bedroom."[58] Marriage thus is viewed by the Supreme Court as early as the mid 1960s in terms of its personal intimacy and the necessity of "privacy" for such a relationship. Yet, there clearly remained some vestige of the institutional quality of marriage in the recognition that it is an association that promotes a way of life for a noble purpose, although that purpose is unspecified. A mere two years later in *Loving v. Virginia*[59], another criminal prosecution and conviction under a Virginia statute prohibiting the marriage of white persons and persons of color offered the opportunity for the court to further articulate its view of marriage and the permissible parameters of state regulation.

The Virginia legislative scheme, which included the criminal statute, comprehensively prohibited white persons from intermarrying with persons of color and with Indians. The Lovings, having been convicted under the Virginia statute, moved to vacate the sentence[60] on the ground that the statute violated both clauses of the Fourteenth Amendment. Chief Justice Warren Burger writing for the majority concluded that the Virginia statute was unconstitutional under both the equal protection and due process clauses of the Fourteenth Amendment. Because the entire statutory scheme of the state of Virginia prohibited marriages of white persons to a person of color, be that person black or Indian, the rather obvious purpose was maintaining "white supremacy." Under the Fourteenth Amendment "[t]he clear and central purpose . . . was to eliminate all official state sources of invidious racial discrimination in the States."[61] Therefore, as the chief justice concludes, "[t]here can be no doubt that restricting the freedom to marry solely because of racial classifications [which are immutable and a consequence of birth] violates the central meaning of the Equal Protection Clause."[62]

Of far greater significance in the years following the decision in *Loving* was the brief discussion of Chief Justice Burger about why the

Virginia statutory scheme also violated the due process clause of the Fourteenth Amendment. The chief justice described the right protected by the due process clause, first, in the following language: "The freedom to marry has long been recognized as one of the vital personal rights essential to the orderly pursuit of happiness by free men."[63] In the very next sentence in the opinion, he opines that "[m]arriage is one of the 'basic *civil rights* of man,' fundamental to our very existence and survival."[64] A *right* described as essential to the existence and survival of mankind implies the unstated "noble purpose" in *Griswold*. Likewise, to the extent that marriage is essential to the orderly pursuit of happiness, this conception of marriage appears entirely consistent with the traditional model of marriage. Unfortunately, the description of marriage as both a personal and, more importantly, a basic *civil* right, rhetorically at least, may have altered the understanding of marriage as a social institution.[65] Recognition of the constitutional right to marry as a personal right essential to the pursuit of happiness focuses on the exercise of an individual's freedom and why he or she desires to marry, which then cannot be restricted unnecessarily by governmental regulation. Furthermore, the use of the adjective "civil," whether deliberately or not[66], suggests a distinction between "civil" and religious, permitting the often heard contemporary argument that the two realms of authority are separate and distinct with no connection one to the other.

Although the United States Supreme Court case of *Zablocki v. Redhail*[67] in 1978 also involved the unconstitutionality of a Wisconsin statute effectively denying a child support obligor the right to marry, the decision is often overlooked as less significant than those preceding or following it because of the uniqueness of the Wisconsin statute.[68] Nonetheless, the opinion's reliance upon the equal protection clause of the Fourteenth Amendment established that if a state statute *significantly* interferes[69] with the exercise of a fundamental right, such as the right to marry, the appropriate level of judicial scrutiny is "critical examination."[70] Citing *Loving v. Virginia* and the language of the chief justice concerning deprivation of the "fundamental liberty" protected by the due process clause, Justice Thurgood Marshall quoted from

Cleveland Board of Education v. LaFleur[71] to the effect that "freedom of *personal choice* in matters of marriage and family life is one of the liberties protected by the due process clause of the Fourteenth Amendment."[72] For, according to Justice Marshall, "it would make little sense to recognize a right of privacy with respect to other matters of family life and not with respect to the decision to enter the relationship that is the foundation of the family in our society."[73] Wisconsin failed to prove that the statute as enacted served to accomplish, in a "closely tailored" manner, sufficiently important state interests; the statute as a "collection device" for child support was both over- and under-inclusive. Thus, even if there was no traditional "classification" drawn by a state statute regulating the right to marry, the equal protection clause of the Fourteenth Amendment applied if the regulation significantly interfered with that fundamental right. Furthermore, the applicable level of scrutiny for the Court to apply was "close examination," arguably less than "strict scrutiny" but more than a mere "rational basis."

The evolving language used to describe marriage in these Supreme Court decisions became "the seed" for the description of the essential components of marriage in *Turner v. Safley,*[74] decided almost twenty years after *Loving v. Virginia.* Justice Sandra Day O'Connor, in determining whether prison regulations denied the fundamental right to marry to incarcerated inmates, examined the "important attributes" that she identified as constituting the core of marriage. That "core" of marriage, not unexpectedly in view of Justice Douglas' opinion in the *Griswold* case, failed to include permanency, but also, for the first time, failed to include in any meaningful way, consummation.[75] By doing so, Justice O'Connor essentially "divorced" marriage from its ordering purpose of procreation. Effective contraception, legalized abortion, and unilateral "no-fault" divorce, reinforced by other cultural trends[76], had by the mid 1980s exacted a toll on the legal and cultural understanding of marriage. According to Justice O'Connor, rather than the "ordering purpose of procreation," the "new" understanding of marriage at its core consisted of (1) "expressions of emotional support and public commitment"; (2) "an exercise of religious faith," thus acknowledging that marriage possessed a spiritual dimension; and (3) "the receipt of government benefits."[77] Justice O'Connor's conception of marriage emphasized almost entirely the perspective of the individual who by the free exercise of his personal choice seeks to pursue and achieve personal happiness and to obtain material benefits from marriage.

Presciently, another justice in a different case decided the same year as *Turner* warned generally against the expansion of constitutional rights by redefining them. That case was *Bowers v. Hardwick*[78], which rejected a claim that a Georgia statute criminally punishing sodomy was unconstitutional because it denied homosexuals their right of personal privacy. *Bowers v. Hardwick* contained extremely important discourse on the "liberty" interest of the Fourteenth Amendment, suggesting the contours of "the outer limits of [the right of personal privacy]" theretofore unmarked.[79] By insisting that the "liberty" interest protected by the due process clause of the Fourteenth Amendment included only those rights deeply rooted in our history and traditions, Justice Byron White marked the outer limits of the "liberty" interest. The right to engage in homosexual sodomy was not a right deeply rooted in our history and traditions, indeed quite the contrary. That demarcation of the "outer limits" subsequently proved determinative for Justice Antonin Scalia who wrote for a plurality in *Michael H. v. Gerald D.*,[80] a decision which upheld the constitutionality of a California statute preventing legal recognition of the biological father of a child if the child was presumed to be that of the husband of the mother.[81] Justice Scalia explicitly relied upon the language and reasoning of the Court in *Bowers v. Hardwick,* that a fundamental right under the due process clause of the Fourteenth Amendment has to be one " 'deeply rooted in this Nation's history and tradition' or 'implicit in the concept of ordered liberty.'"[82] Considering the history and traditions of our country, according to Justice Scalia, the biological father of a child conceived in adultery and presumed to be the child of the husband of his mother has no deeply rooted "right" to legal recognition of his relationship. Subsequently, the same language was invoked in *Washington v. Glucksberg.*[83]

By 2003 the United States Supreme Court was poised to reconsider in the same context as *Bowers*—the prosecution of two consenting homosexual adults for sodomy—the demarcation of the right to privacy afforded a person under the due process clause. During the 1990s the Court decided two other extremely influential cases in which the "right to privacy" and equal protection were invoked: *Planned Parenthood of Southeastern Pa. v. Casey*[84] involving restrictions in state abortion legislation, and *Romer v. Evans*[85] involving Colorado legislation that prohibited all legislative, executive, and judicial action designed to protect homosexuals from discrimination. Although not the holding in the *Casey* case, which reaffirmed *Roe v. Wade*,[86] *dicta* in the opinion included language, often referred to as "the sweet-mystery-of-life passage,"[87] that if applied would significantly expand the privacy right beyond rights deemed fundamental because deeply rooted in our country's history and tradition. *Romer* contributed the notion that state legislation directed at a class of politically unpopular persons, such as homosexuals, with no obvious "legitimate" governmental interest [and imposition of "our moral code" is not legitimate] must be the result of deep animosity and of reliance on harmful stereotypes that serve no purpose other than to demean such persons.[88] Justices O'Connor and Kennedy, respectively, wrote these two opinions, and not surprisingly, these two strands of constitutional interpretation united in *Lawrence v. Texas* to slip the noose of demarcation for the "liberty" interest drawn in *Bowers*, which since 1986 had arguably marked the outer limits of the due process clause.

In *Lawrence v. Texas*[89] the Court found a Texas criminal statute punishing sodomy unconstitutional and specifically overruled the earlier case of *Bowers v. Hardwick*.[90] By so doing the Court rejected Justice White's warning against continually expanding constitutional rights by redefinition. The "liberty" interest protected by the due process clause of the Fourteenth Amendment "protects the person from unwarranted government intrusions into a dwelling or other private places."[91] This "[f]reedom extends [however] beyond those spatial bounds. *Liberty presumes an autonomy of self that includes freedom of thought, belief, expression, and certain intimate conduct* [earlier identified as adult, consensual sexual intimacy[92]]."[93] Yet the Court refused to classify the "right to homosexual sodomy" as a fundamental right.[94] Borrowing from the reasoning in the *Romer* case Justice Kennedy identified the special offensiveness of the Texas statute as the stigma attached to making certain conduct criminal: "When homosexual conduct is made criminal by the law of the State, that declaration in and of itself is an invitation to subject homosexual persons to discrimination both in the public and in the private spheres."[95] It in essence "demeans the lives of homosexual persons."[96]

Quite naturally, and reinforced by the warning in Justice Scalia's dissenting opinion[97], the language of *Lawrence* logically suggests that because an individual has a "liberty" interest in adult, consensual sexual intimacy which is entitled to protection under the Fourteenth Amendment, a redefinition of the "right to marry" to include sexual non-complementarity looms ahead. Furthermore, since sexual complementarity is the immutable biological feature of traditional marriage, no other "significant" governmental restriction on the "right to *marry*" imposed by a state could withstand constitutional scrutiny if it couldn't. The rational fear engendered by the language used in the majority opinion in *Lawrence* is further heightened by the rejection of a definition of "liberty" anchored in our history and traditions, as *Bowers* held, and by the Court's overt resort to and reliance upon international law.[98] Although a matter of domestic civil law rather than international law, it is worth noting that some European countries since the early 1990s have recognized the equivalent of same-sex "marriage"[99] and have experimented with different legal statuses afforded some or all of the benefits of marriage. Even more recently, two European countries, the Netherlands and Belgium, have accepted same-sex "marriage" by enacting legislation, and Spain recently became the third.[100]

No doubt anticipating such speculation, Justice Kennedy sought to reassure the American public that *Lawrence* "does not involve whether the government must give formal recognition to any relationship that homosexual persons seek to enter."[101]

> The statutes do seek to control a personal relationship that, whether or not entitled to formal recognition in the law, is within the liberty of persons to choose without being punished as crimi-

nals. *This, as a general rule, should counsel against attempts by the State, or a court, to define the meaning of the relationship or to set its boundaries absent injury to a person or abuse of an institution the law protects.* It suffices for us to acknowledge that adults may choose to enter upon this relationship in the confines of their homes and their own private lives and still retain their dignity as free persons. When sexuality finds overt expression in intimate conduct with another person, the conduct can be but one element in a personal bond that is more enduring. *The liberty protected by the Constitution allows homosexual persons the right to make this choice.*[102]

Explicitly unanchored from our history and traditions, the "liberty" interest Justice Kennedy found in the Fourteenth Amendment "presumes an autonomy of self that includes freedom of thought, belief, expression, and certain intimate conduct."[103] That "liberty" interest as he describes it is both spatial and transcendent. The transcendental dimension of the "liberty" from governmental intrusion to which Justice Kennedy refers includes personal decisions relating to marriage (including entry into marriage), procreation, contraception, family relationships, childrearing and education—decisions "involving the most intimate and personal choices a person may make in a lifetime, choices central to personal dignity and autonomy."[104] Yet the most radical of Kennedy's statements contained in this opinion was quoted from the *dicta* in *Planned Parenthood of Southeastern Pa. v. Casey*: "At the heart of liberty is the right to define one's own concept of existence, of meaning, of the universe, and of the mystery of human life,"[105] the so-called "sweet-mystery-of-life" passage: *Individual autonomy in its most breathtakingly radical form.*

At the same time that Kennedy recognizes this radical individual autonomy as a constitutional right, he explicitly rejects as a consideration "religious beliefs, conceptions of right and acceptable behavior, and respect for the traditional family."[106] Although recognizing that these considerations are not "trivial," but indeed are "profound and deep convictions accepted as ethical and moral principles to which [citizens] aspire and which thus determine the course of their lives, ... [we must not] mandate our own moral code."[107] Justice Sandra O'Connor rather unconvincingly attempts to distinguish laws that "preserve the traditions of society" which are acceptable, from those that "express moral disapproval," which are unacceptable.[108]

With radical individual autonomy at the heart of the "liberty" interest of the due process clause, there appear to be *no* parameters within which that "liberty" is contained. In essence, "liberty" is constantly evolving. Furthermore, in identifying and protecting this *evolving* "liberty" interest, there appears to be no consideration of the impact of decisions made by the individual exercising his "liberty" upon others, not even upon an existing spouse or child. Nor does there appear to be any hesitation or reluctance to create a broad right of autonomy that attaches to one individual which inevitably will come into conflict with the same right of autonomy exercised by other individuals. How those conflicts are to be resolved, whether one individual's right to autonomy prevails over another, is left unanswered. Autonomy of *all* the individuals in the family, constitutionally guaranteed, destroys the conception of the family as a unit, a system, and raises the ultimate question of the continued viability of family law.

LAWRENCE V. TEXAS

Even before the United States Supreme Court rendered its decision in *Lawrence v. Texas*, marriage was increasingly viewed by legal elites and the judiciary as an individual *civil* right, a form of "individual self-expression."[109] That view after all had evolved through a series of United States Supreme Court decisions preceding *Lawrence* and had found its most directly applicable articulation of the "new" meaning of *civil* marriage[110] in *Turner v. Safley* in 1986.[111] Although any selection of significant state court decisions and other legal developments in the evolution of the definition and purpose of marriage may be arbitrary, two decisions and one proposal for marriage legislation merit discussion, principally because of their chronological proximity to *Lawrence v. Texas*: the decisions of the Vermont and Massachusetts supreme courts in *Baker v. Vermont*[112] and *Goodridge v. Department of Public Health Massachusetts*[113] and the American Law Institute's *Principles of the Law of Family Dissolution.*

The choice of these two cases does not in any way minimize the importance of two cases decided at the beginning of the 1990s, *Baehr v. Lewin*[114] in Hawaii and *Brause v. Bureau of Vital Statistics*[115] in Alaska. Both of these decisions involved the constitutionality of their marriage license statutes under their state constitutions, but in each case the people of Hawaii and Alaska quickly voted to amend their constitutions to essentially define marriage as being between a man and a woman.[116] These decisions and the immediate response of the people in each state to preclude a redefinition of marriage no doubt prompted Congress to pass the Defense of Marriage Act[117], which defines marriage for purposes of federal law as a union of one man and one woman and explicitly permits states to refuse to recognize a same-sex "marriage" celebrated in another state. Forty-two states have followed suit with their own defense of marriage acts (a total of forty-four states).[118] Once again, the pattern of judicial decision of unconstitutionality, amendment of the affected state constitution to overrule it, preemptive legislation by other states, and finally, federal legislation sounds both current and familiar. Furthermore, by including the American Law Institute's *Principles* as part of the context surrounding *Lawrence*, one recognizes that an almost identical set of circumstances occurred with the enactment of California's "no-fault" divorce law in 1969 and the proposal of a virtually identical divorce law by legal academicians in the Uniform Marriage and Divorce Act in 1971.[119]

Even though the decision in *Baker v. Vermont*, holding unconstitutional a state statutory restriction of marriage licenses to heterosexual couples only (thus necessarily the "benefits" of marriage), was rendered first, the opinion relied upon a unique provision of the Vermont constitution, the common benefits clause.[120] The Vermont constitution guarantees "that government should be for the 'common benefit' of all citizens"[121]; and that clause, according to the Vermont supreme court in *Baker*, required the legislature to either recognize same-sex "marriage" or create a new legal status with the same legal benefits afforded marriage within six months after judgment.[122] In a phrase reminiscent of Justice O'Connor's examination of the "core" of the "right to marry" in *Turner v. Safley*, the Vermont supreme court opined: "The legal benefits and protections flowing from a marriage license are of such significance that any statutory exclusion must necessarily be grounded on public concerns of sufficient weight, cogency, and authority that the justice of the deprivation cannot seriously be questioned. Considered in light of the extreme logical disjunction between the classification and the stated purpose of the law—protecting children and 'furthering the link between procreation and child rearing'—the exclusion falls substantially short of this standard."[123] Ultimately, the Vermont court reduced marriage to a bundle of material benefits: "[w]hile many have noted the symbolic or spiritual significance of the marital relation, it is plaintiffs' claim to the secular benefits and protections of a singularly human relationship that, in our view, characterizes this case."[124]

The significance of the *Baker* decision and its impact on later legal developments lay in (1) the use of a unique state constitutional clause to permit the assertion of a "right to marry" by persons of the same sex and (2) the technique of essentially ordering the state legislature to enact legislation[125] affording same-sex couples the same rights and material benefits as married persons.[126] Although the Massachusetts supreme court in 2003 in the *Goodridge* case relied upon familiar state constitutional provisions to declare a statute restricting marriage licenses to a man and a woman unconstitutional, the court interpreted its due process and equal protection clauses as more protective of individual rights than the United States Constitution.[127] Furthermore, the Massachusetts supreme court also adopted the same technique for the enforcement of its judgment as that chosen by the Vermont supreme court, yet it was far bolder in its content.[128] The court both in its opinion and a subsequent advisory opinion[129] directed the Massachusetts legislature to provide same-sex couples "the right to marry" identical to the right enjoyed by heterosexual couples. For the Massachusetts supreme court no alternative legal status, such as civil unions adopted in Vermont[130], would suffice. After all, according to the Massachusetts Supreme Court the "four purposes of marriage laws" included: "1) encouraging stable relationships over transient ones; 2) providing for orderly property distribution; 3) decreasing the state's obligation to provide for the needy; and 4) providing a way to track 'important epidemiological and demographic data.'"[131] Marriage defined down even further.

"Gay" activists had targeted state constitutions in friendly states because they believed conservative United States Supreme Court opinions about the meaning of the equal protection and due process clauses had pragmatically foreclosed success under the United States Constitution. After having been successful in obtaining judgments of unconstitutionality of state marriage laws in judicial decisions in Hawaii[132] and Alaska[133], "gay" activists suffered defeat when the implementation of those decisions was preempted by amendments to both state constitutions which essentially defined marriage as between a man and a woman.[134] By contrast to Hawaii and Alaska, the state constitutions of Vermont[135] and Massachusetts[136] contained difficult and lengthy amendment processes, each different but equally cumbersome. Thus, any judicial decision of unconstitutionality could be neither preempted nor overruled by a quick amendment to their state constitutions. As a consequence, the people in Vermont and Massachusetts, unlike those in Hawaii and Alaska, would have the opportunity to become comfortable with the redefinition of marriage and less likely to react by proposing a constitutional amendment to overrule their state court decisions. Because of the lapse of time during which same-sex "marriages" could occur, any proposed constitutional amendment to preempt the effect of these decisions would have to consider the "marriages" contracted in the interim. Between the decision rendered by the Vermont court in 1999 and that rendered by the Massachusetts court in 2003, *Lawrence v. Texas* was settled by the United States Supreme Court and its broad language about the right of "privacy" afforded to intimate sexual conduct between consenting adults, including two persons of the same sex, opened a potential route to same-sex "marriage" most had previously considered closed. As might be expected, the Massachusetts court in *Goodridge* cited the language of the opinion in *Lawrence*, a decision rendered a mere five months before that in *Goodridge*.[137]

Two years after the enactment of civil unions in Vermont, the American Law Institute, "a prestigious group of judges, lawyers and scholars,"[138] announced to media fanfare, which is itself unusual, the completion of its project *Principles of the Law of Family Dissolution*. The avowed purpose of the project is to "solidify the 'no-fault' divorce revolution."[139] Consequently, the vision or theory of marriage implied by the *Principles*, especially in its proposals for the division of marital property and compensatory spousal payments, constitutes the legal equivalent of "a joint venture for a limited purpose,"[140] inherently temporary and subject to renewal at the completion of each stage of the project of family life,[141] a result of unilateral "no-fault" divorce. In this view of marriage, moral relations between the spouses deserve no consideration. Whether the husband committed adultery because the wife "got fat" or the wife "got fat" because the husband was committing adultery establishes that it is impossible to judge the complex psychological interaction of spouses so as to determine whose conduct *caused* the marriage to fail and, thus, to assign blame to one of the spouses.[142] Clairvoyantly, the reporters for the *Principles* predicted that the "privacy" interests of the spouses in a marital relationship under the due process clause of the Constitution might preclude the ability of a state to punish marital misconduct by imposing "fixed societal standards of conduct on intimate personal relationships."[143] So there goes another element of the traditional understanding of marriage—mutual fidelity.

Furthermore, by proposing principles for application when a cohabiting relationship, labeled a domestic partnership, terminates, the *Principles*, as Maggie Gallagher observes, builds "upon this new view of marriage as primarily symbolic expressive conduct. . . . Marriage is reduced to a rite, which carries rights."[144] The view the *Principles* reflects is that the only difference between marriage and cohabitation is one of *form*, not *substance*.[145] The proposed legislative provisions recognizing domestic partnerships,[146] whether the partners are heterosexual or homosexual, affords to them legal rights and responsibilities at the dissolution of their relationship, if terminated for a reason other than death. By utilizing "default rules" which apply absent a contrary agreement between the parties, persons who "for a significant period of time share a primary residence and life together as a couple"[147] have marriage-like rights and obligations at the dissolution of their relationship. These proposals essentially recognize that "the fundamental underlying social institution which gives rise to legal benefits is no longer marriage, but domestic partnership."[148] Drafted by three law professors[149] who were appointed by the executive committee of the American Law Institute and granted significant editorial discretion, the proposal for the extension of rights and obligations to domestic partners, particularly to same-sex partnerships, represented a significant departure from most of the previous projects of the American Law Institute. In commenting upon the adoption of civil unions in Vermont and domestic partnerships by the ALI, the late David Coolidge commented: "It is striking that the adoption of Chapter 6 of the *Principles of the Law of Family Dissolution* . . . on 'Domestic Partnerships' took place within a month after the State of Vermont created 'civil unions.'"[150]

Furthermore, its announcement in December 2002—six months before *Lawrence* and eleven months before *Goodridge*, while both cases were pending—appeared intended to influence legal developments, particularly those initiated by judicial decisions.[151] Any long-term effect that the *Principles* may have is less clear, although it remains a legal source permeated throughout with the "new" view of marriage–a close intimate, personal, and essentially private relationship with virtually no moral content, which offers little if any security or sanctuary for a man and a woman desirous of a stable relationship for the purpose of child rearing. In somewhat of an understatement, Maggie Gallagher posits: "There are many problems with this vision of marriage and its relationship to law."[152]

THE "FALLBACK" PROPOSAL

With the creation of alternative legal statuses, such as the Vermont "civil union,"[153] the Hawaiian "reciprocal beneficiaries"[154], and the ALI "domestic partnerships," there exists a "smorgasbord" of legal relationships which afford few, some, or virtually all of the material benefits of marriage to two persons. Some of these legal relationships are open to those who are prohibited from marrying or those who do not marry. Critics of these various statuses refer to them as "marriage-lite"[155] or "quasi-marital"[156] relationships. Of course, as of May 2004, same-sex couples can marry in Massachusetts as a result of the *Goodridge* case, a case whose result was subsequently challenged in *Largess v. S.J. Ct. of Massachusetts,* which the United States Supreme Court refused to hear on a writ of certiorari.[157] Yet the inherent and inextricable connection between alternative legal statuses and marriage escapes most Americans and even most Europeans—who have experimented for a longer period of time and with more different forms than current American experiments.[158] Developing piecemeal and often in response to judicial decisions, a new system of family law is being created "in which 'union' or 'partnership' is the central organizing principle, and marriage becomes a private term that some people may use to describe the meaning of their relationship"[159]: "[T]here are reasons to believe that civil unions and domestic partnerships, understood as quasi-[ALI proposal] or virtually-marital [Vermont legislation] categories, will weaken the institution of marriage."[160]

Remarkably, there is some agreement at both ends of the ideological spectrum that indeed alternatives to marriage, especially as traditionally understood, present a serious threat to marriage. There is agreement about the threat of these alternatives even if marriage is ultimately "re-imagined" to conform to assumptions about behavior that more closely mirror that of "gay" couples.[161] "Gay" activists William Eskridge and Jonathan Rausch both argue that a "smorgasbord"[162] of legal systems from which couples may choose their level of commitment "are likely to weaken marriage."[163] Rauch is very explicit: "There are two ways to erode and perhaps eliminate the special status of matrimony. [one is to take away government endorsement and privatize marriage which is a non-starter] So the ticket (goes the argument) is to extend the benefits of marriage to the unmarried. Give the benefits to committed partners of whatever gender. . . . [M]arriage-lite is an arrow aimed at the very heart of Rule 1: 'If you want the benefits of marriage, *get married*. To whatever extent they mimic marriage, domestic-partner programs send the message that, from the *law's and thus society's point of view*, marriage is no longer unique.'"[164]

Evidence from European experiments with registered partner-ships[165], same-sex "marriage"[166], marriage to domestic partnership con-versions[167], and the *PAC* in France[168] would suggest that given an option of lesser commitment, many couples seize it, including heterosexual couples who biologically can have children whose welfare is a vital and undeniable *public* concern.[169] As Jonathan Rauch observes, "[a]ctually, a lot of people, gay and straight, would like a halfway house ["a way to get health insurance without having to say, 'till death us do part.'"]; or, to be more blunt about it, a free ride."[170] Careful attention to the language deployed by most activists as well as the courts reveal a focus primarily, if not exclusively, upon the "benefits" conferred by marriage,[171] without a discussion and explicit consideration of the obligations of marriage. Perhaps this rhetoric explains the rush in California to "unregister" as domestic partners before the effective date of state legislation (January 1, 2005) that extends the "rights" and "benefits" of marriage to domestic partners, but also imposes the "obligations" of marriage.[172]

Charles Murray, generally considered to occupy the other end of the ideological spectrum from Rausch, argues to the same effect in his summer 2004 article in the *Public Interest*.[173] After acknowledging that Jonathan Rauch has argued that marriage-lite in the form of alternative legal statuses that compete with marriage, will be "seriously damaging to heterosexual marriage," Murray agrees that "[h]e is right"[174]: "Civil unions that are even easier to get out of than marriage is now, that enable people to get the economic and statutory goodies of marriage without taking on the full symbolic[175] and legal obligations of marriage, will become an increasingly common alternative for heterosexuals. They will remove the last vestiges of stigma about cohabitation as a framework for having children.[176] . . . [W]ill the reality that faces us—increased use of civil unions for straights as well as gays—be good for straights? No. It is a looming disaster."[177]

Ultimately, as these authors from different ends of the spectrum argue, a status that is marriage in all but name, or is a status that permits couples to pick only the benefits and privileges of marriage forgoing its obligations, undermines heterosexual marriage. Furthermore, such legal approaches confirm the current cultural understanding that marriage is about an essentially private, intimate relationship publicly recognized, not about society's need to assure a child a committed mother and father.[178] Marriage *alone* has been the unique publicly privileged intimate relationship. The law privileges marriage so that men and women will be channeled into this vital social institution to continue to perform the very *public* function of producing and acculturating the next generation of citizens[179]—a long-term enterprise, expensive in both time and economic resources.[180] Marriage law serves, as Maggie Gallagher argues, to draw clear boundaries with fixed clear rules between marriage and other ambiguous intimate relationships. Legal recognition of marriage also serves the two parties to an intimate relationship by offering them a means to signal each other concerning his or her level of commitment.[181] There must be no other *faux* competitor if marriage, properly understood, is to be protected: "the surest way to break marriage's status as the norm is to surround it with competitors which offer most of the benefits but few of the burdens, as is happening with domestic-partner programs intended for gay couples but extended to straight couples as well. . . . Go back to Rule 1. In fact *reinforce* 'If you want the benefits of marriage, *get married.*'"[182]

The undermining effect of other legal statuses upon marriage lies at the heart of the current litigation in states enacting constitutional amendments that define marriage traditionally and also prohibit recognition of any legal status substantially similar to marriage for any unmarried couple.[183] Opponents of these amendments in the states that constitutionally restrict amendments to a single "object,"[184] argue that combining a definition of marriage with a prohibition of other statuses similar to marriage violates the "single object" rule. Some judges fail to recognize what legislatures clearly did, that is, that same-sex "marriage" is only one of the perceived contemporary threats to traditional marriage.[185] Other legal statuses which undermine the uniqueness of marriage likewise threaten the institution. Jonathan Rauch, a proponent of gay "marriage," knows that "[t]he potential market for same-sex marriages is probably no more than 5 percent of the population; but the potential market for partner programs encompasses the whole population. Although no one can be sure, eventually enough employers and government jurisdictions might adopt straight-inclusive domestic-partner programs to make legal partnership widely competitive with marriage."[186]

CONCLUSION

Marriage? Will it continue to possess a recognizable identity and traditional understanding? Law, which jettisoned the element of "permanency" as a component of the received model of marriage, assisted over time in the redefinition of marriage as simply an intimate personal relationship. Easy divorce and frequent remarriage among heterosexual couples subtly shaped cultural attitudes that now accept marriage as disconnected from procreation, both of which (marriage and procreation) fall within a protected zone of personal "privacy."[187] By abandoning the public interest in the stability and protection of the marital relationship, state legislatures and state judicial opinions contributed to the current cultural understanding of marriage. Evolving notions of a form of radical individual autonomy fueled by United States Supreme Court decisions and encouraged by intellectual elites in the academy and the media threaten the remaining two elements of traditional marriage—sexual complementarity and sexual fidelity.

The people of the United States, particularly over the last ten years, have begun to examine the consequences of a weakened "marriage culture": its effect on the quality of life in a community and its impact on the most vulnerable of our citizens—our children. A nascent "marriage movement" has emerged[188], composed of a loose coalition of public intellectuals, psychologists, social workers, marriage educators, government employees, public officials, academicians, and members of the faith-based community. Much of the emphasis of the "marriage movement" concerns marriage education, teaching married couples the skills that prove useful in maintaining and nurturing their marital relationship. The Department of Health and Human Services, Administration of Children and Families, under the leadership of Wade Horn, has requested and obtained money from Congress for "marriage initiatives," money likely to be appropriated in view of the re-election of President George W. Bush.

Perceiving a threat to the understanding and promotion of marriage as a lifelong commitment of a father and a mother and the ideal environment for rearing children, Americans in some states have proposed amendments to their state constitutions to deny "marriage" to same-sex couples and more such amendments can be expected.[189] Even more remarkably, in a majority of those states, the amendments also deny recognition to any *legal status* designed for same-sex or heterosexual couples that is identical to or substantially similar to marriage, so-called "marriage-lite."[190] In every state in which a constitutional amendment has appeared on the ballot, the amendment has passed handily. These amendments presented directly to the people are also calculated to send a message to the United States Supreme Court—unlike criminal sodomy statutes repealed by a large majority of the states at the time of *Lawrence* and relied upon in that opinion[191], same-sex "marriage" has recently been rejected by an average of 67 percent of the American people who voted on the measures.[192] Furthermore, in what has become a predictable pattern of judicial opinion and the democratic response, members of Congress have proposed a Federal Marriage Amendment, which would define marriage as a union of one man and one woman.[193]

In virtually all of the public debate over same-sex "marriage," proponents argue that permitting two men or two women to marry is not the biggest threat to marriage, divorce is. That message has been received. One extraordinary fruit of the debate and legislative battles has been a renewed effort and commitment by deeply concerned Americans and Christian leaders like the National Conference of Catholic Bishops to strengthen the institution of marriage.[194] Unlike relatively weak and intermittent opposition to eliminating "permanency" from the understanding of marriage as a *legal* institution, there has been widespread, consistent opposition to judicial elimination of "sexual complementarity." That principled opposition has spawned renewed commitment to the strengthening of traditional marriage, the result of the harsh spotlight on marriage and a current assessment of the institution's fragility. Can restoration of "permanency," *or at least quasi-permanency*, be far behind?[195]

Suffer the Little Children
Marriage, the Poor, and the Commonweal

W. Bradford Wilcox*

I N 2000, then-Minnesota Governor Jesse Ventura offered this explanation for his veto of a bill that would have awarded Minnesota
couples who take a premarital preparation class a fifty-dollar re-
duction in the fee for their marriage license: "Marriage is a private
affair and the government should stay out." Ventura's comments are
indicative of a libertarian view of marriage, and relationships more
broadly, that has considerable cachet in American public life. This view
is not without warrant, especially since most Americans would agree
that marriage serves important private goods, especially emotional
and sexual intimacy, that require a measure of autonomy from state
interference for their proper realization.

But this view fails to appreciate the ways in which marriage also
functions as a public institution that serves important public purposes,
broadly understood. Marriage is a public institution insofar as it is
governed, in part, by legal norms set at the state and federal levels of

* This essay is adapted from two publications: W. Bradford Wilcox. 2002. *Sacred Vows, Public
Purposes: Religion, the Marriage Movement and Public Policy.* Washington, DC: The Pew Forum
on Religion and Public Life; and, W. Bradford Wilcox. 2005. "The Facts of Life & Marriage:
Social Science & the Vindication of Christian Moral Teaching," *Touchstone* 18: 38-44.

government. State law is particularly important in setting the terms of entry into and exit from marriage, but even the federal government confers over one thousand rights, benefits, and special statuses on marriage, largely to the benefit of married citizens.[1] On the other hand, many federal and state welfare policies unintentionally penalize marriage among low-income couples, insofar as means-tested programs tend to treat low-income single parents better than low-income married couples.[2] Thus, for better and worse, public policy has influenced and continues to influence the economic benefits, cultural understanding, and normative meaning of marriage.

Why is the state so interested in marriage? What uniquely public purposes does it serve? The Founders, including John Witherspoon and John Adams, saw marriage as a bulwark of social order and a "seedbed of virtue" that the new republic could not do without. Witherspoon argued that marriage awakens a spirit of benevolence and duty in its members that is then extended to their local communities and the nation as a whole. Adams believed that "the foundations of national Morality must be laid in private families" and that the virtues lived out in marriage—for instance, fidelity—were crucial to the welfare of children. And both maintained that marriage played a uniquely salutary role in engendering virtuous behavior among men.[3]

What is striking about the Founders' reflections on this topic is that so much of their wisdom has been vindicated by contemporary social science. Marriage promotes social order by regulating sexual and romantic relations, providing a long-term vehicle for the accumulation of property, and—most importantly—fostering a strong, life-long bond between men and women that confers considerable social, economic, and spiritual benefits on any children that they have.[4] Likewise, marriage can play a unique role in turning single men away from the selfish and dangerous pursuits that often occupy them and toward the needs of their families and communities, as evidenced by increases in hard work, sobriety, and religious attendance among newly-married men.[5]

More generally, studies suggest that the virtues and dependencies cultivated between men and women in marriage, and between parents and children in married families, radiate outward into the commonweal, generating higher levels of civic engagement and lower levels of state spending.[6] Among other things, a strong marriage culture limits the size and scope of government, insofar as it limits the need for welfare programs aimed at single-parent families and for police and penal policies aimed at criminals, who disproportionately hail from the ranks of unmarried men and from men who grew up in broken families.[7]

Perhaps most importantly, studies indicate that a strong marriage culture protects the poor, especially poor children. Marriage provides poor adults and their children with access to two potential earners and better economies of scale, greater incentives for men to work, two families to whom they can turn for social, financial, and emotional support, and two parents who can support and spell one another amidst the challenges of childrearing. Studies indicate, among other things, that adults who begin adulthood in poverty are 66 percent less likely to remain poor if they get and stay married; that low-income married families are less than half as likely to experience material hardship—missing a meal or failing to pay bills—than are cohabiting or single parents; and that single mothers who marry shortly after a nonmarital birth experience an increase of more than 50 percent in their standard of living relative to single parents and 20 percent relative to cohabiting families.[8] Similarly, studies suggest that low-income children who grow up outside an intact, married family are more likely to experience delinquency, serious psychological problems, and health problems than low-income children in intact, married families.[9] Moreover, low-income couples who marry and have children are much less likely to remain poor than are low-income single-parent families.[10]

Clearly, then, a strong marriage culture serves the common good. This is why the vast majority of cultures, and virtually all of the great civilizations of the world, have sought to unite the goods of sexual intimacy, childbearing and childrearing, and lifelong love between adults in the institution of marriage. Unfortunately, the last five decades have witnessed the deinstitutionalization of marriage, where these goods are separated one from the other, throughout the developed West.

Since the 1960s, from Sweden to Spain, Germany to Great Britain, and Norway to New Zealand, the West has witnessed dramatic increases in divorce, illegitimacy, single parenthood, and voluntary childlessness. All these indicators point to the declining power and authority of the institution of marriage as the primary vehicle for the social organization of adult sexual and emotional intimacy, childbearing and childrearing, and the civilization of men. Because of its signal impact on the poor and the commonweal, the deinstitutionalization of marriage amounts to one of the most disturbing developments of our time.

This essay proceeds in two steps. First, I argue that contraception and abortion helped to separate sex and then procreation from marriage, with dramatic consequences for the institution of marriage and the society at large. Second, I consider how out-of-wedlock childbearing and divorce—viewed here as consequences of the deinstitutionalization of marriage—harm the commonweal and particularly the poor. This essay focuses on the United States, but the general argument offered in this essay is equally applicable to most modern countries. (For similar arguments on family trends in Great Britain, for instance, see research by Steven Nock, a sociologist at the University of Virginia, and Charles Murray, a fellow at the American Enterprise Institute.)[11]

CONTRACEPTION AND ABORTION

The introduction of the Pill in the 1960s and legal abortion in the 1970s separated sex from procreation in ways that had serious consequences for sexual norms, childbearing, divorce, and the prevalence of marriage. Scholars from Robert Michael at University of Chicago to George Akerlof at the University of California at Berkeley argue that contraception played a central role in launching the sexual and divorce revolutions of the late twentieth century. Michael, an economist, has written that about half of the increase in divorce from 1965 to 1976 can be attributed to the "unexpected nature of the contraceptive revolution"—especially in the way that the introduction of the Pill in the

1960s made marriage and sex less child-centered. Specifically, Michael argues that contraception made adulterous relationships less costly for married persons, allowed many married women to turn their focus from childbearing and childrearing to careers (which were less intrinsically connected to the marital bond), and, as a consequence, decreased wives' economic dependence on husbands and wives' investments in a good held in common with their husband, that is, children. More fundamentally, contraception changed men and women's basic assumptions about the nature and character of marriage by allowing men and women to focus more on their relationship, leisure, consumerism, and careers, and less on children.[12]

George Akerlof's scholarship on the effects of contraception and abortion is even more provocative. He argues that the availability of contraception and then abortion in the 1960s and 1970s was one of the crucial factors fueling the sexual revolution and the collapse of marriage among the working class and the poor. Akerlof is a Nobel-prize winning economist, a professor at Berkeley, and a former fellow at the Brookings Institution. In two articles in leading economic journals, Akerlof details findings and advances arguments that suggest the social costs of contraception and abortion for sexual morality and men have been high indeed.[13]

In his first article, Akerlof begins by asking why the U.S. witnessed such a dramatic increase in illegitimacy from 1965 to 1990—from 24 percent to 64 percent among African-Americans, and from 3 percent to 18 percent among whites. He notes that public health advocates had predicted that the widespread availability of contraception and abortion would reduce illegitimacy, not increase it. So what happened?

Using the language of economics, Akerlof points out that "technological innovation creates both winners and losers."[14] In this case the introduction of widespread effective contraception—especially the Pill—put traditional women with an interest in marriage and children at "competitive disadvantage" in the relationship "market" compared to modern women who took a more hedonistic approach to sex and relationships; the contraceptive revolution also reduced the costs of sex for women and men, insofar as the threat of pregnancy was taken off the table—especially as abortion became widely available in the 1970s.

The consequence? Traditional and moderate women could no longer hold the threat of pregnancy over their male partners, either to avoid sex or to elicit a promise of marriage in the event that pregnancy resulted from sexual intercourse. And modern women no longer worried about getting pregnant. Accordingly, more and more women gave in to their boyfriends' entreaties for sex.

In Akerlof's words, "the norm of the premarital sexual abstinence all but vanished in the wake of the technology shock."[15] Women felt free (or pressured) to have sex before marriage. For instance, Akerlof finds that the percentage of girls sixteen and under reporting sexual activity surged in 1970 and 1971 as contraception and abortion became common in many states throughout the country.

Thus, the sexual revolution left traditional or moderate women who wanted to avoid premarital sex or contraception "immiserated" because they could not compete with women who had no serious objection to premarital sex, and they could no longer elicit a promise of marriage from boyfriends in the event they got pregnant. Boyfriends, of course, could say that pregnancy was their girlfriends' choice. So men were less likely to agree to a shotgun marriage in the event of a premarital pregnancy than they would have been before the arrival of the Pill and abortion.

Thus, many of the traditional and especially moderate women ended up having sex and having children out of wedlock, while many of the permissive women ended up having sex and contracepting or aborting so as to avoid childbearing. This explains in large part why the contraceptive revolution was associated with both an increase in abortion and illegitimacy.

In his second article, Akerlof argues that another key outworking of the contraceptive revolution was the disappearance of marriage—shotgun and otherwise—for men. Contraception and abortion allowed men to put off marriage, even in cases when they had fathered a child. Consequently, the fraction of young men who were married in the

U.S. dropped precipitously. Between 1968 and 1993 the percentage of men 25 to 34 who were married with children fell from 66 percent to 40 percent. Accordingly, young men did not benefit from the civilizing influence of wives and children.

Instead, they could continue to hang out with their young male friends, and were thus more vulnerable to the drinking, partying, tom-catting, and worse that is associated with unsupervised groups of young men. Absent the civilizing influence of marriage and children, young men—especially men from working class and poor families without access to educational and professional opportunities that would foster devotion to the legitimate economy—were more likely to respond to the lure of the street. Akerlof notes, for instance, that substance abuse and incarceration more than doubled from 1968 to 1998. Moreover, his statistical models indicate that the growth in single men in this period was indeed linked to higher rates of substance abuse, arrests for violent crimes, and drinking.

From this research, Akerlof concludes by arguing that the con-traceptive revolution played a key, albeit indirect, role in the dramatic increase in social pathology and poverty this country witnessed in the 1970s; it did so by fostering sexual license, poisoning the relations be-tween men and women, and weakening the marital vow. In Akerlof's words: "Just at the time, about 1970, that the permanent cure to poverty seemed to be on the horizon and just at the time that women had ob-tained the tools to control the number and the timing of their children, single motherhood and the feminization of poverty began their long and steady rise."[16] Furthermore, the decline in marriage caused in part by the contraceptive revolution "intensified . . . the crime shock and the substance abuse shock" that marked the 70s and 80s.[17]

As suggested above, these shocks fell disproportionately on the ranks of the poor and working classes. Two pairs of statistical trends illustrate the way in which the social pathologies of the late twentieth century fell disproportionately on the poor. About 5 percent of col-lege-educated mothers have had a child outside marriage (little change since the early 1960s) and about 20 percent of women with high school education or less now have a child outside marriage (up from about 5 percent in the early 1960s). Similarly, the percent of divorced or separated mothers with a college education is about 7 percent (up from about 5 percent in the early 1960s), while the percentage of divorced or separated mothers without a college education is about 16 percent (up from about 7 percent in the early 1960s).[18]

Why were family decline and attendant social pathologies concentrated among poor and working class Americans? Marriage as an institution is dependent upon two pillars: socioeconomic status and normative commitment. In terms of socioeconomic status, the poor have less of an economic stake in marriage (e.g., a family home owned by both spouses) and a lesser ability to possess the material accoutrements of marriage (e.g., sufficient income to purchase a family home). So they depend more on religious and moral norms regarding marriage to maintain their commitment to the institution (e.g., children should be born and reared in a married home). Middle and upper class Americans remain committed to marriage in practice because they continue to have an economic and social stake in marriage, and because they have the means to possess the material accoutrements of marriage. They recognize that their lifestyle, and the lifestyle of their children, will be markedly better if they form a long-term social and economic partnership—that is, marriage—with one person.

So the bottom line is this: the research of Nobel laureate George Akelof suggests that the tragic outworkings of the contraceptive revolution—marked especially by the ready availability of the Pill and abortion—were sexual license, family dissolution, crime, and poisoned relations between the sexes—and that the poor have paid the heaviest price for this revolution.

DIVORCE AND OUT-OF-WEDLOCK CHILDBEARING

As we have seen, the deinstitutionalization of marriage in the late twentieth century, in which the contraceptive revolution played a central part, also played an important indirect role in fostering a surge in male misbehavior in the 1970s and 1980s, insofar as poor and working class men were much less likely to experience the civilizing influence of married family life. Now, I turn to a consideration of the ways in which increases in divorce and nonmarital childbearing—key consequences of the deinstitutionalization of marriage—have affected the lives of children and the welfare of the commonweal.

I focus first on the consequences for children of growing up apart from an intact, married family. Note, of course, that poor and working class children are much more likely to spend time in a single- or step-family because illegitimacy and divorce are concentrated at the lower end of the socioeconomic ladder. I focus on the research of Sara McLanahan, a sociologist at Princeton University. In the 1970s, as a divorced, single mother she set out to show that the negative effects of divorce could be attributed solely to the economic dislocation caused by divorce. But after spending twenty years researching the subject, she came to the conclusion that the social and emotional consequences of divorce also played a key role in explaining the negative outcomes of divorce. She also found that remarriage was, on average, no help to children affected by divorce.

Before turning to her findings about the negative effects of growing up apart from an intact, married family, let us first focus on the positive goods that intact, married families typically provide their children. McLahanan argues that the intact, two-parent family does four key things for children. First, children benefit from the economic resources that mothers and particularly fathers bring to the household through work and sometimes family money. Second, children see their parents model appropriate male-female relations, including virtues like fidelity and self-sacrifice in the context of a marital relationship. Third, because both parents are invested in the child, they spell one another in caring for their children, and they monitor one another's parenting. This reduces stress, helps to insure that parents are not too strict, or too permissive, and makes it much more likely than other family arrangements to forestall abuse. Finally, fathers often serve as key guides to children seeking to negotiate the outside world as adolescents and young adults. Fathers introduce them to civic institutions, the world of work, and provide them with key contacts in these worlds.

McClanahan also argues that stepfathers do not have the history, the authority, and the trust of the children to function—on average—as well as biological fathers. "From the child's point of view, having a new adult move into the household creates another disruption. Having adjusted to the father's moving out, the child must now experience a second reorganization of household personnel. Stepfathers are less likely to be committed to the child's welfare than biological fathers, and they are less likely to serve as a check on the mother's behavior."[19]

So how are children who grow up apart from an intact family affected by this experience? Children in single-parent families are about twice as likely to drop out of high school. Data from the National Survey of Families and Households showed that children in divorced families had a 17 percent risk of dropping out of school, compared to a 9 percent risk for children in married families, even after controlling for parents' education and race. Other surveys found similar results.[20] Girls raised in single-parent families are almost twice as likely to have a nonmarital birth as teens. In the National Survey of Families and Households the risk for children in divorced families is 15 percent compared to 9 percent for those with married parents. Again, this survey is typical.[21] McLanahan also finds that boys raised outside of an intact nuclear family are more than twice as likely as other boys to end up in prison, even controlling for a range of social and economic factors.[22]

McLanahan also explored whether children in stepfamilies did better than children in single-mother families. Bear in mind that by the time she was conducting this latest round of research she had remarried. Here is what she found: "remarriage neither reduces nor improves a child's chances of graduating from high school or avoiding a teenage birth."[23] In other words, remarriage *does not* mitigate the devastating social effects of divorce; her work also suggests that marriage to an adult who is not related to the child does not mitigate the effects of a nonmarital childbirth.

So, after spending twenty years researching the effects of family structure on children, McLanahan came to this conclusion with her colleague, Gary Sandefur at the University of Wisconsin: "If we were asked to design a system for making sure that children's basic needs were met, we would probably come up with something quite similar to the two-parent ideal. Such a design, in theory, would not only ensure that children had access to the time and money of two adults, it also would provide a system of checks and balances that promoted quality parenting. The fact that both parents have a biological connection to the child would increase the likelihood that the parents would identify with the child and be willing to sacrifice for that child, and it would reduce the likelihood that either parent would abuse the child."[24] This, of course, sounds quite similar to the perennial wisdom of the Western moral tradition, articulated by figures as various as Aristotle, Calvin, and St. Thomas Aquinas. Sadly, many in the West have lost sight of this wisdom, and our children—especially children in poor and working class homes—are paying the price.

Of course, the poor are not the only ones paying the price for the deinstitutionalization of marriage. The commonweal is also paying a heavy price for the breakdown of a strong marriage culture in the United States. The work of Isabel Sawhill, director of economic studies at the Brookings Institution, is suggestive in this regard. Sawhill argues that the growth in single-parent families over the latter half of the twentieth century was deeply implicated in increases in poverty and state spending. For instance, the child poverty rate rose one-third from 15 percent in 1970 to 20 percent in 1997; almost all of the increase in child poverty in this period can be attributed to the financial fallout of divorce and nonmarital childbearing, since children in single-parent homes do not benefit from the income and economies of scale associated with marriage.[25]

These family trends have been equally important for the public purse. Sawhill estimates that the growth in single-parent families between 1970 and 1996 increased welfare spending alone by $229 billion.[26] This estimate would increase exponentially if the costs of family breakdown for medicaid, housing, family courts, and the criminal justice system were factored into analyses of the public costs of the deinstitutionalization of marriage. Of course, increases in divorce and nonmarital childbearing have also been associated with increases in the size and invasive reach of government. For instance, in the last forty years, family courts have taken a large role in monitoring and determining the nature of parent-child relationships since approximately one million children are affected by divorce every year, a Federal Office of Child Support Enforcement was founded to help state agencies track fathers who have fallen behind in child support payments, and police departments have added officers to deal with high crime rates in communities dominated by fatherless families. The bottom line is this: as the Founders would have predicted, when the habits and virtue that sustain a strong marriage culture weaken, Leviathan moves into the breach.

CONCLUSION

The portrait this chapter paints is sobering. By virtually any measure, in the U.S. the institution of marriage—in which virtually every culture in the world has sought to unite the goods of sexual intimacy, procreation, and lifelong love between adults who are also parents together—weakened markedly from 1960 to 1995. The sources of this decline are numerous, but this chapter argues that contraception and abortion played key roles, insofar as they helped separate sex, procreation, and marriage from one another. This chapter also argues that high rates of divorce and nonmarital childbearing are important consequences of the weakening of marriage, and have profoundly affected for worse the commonweal, the society, and especially the poor. In all these ways, the deinstitutionalization of what many view as a private institution, marriage, has had very public consequences.

But I would like to conclude on two hopeful notes. First, we are beginning to see a new openness among intellectuals to the importance of marriage and to the perils of divorce. For a long time intellectuals were not willing to acknowledge the importance of marriage for children. But the intellectual tide is now turning towards a refreshing willingness to grapple with our children's toughest social problems in a probing and open-minded manner. Besides Akerlof, McLanahan, and Sawhill, scholars like Linda Waite at the University of Chicago, Robert Lerman at the Urban Institute, and Norval Glenn at the University of Texas have all underlined the importance of marriage in recent years. Their willingness to speak up on behalf of the unvarnished truth—a truth which is evident for all to see in our statistical models—suggests that the intellectual foundations of marital deinstitutionalization may be crumbling before our very eyes.

Second, the latter half of the 1990s witnessed the stabilization of many marriage-related trends. Divorce fell slightly, teenage sexual activity also fell, cohabitation rates stabilized, and the percentage of children living in a single-parent family also stabilized.[27] These demographic trends suggest that Americans may have had enough with our failed family experiment of the last four decades and are ready to chart a new path when it comes to family life, especially if they learn more about what social scientists have discovered about the merits of marriage (most Americans seem unaware of recent social science regarding the family). Both of these developments must be viewed as good news for our society, the commonweal, and especially the poor, who have borne the heaviest burden for our rejection of the perennial wisdom of humankind that sex, childbearing and childrearing, and parenthood should be united together by marriage. And, finally, let us hope that the social scientific wisdom we have gained in the last decade will help the United States resist the temptation to launch yet another social experiment that further divorces these goods one from the other.

Notes

Foreword

1 Robert Schoen and Nicola Standish. 2001. "The Retrenchment of Marriage: Results from Marital Status Life Tables for the United States, 1995." *Population and Development Review* 27-3: 553-563.

2 W. Bradford Wilcox *et al.* 2005. *Why Marriage Matters: Twenty-Six Conclusions from the Social Sciences*. New York: Institute for American Values.

1 *Sacrilege and Sacrament*

1 See James Q. Wilson, *The Moral Sense*, New York, 1994; Charles Murray, *Losing Ground: American Social Policy* 1950-1980, New York, 1984.

2 On this point, and the subsequent history of marriage, see John Witte, *From Sacrament to Contract: Marriage, Religion and Law in the Western Tradition*, Louisville KY, 1997.

3 G.W.F. Hegel, *Philosophy of Right*, tr. T.M. Knox, London 1952, §161.

4 *Kant's Philosophical Correspondence:* 1755-99, ed. and tr. Arnulf Zweig, Chicago 1967, p. 235, *The Metaphysic of Morals*, Academy Ed., 277.

5 R. Scruton, *Perictione in Colophon*, South Bend Indiana, 2000, pp 30-32. On the real identity of Archeanassa, see R. Scruton, *Xanthippic Dialogues*, South Bend Indiana, 1998, pp 269-70.

6 Sir Henry Maine, *Ancient Law*, Oxford 1861.

7 Margaret Mead, *Coming of Age in Samoa*, New York 1928.

8 Actually *l'amour courtois*, so named by Gaston Paris in a seminal article of 1883: 'Lancelot du Lac: *Le Conte de la Charrette*', *Romania* 12, 459-534.

9 Andreas Capellanus, *De arte honesti amandi*, tr. John Jay Parry as *The Art of Courtly Love*, New York 1941.

10 *Sexual Desire*, New York and London 1986; *Death-Devoted Heart: Sex and the sacred in Wagner's Tristan and Isolde*, New York 2003.

11 The research necessary to back up these claims (at least in the case of England and Wales) is available in Valerie Riches, *Sex Education or Indoctrination: how ideology has triumphed over facts*, with additional research by Norman Wells, London, Family and Youth Concern, 2004. Americans will be familiar with the research of Kay Hymowitz and others to the same effect.

12 Richard Rorty, *Achieving our Country: Leftist Thought in Twentieth Century America*, New York 2002.

13 Still, it is worth pointing out that societies where marriage has broken down or where children are routinely born out of wedlock are now dying: in Europe because the children are not born, in sub-Saharan Africa because the children die of AIDS. In societies where marriage is the norm and children are born in wedlock, population is increasing, notably in the Islamic world.

14 See Alan Sokal and Jean Bricmont, *Intellectual Impostures*, London 1998 (published in the USA as *Fashionable Nonsense*, NY 1998), an Frederick Crews, *Postmodern Pooh*, NY 2001, London 2002.

15 I have benefited greatly from Seana Sugrue's comments on an earlier draft of this paper.

2 *What About the Children?*

1 Max Weber, *The Protestant Ethic and the Spirit of Capitalism* (New York: Charles Scribner's Sons, 1958), p. 181; Jürgen Habermas, *The Theory of Communicative Rationality II* (Boston, Mass.: Beacon Press, 1987, p. 333.

2 Ralf Dahrendorf, "A Precarious Balance: Economic Opportunity, Civil Society, and Political Liberty," *The Responsive Community* (Summer 1995), pp. 28-32.

3 Barbara Dafoe Whitehead and David Popenoe, "Why Men Won't Commit: State of Our Unions: The Social Health of Marriage in America 2002," (New Brunswick, NJ.: Rutgers, The National Marriage Project, 2002), p. 8.

4 Gary Becker, *Treatise on the Family* (Cambridge, Mass.: Harvard University Press, 1991), pp. 356, 357.

5 Ibid.; Charles Murray, *Losing Ground* (New York: Basic Books, 1984). pp. 129-133.

6 For reviews of these trends in both the U.S. with its strong market economy and Sweden with its emphasis on the state-supported family, see David Popenoe, *Disturbing the Nest* (New York: Aldine De Gruyter, 1988); Alan Wolfe, *Whose Keeper* (Berkley, CA.: University

of California Press, 1989).

7   Nancy Cott, *Public Vows: A History of Marriage and the Nation* (Cambridge, Mass.: Harvard University Press, 2000), p. 198.

8   Ibid., p. 199.

9   William N. Eskridge, *Equality Practice: Civil Unions and the Future of Gay Rights* (New York: Routledge, 2002).

10 John Witte, *From Sacrament to Contract: Marriage, Religion, and Law in the Western Tradition* (Louisville, KY: Westminster John Knox Press, 1997), p. 2.

11 For a philosophical and theological exposition of the unitive goods of marriage, see Karol Wojtyla (the future Pope John Paul II) *Love and Responsibility* (New York: Farrar, Straus, and Giroux, 1981), pp. 40-44.

12 Daniel Cere, "Redefining Marriage and Family: Trends in North American Jurisprudence," (Family Law Project: Harvard University, 2003), p. 24.

13 This position is often associated with the organizations called Focus on the Family and Promise Keepers. See James Dobson, *Dr. Dobson Answers Your Questions about Marriage and Sexuality* (Wheaton, IL.: Tyndale House Publishers, 1974), pp. iii, 65-71; James Dobson and Gary Bauer, *Children at Risk* (Dallas, TX.: Word Publishing, 1990), p. 156; Tony Evans, "A Man and His Integrity," *Seven Promises of a Promise Keeper* (Colorado Springs, Colo.: Focus on the Family Publishing, 1994), p. 73.

14 Martha Fineman, *The Illusion of Equality* (Chicago, IL.: The University of Chicago Press, 1991) and *The Neutered Family and Other Twentieth Century Tragedies* (New York: Routledge, 1995).

15 Jonathan Rauch, *Gay Marriage: Why It is Good for Gays, Good for Straights, and Good for America* (New York: Henry Holt and Company, 2004).

16 Martin Daly and Margo Wilson, "The Evolutionary Psychology of Marriage and Divorce," *The Ties that Bind* (New York: Aldine De Gruyter, 2000), pp. 91-110.

17 Aristotle, *Politics* in *The Basic Words of Aristotle* (New York: Random House, 1941), Bk. I, ii.

18 Plato, *Republic* (New York: Basic Books, 1968), Bk. v, par .462.

19 Aristotle, *Politics*, Bk. I, ii.

20 Ibid.

21 Thomas Aquinas, "Supplement," *Summa Theologica* III (London: T. and T. Washbourne, 1917), Q. 41, A. 1.

22 Ibid.

23 Ibid. Q. 42, A. 3.

24 For a discussion of how metaphors of characterizing the ultimate context of experience unwittingly pervade the social sciences, see Don Browning, *Religious Thought and the Modern Psychologies* (Minneapolis, MN.: Fortress Press, 1987, 2004).

25 Aquinas, "Supplement," *Summa Theologica* III, Q 41, A. 1.

26 Ibid.

27 Ibid.

28 For a summary of these four conditions as they can be found in the literature of evolutionary psychology, see Don Browning, Bonnie Miller-McLemore, Pamela Couture, Bernie Lyon, and Robert Franklin, *From Culture Wars to Common Ground: Religion and the American Family Debate* (Louisville, KY: Westminster John Knox, 1997, 2000), pp. 111-114. See also Don Browning, *Marriage and Modernization: How Globalization Threatens Marriage and What to Do about It* (Grand Rapids, MI: Wm. B. Eerdmans, 2003), pp. 109-111.

29 Aquinas, "Supplement," *Summa Theologica*, III, Q 41.

30 Aquinas, *Summa Theologica*, II-II, Q 10, A12.

31 *Rerum Novarum*, in *Proclaiming Justice and Peace: Papal Documents from* Rerum Novarum *through* Centisimus Annus, Michael Walsh and Brian Davies (eds.) (Mystic, CN: Twenty-Third Publications), para. 11 and 12: Pius XI, *Casti Connubii* (New York, NY: The Barry Vail Corporation, 1931) and Pius XI, *Quadragesimo Anno*, The Papal Encyclicals (McGrath, 1981).

32 Mary Midgley, *Beast and Man* (Ithaca, NY: Cornell University Press, 1978).

33 Jean Porter, *Natural and Divine Law* (Ottawa, Ontario: Saint Paul University Press, 1999).

34 Stephen Pope, *The Evolution of Altruism and the Ordering of Love* (Washington, D.C.: Georgetown University Press, 1994).

35 Larry Arnhart, *Darwinian Natural Right* (Albany, NY: State University of New York, 1998).

36 Lisa Sowle Cahill, *Sex, Gender and Christian Ethics* (New York: Cambridge University Press, 1996).

37 Midgley, *Beast and Man*, p. 81.

38 Rauch, *Gay Marriage*, p. 52.

39 Ibid., p. 42.

40 Ibid., p. 22.

41 Ibid., p. 108.

42 Ibid., p. 111.

43 *Goodridge v. Department of Public Health*, 798 N.E.2d 941 (Mass. 2003), majority opinion, p. 1, 5.

44 Ibid., p. 5.

45 Ibid., p. 14.

46 Ibid., p. 10.

47 Andrew Sullivan, *Virtually Normal* (New York: Vintage Books, 1995); Evan Wolfson, "All Together Now," *Marriage and Same-Sex Unions: A Debate*, ed. by Lynn Wardle, Mark Strasser, William Duncan, and David Coolidge (Westport, CT: Praeger, 2003), pp. 3-10.

48 Cere, "Redefining Marriage and Family: Trends in North American Jurisprudence," p. 24.

49 The United Nations Convention on the Rights of the Child, Article 7.

50 Elizabeth Marquardt's forthcoming book is based on a new, national study that includes a nationally representative telephone survey of young adults from divorced and intact families, conducted with Dr. Norval Glenn at the University of Texas-Austin. See *Between Two Worlds: The Inner Lives of Children of Divorce* (Crown Publishers, September 2005) Also see www.americanvalues.org, scroll down to "children of divorce" and be sure to click on "archives" in that section as well.

51 *Goodridge v. Department of Public Health*, pp. 10-11.

52 Marquardt asks whether children of same-sex couples could be all that different from children in every other alternative family form we've tried, in "Gay Marriage: A fine idea in principle, but what about the kids?" *Chicago Tribune* (December 7, 2003), p. 4. Also available on the www.americanvalues.org website.

53 Fineman's most mature theory of dependency can be found in her recent book, *The Autonomy Myth: A Theory of Dependency* (New York: The New Press, 2004).

54 Fineman, *The Neutered Mother and the Sexual Family*, pp. 143-144.

55 Ibid., p. 229.

56 Ibid., pp. 164-166.

57 Richard Posner, *Sex and Reason* (Cambridge, Mass.: Harvard University Press, 1992), p. 298.

58 David Greenberg, *The Construction of Homosexuality* (Chicago: The University of Chicago Press, 1988).

59 Rauch, *Gay Marriage*, pp. 129-130.

60 Ibid., p. 88.

61 Richard Goldstein, *The Attack Queers: Liberal Society and the Gay Right* (New York: 2002), pp. 35, 50-56. Michael Warner (ed.), *Fear of A Queer Planet* (Minneapolis, MN.: University of Minnesota Press, 1993), p. xiii, and Michael Warner, *The Trouble with Normal: Sex, Politics, and the Ethics of Queer Life* (Cambridge, Mass.: Harvard University Press, 1999), pp. 9, 22.

62 Warner, *The Trouble with Normal*, pp. 88-89.

63 Don Browning, *From Culture Wars to Common Ground: Religion and the American Family Debate*, pp. 37-38.

64 Ibid., p. 2.

65 Ibid., pp. 287-288.

66 For a fuller discussion of the practical proposals connected with critical familism, see Browning, et.al., *From Culture Wars to Common Ground*, pp. 307-334; see also, Don Browning and Gloria Rodriguez, *Reweaving the Social Tapestry: Toward a Public Philosophy and Policy of Families* (New York: W. W. Norton, 2002), esp. chpts. 6-8.

67 For a discussion about the need for an interfaith dialogue on the reconstruction of marriage, see Don Browning, *Marriage and Modernization*, pp. 223-244.

3 *Changing Dynamics of the Family*

1 Alfred D. Chandler, Jr., *The visible hand: the managerial revolution in American business*, Cambridge, Mass.: Belknap Press, 1977.

2 The concept of Rhineland capitalism as a special path was popularized by Michel Albert, *Capitalism versus Capitalism*, London: Whurr, 1993 (original French edition 1991).

3 Peter Payne, "Family business in Britain: An historical and analytical survey", in (eds.) Akio Okochi, Shigeaki Yasuoka, *Family business in the era of industrial growth: its owner-ship and management: proceedings of the Fuji Conference. The International Conference on Business History*, 10, Tokyo: University of Tokyo Press, 1984.

4 Jeffrey Fear, "August Thyssen and German Steel", in (ed.) Thomas K. McCraw, *Creating modern capitalism: How entrepreneurs, companies, and countries triumphed in three industrial revolutions*, Cambridge and London: Harvard University Press, 1997, pp. 185-226

5 See Edward S. Herman, *Corporate Control, Corporate Power*, Cambridge: Cambridge University Press, 1981, p. 352.

6 Jack Goody, *The East in West*, Cambridge: Cambridge University Press, 1996, pp. 199, 201.

7 See for instance the entertaining recent book by Adam Bellow, *In Praise of Nepotism*, New York: Random House, 2003.

8 Johann Wolfgang von Goethe, *Goethes Werke herausgegeben im Auftrage der Grossherzogin Sophie von Sachsen, Tag- und Jahres-Hefte als Ergänzung meiner sonstigen Bekenntnisse. [1749-1806], I. Abtheilung: 35. Band*, Weimar: H. Böhlau, 1892, pp. 57-59 (1795).

9 Cited in René Sédillot, *Deux cent cinquante ans d'industrie*, p. 122.

10 See Shigeaki Yasuoka, "Capital ownership in family companies: Japanese firms com-pared with those in other countries", in (eds.) Akio Okochi, Shigeaki Yasuoka, *Family business in the era of industrial growth: its ownership and management: proceedings of the Fuji Conference. The International Conference on Business History*, 10, Tokyo: University of Tokyo Press, 1984, pp. 1-32.

11 Notably those in Germany directed by Lothar Gall and by Jürgen Kocka.

12 See the model evolved by Yoram Ben-Porath, "The F-connection, families, friends and the organization of exchange," *Population Development Review*, 6 (1980), pp. 1-30.

13 Tarun Khanna and Krishna Palepu, "Policy shocks, market intermediaries, and corporate strategy: The evolution of business groups in Chile and India", Journal of Economics and Management Strategy 8/2, 1999, pp. 271-310.

14 See for instance the session of the International Economic History in Budapest, 1982: (ed.) Leslie Hannah, *From Family Firm to Professional Management: Structure and Per-formance of Business Enterprise*, Budapest: Akadémiai Kiadó, 1982.

15 *Financial Times*, Feb. 3, 2003: "The Complex Evolution of Family Affairs" (p. 6).

16 Frédéric Lemaître, "La France: championne du capitalisme familial", *Le Monde*, April 18, 2003.

17 Mara Faccio, Larry H.P. Lang, The ultimate ownership of Western European corpora-tions, *Journal of Financial Economics* 65, 2002, p. 393.

18 Knut Borchardt, "Der Unternehmerhaushalt als Wirtschaftsbetrieb", in (ed.) Tilmann Buddensieg, *Villa Hügel: Das Wohnhaus Krupp in Essen*, Berlin: Siedler, 1994, p. 12.

19 R. Passow, "Aktiengesellschaften", in (eds.) Ludwig Elster, Adolf Weber, Friedrich Wieser, *Handwörterbuch der Staatswissenschaften*, 4th ed., Jena: G. Fischer, 1923, Vol. I, p. 134.

20 Pierre Bourdieu, Monique de Saint Martin, "Le patronat," in *Actes de la Recherche en sciences sociales* 20-21, 1978, p. 27.

21 *Family Business, Business Families*, Harvard University Press, 2005.

22 Thomas Malthus, *An Essay on the Principle of Population*, reprinted Harmondsworth, 1970, pp. 67, 124.

23 Ibid., 118, 142.

24 *The Times* (London), September 16, 2004; *Financial Times*, September 30, 2004.

25 Lawrence Stone, "Passionate Attachments in the West in Historical Perspective", in (eds.) Willard Gaylin and Ethen Person, *Passionate Attachments: Thinking About Love*, New York: The Free Press, 1988, p. 19.

26 Quoted in Sue Shellenbarger, "And Baby Makes Stress", *Wall Street Journal*, December 16, 2004, p. D1.

27 Hendrik Hartog, "What Gay Marriage Teaches About the History of Marriage", History News Network, April 5, 2004. http://www.hnn.us/articles/4400.html

28 Fyodor Dotoyevsky (transl. David Magarshack), *The Brothers Karamazov*, Harmondsworth: Penguin, 1958, p. 878.

4 *Unilateral Divorce*

1 For an elegant exposition of the pre-political character of marriage, see Seana Sugrue, "Soft Despotism and Same-Sex Marriage," this volume.

2 Adam Smith, *An Inquiry into the Nature and Cause of the Wealth of Nations*, edited by Edwin Canna, (Chicago: University of Chicago Press, 1976), Vol. I, Book 1, Chapter II, (pg. 17).

3 The causal factor in women's attachment appears to be the hormone oxytocin, which bonds a woman both to her sex partner and to her offspring. The title of the classic paper in the field describes the basic point: "The Role of Oxytocin Reflexes in Three Interpersonal Reproductive Acts: Coitus, Birth and Breast Feeding," by Niles Newton, in *Clinical Psychoneuroendocrinology in reproduction*, L. Carenza, P. Pancheri,and L. Zichella, eds. (New York: Academic Press, 1978), PP. 411-18. On the attachment of mothers to their babies, see generally, Steven E. Rhoads, *Taking Sex Differences Seriously*, (San Francisco: Encounter Books, 2004) pp. 190- 222. On women's demand for stability and depend-ability, see David M. Buss, *The Evolution of Desire: Strategies of Human Mating*, (New York: Basic Books, 1994) pp. 32-34. On the attachment of women to their sex partners, see generally, Rhoads, *Taking Sex Differences Seriously*, pp 46-78.

4   On male possessiveness, see David M. Buss, *The Dangerous Passion: Why Jealousy is as Necessary as Love and Sex*, (New York: Free Press, 2000), and *The Evolution of Desire: Strategies of Human Mating*, (New York: Basic Books, 1994) pp. 66-70.

5   See for instance, the testimony of Dr. David Brodzinsky in the Hawaiian same-sex marriage case, *Baehr v. Miike*, No. 91-1394, 1996 WL 694235 at 11 (Haw.Cir.Ct. Dec. 3, 1996), responding to the possibility that the state would prefer one family structure over another, "I find that offensive truthfully. I find it offensive because it tends to suggest that there's only one way of being a parent. It excludes all nonbiological parenting which would be adoptive parenting, stepparenting, foster parenting, parenting by gays and lesbians. It suggests that if there are some additional issues that come with some of these nontraditional families that should be reason for excluding rather than taking that information and using it not in a punitive way but in a proactive, kind of supportive way to help families deal with the inevitable issues that come up in life." Quoted by Maggie Gallagher and Joshua Baker in "Do Moms and Dads Matter? Evidence from the Social Sciences on Family Structure and the Best Interests of the Child," 4 *Margins Law Journal* 166-7 (2004).

6   The General Accounting Office Report "Categories of Laws Pertaining to Marital Status," (GAO/OGC -97-16 Defense of Marriage Act) describes 1049 areas in which marital status matters in federal law. Advocates of extending marriage rights to same-sex couples cite this report as evidence that the federal government bestows benefits on married couples, and that these benefits should be extended to same-sex couples as well. However, many of these provisions are not benefits at all, but rather situations in which married couples are treated distinctly in federal law. For a critique of this common interpretation of the GAO report, see Joshua K. Baker, "1000 Benefits of Marriage? An Analysis of the 1997 GAO Report, *iMAPP Policy Brief*, (Washington D.C.: Institute for Marriage and Public Policy, May 26, 2004), available on-line at http://www.marriagedebate.com/pdf/iMAPP.GAO.pdf.

7   See for instance, Richard Posner, *Sex and Reason*, (Cambridge, MA: Harvard University Press, 1992), who describes his laissez-faire approach to sex as one that would treat "sex as morally indifferent, (and) would limit sexual freedom only to the extent required by economic or other utilitarian considerations," at pg. 181.

8   Theresa Crenshaw, *The Alchemy of Love and Lust: how our Sex Hormones Influence our Relationships*, (New York: Pocket Books, 1996), 93-100.

9   For useful summaries of the voluminous literature on this topic, see generally, William J. Doherty et.al., *Why Marriage Matters: Twenty-One Conclusions from the Social Sciences*, (Washington D.C.:Institute for American Values, 2002); Linda J. Waite and Maggie Gallagher, *The Case for Marriage: Why Married People are Happier, Healthier and Better Off Financially*, (New York: Doubleday, 2000), pp. 124-149; Paul R. Amato and Alan Booth, *A Generation at Risk: Growing Up in an Era of Family Upheaval*, (Cambridge MA: Harvard University Press, 1997); Judith S. Wallerstein, Julia M. Lewis and Sandra

Blakeslee, *The Unexpected Legacy of Divorce: A 25 Year Landmark Study*, (New York: Hyperion, 2000).

10 Richard Epstein, for instance, made this argument in a column in the *Wall Street Journal*, "Live and Let Live," July 13, 2004. I think it is fair to say that this column, brief though it is, summarizes the position of many modern thinkers.

11 Family courts have ruled on an astonishing range of conflicts between estranged parents. A Nebraska judge ruled on how much English a father must speak when visiting his daughter, (Associated Press, October 14, 2003) (accessed at www.foxnews.com on October 15, 2003); another judge in Amarillo Texas overseeing a child-custody case told a Mexican native that speaking only Spanish at home constituted abuse of her 5 year old daughter; *Austin American Statesman* August 29, 1995.

12 Lest the reader think this statement an exaggeration, consider this comment by feminist law professor Joan Williams: "Like most women of my class, I view an active sexual life as an entitlement and children in part in terms of opportunity costs." Joan Williams, *Unbending Gender: Why Family and Work Conflict and What to do About It*, (New York: Oxford University Press, 2000), pg. 261. I analyze and critique this position in *Smart Sex: Finding Life-Long Love in a Hook-Up World*, (Dallas, TX: Spence Publishing, 2005).

13 "Parental divorce on mental health throughout the life course," *American Sociological Review*, 63 (April 1998) 239-249, showing negative effects of parental divorce on their children's mental health, well into adulthood; Michael Workman and John Beer, "Depression, suicide ideation and agression among high school students whose parents are divorced and use alcohol at home," *Psychological Reports*, 70 (1992) 503-511, showing that children from divorced homes are more aggressive than children from non-divorced homes; Nancy Vadne-Kiernan, Nicholas S. Ialongo, Jane Pearson and Sheppard Kellam, " Household Family Structure and Children's Aggressive Behavior: A Longitudinal Study of Urban Elementary School Children, *Journal of Abnormal Child Psychology*, 23:5 (1995) 553-68 showing that boys in mother-only families are more likely to be aggressive than boys with fathers present; Stephanie Kasen, Patricia Cohen, Judith S. Brook and Claudia Hartmark, " A Multiple-Risk Interaction Model: Effects of Temperament and Divorce on Psychiatric Disorders in Children," *Journal of Abnormal Child Psychology*, 24:2 (1996) 121-150 showing that children of single mothers are higher risk for psychiatric disorders; Gunilla Ringback Weitoft, Anders Hjern, Bengt Haglund and Mans Rosen, "Mortality, severe morbidity, and injury in children living with single parents in Sweden: a population-based survey," *Lancet*, 361: 9354 (25 January 2003) showing children of single parent families have higher rates of mortality and psychiatric diseases; Patrick F. Fagan and Robert Rector, "The Effects of Divorce in America, *Heritage Foundation, Backgrounder,* No. 1373, (Washington D.C., 2000); McLanahan, Sara and Karen Booth, "Mother-Only Families: Problems, Prospects and Politics," *Journal of Marriage and the Family*, 51, no. 3 (August 1989): 557-80; Dawson, Deborah, A. "Family Structure and Children's Health and Well-Being: Data from the 1988 National Heath Interview

Survey on Child Health," *Journal of Marriage and the Family*, Vol. 53, (Aug. 1991), 573-584; Ronald L Simons, Kuei-Hsiu Lin, Leslie C. Gordon, Rand D Conger, and Federick O. Lorenz, "Explaining the Higher Incidence of Adjustment Problems Among Children of Divorce Compared with Those in Two-Parent Families," *Journal of Marriage and the Family*, 61 (November 1999): 1020-1033.

14 Robert Whelan, *Broken Homes and Battered Children: A study of the relationship between child abuse and family type* (London: Family Education Trust, 1993). See also Martin Daly and Margo Wilson, "Discriminative Parental Solicitude: A Biological Perspective," *Journal of Marriage and the Family*, May 1980, pg. 282; Michael Gordon and Susan Creighton, "Natal and Non-natal Fathers as Sexual Abusers in the United Kingdom: A Comparative Analysis," *Journal of Marriage and the Family*, 50 (February 1988): 99-105. See also the information contained in David Blankenhorn, pg. 40, footnote 58. Leslie Margolin, "Child Abuse by Mothers' Boyfriends: Why the Overrepresentation?" *Child Abuse and Neglect*, 16, (1992) 541-551 finds similar results for the U.S.

15 Elizabeth C. Cooksey, and Michelle M. Fondell, "Spending Time With His Kids: Effects of Family Structure on Fathers' and Children's Lives," *Journal of Marriage and the Family*, 58 (August 1996): 693-707. For pre-teens, there was a statistically significant negative impact on grades of living in a single father household, or living with a step-father who has biological children living in the same household. For teens, the statistically significant negative impact came from living either in a single father household, or in a household with a step-father who does not have biological children in the household. Pong, Suet-Ling, "Family Structure, School Context, and Eighth Grade Math and Reading Achievment," *Journal of Marriage and the Family*, 59 (August 1997): 734-746. Doris R. Enwisle and Karl L. Alexander, "Family Type and Children's Growth in reading and Math over the Primary Grades," *Journal of Marriage and the Family*, 58 (May 1996): 341-355. Karen Bogenschneider, "Parental Involvement in Adolescent Schooling: A Proximal Process with Transcontextual Validity," *Journal of Marriage and the Family*, 59 (August 1997): 718-733.

16 Douglas A. Smith and G. Roger Jarjoura "Social Structure and Criminal Victimization," *Journal of Research in Crime and Delinquency*, 25, no.1 (February 1988) 27-52. (See especially Table 2, pg. 41) showing that neighborhoods with high densities of single parent households have higher crime rates; Gunilla Ringback Weitoft, Anders Hjern, Bengt Haglund and Mans Rosen, "Mortality, severe morbidity, and injury in children living with single parents in Sweden: a population-based survey," *Lancet*, 361: 9354 (25 January 2003) showing children of single parents are more likely to abuse drugs and alcohol; Chris Coughlin and Samuel Vuchinich, "Family Experience in Preadolescence and the Development of Male Delinquency," *Journal of Marriage and the Family*, 58 (May 1996): 491-501, showing that experience in stepfamilies or single parent families more than doubled the risk of delinquency that began by age 14.

D. Wayne Osgood and Jeff M. Chambers, "Social Disorganization Outside the Metropolis: an Analysis of rural youth violence," *Criminology*, 38: 1 (2000) 81-115, showing that the percentage of female-headed households has a greater impact on the rates of juvenile violence than race or poverty.

17 Irwin Garfinkel and Sara S. McLanahan, *Single Mothers and Their Children*, (Washington, D.C.: Urban Institute Press, 1986) pp. 30-31 cites research showing that daughters of single parents are 53 percent more likely to marry as teenagers, 111 percent more likely to have children as teenagers, 164 percent more likely to have a premarital birth, and 92 percent more likely to dissolve their own marriages.

18 *Goodridge v. Dept of Publ Health*, 798 N.E. 2nd 941, 954 (Mass. 2003) "Simply put, the government creates civil marriage."

19 Duggan, Lisa, "Holy Matrimony," *Nation*, March 22, 2004.

20 The reverse is not true: enemies of the market are not all opponents of marriage. This should not be surprising, since supporting marriage amounts to supporting an organic, non-ideological, pre-political institution. People from all across the political, ideological and religious spectrum can and do support marriage, without any damage to their other beliefs. In a sense, the support of the institution of marriage does not require an explanation. The position that cries out for explanation is the radical redefinition of marriage or the denial that society requires an institution like marriage.

21 See note 6, *supra*.

22 Morse, Jennifer Roback, *Love and Economics: Why the Laissez-Faire Family Doesn't Work*, (Dallas, TX: Spence Publishing, 2001), Chapter 4, "Why the Family isn't a contract."

23 As recounted by Sanford Braver with Diane O'Connell, *Divorced Dads: Shattering the Myths*, (New York: Putnam, 1998), pp. 241-3. This argument is being revived in New York State, which technically does not have no-fault provisions to its divorce law. ("A New Push to Loosen New York's Divorce Law," *New York Times*, November 30, 2004.) This article recounts the difficulties of obtaining divorces, and argues that including a no-fault provision would be desirable. However, the article also reports that over the last 12 months, about six divorces were denied. Out of a total of over 50, 000 divorces, denying 6 divorces is close to zero. Considering that New York has the third lowest divorce rates in the country (tied with CT at 3.2 per 1000 population), denying 6 divorces per year may be a socially acceptable price to pay.

24 An alternative term that tends to shed a more favorable light on the legal institution of no-fault divorce, is "non-adversary divorce." See for instance, R. Schoen et.al, "California's experience with non-adversary divorce," *Demography*, 12:223 (1975).

25 On the theory of the firm, see Oliver E. Williamson, *The Economic Institutions of Capitalism*, (New York: Free Press, 1998), and Oliveer E. Williamson and Sidney G. Winter, *The Nature of the Firm: Origins, Evolution and Development*, (New York: Oxford University Press, 1991); R. H. Coase, "The Nature of the Firm," *Economica* (1937): 386-405; M.C. Jensen and W.H. Meckling, "Theory of the Firm: Managerial Behavior, Agency Costs and Ownership Structure," *Journal of Financial Economics* (October 1976): 305-360; for a textbook treatment on losses from shirking on contractual performance, see David Kreps, *A Course in Microeconomic Theory*, (Princeton: Princeton University Press, 1990).

26 For a discussion of the "privatization" model of the family, see my "Who Puts the Self into Self-Interest?" *Religion and Liberty*, Vol. 8, no. 4, (Nov./Dec. 1998).

27 Brinig, Margaret and Douglas W. Allen. (2000). "'These Boots are Made for Walking:' Why Most Divorce Filers are Women," *American Law and Economics Review*, 2, 126-7.

28 Sanford Braver with Diane O'Connell, *Divorced Dads: Shattering the Myths*, (New York: Putnam, 1998), pp. 124-145.

29 "Split Shift: Later in Life, a gender role reversal shows husbands more dependent, wives yearning to be free," *San Diego Union-Tribune*, October 2, 2004, E1.

30 Alexis de Tocqueville, *Democracy in America*, George Lawrence, translator, J.P. Mayer, editor, (Garden City, New York: Doubleday Books, 1969), pg. 291.

31 Sanford Braver with Diane O'Connell, *Divorced Dads: Shattering the Myths*, (New York: Putnam, 1998), pp. 139-40.

32 Brinig, Margaret and Douglas W. Allen. (2000). "'These Boots are Made for Walking:' Why Most Divorce Filers are Women," *American Law and Economics Review*, 2, pp. 149, 158.

33 Kersti Yllo and Murray A. Strauss, "Interpersonal Violence Among Married and Co-habiting Couples," *Family Relations*, 30 (1981) 339-47. Jan E. Stets and Murray A. Straus, "The Marriage License as a Hitting License: A Comparison of Assaults in Dating, Cohabiting and Married Couples," *Journal of Family Violence*, Vol. 4, No. 2, (1989) shows that cohabiting couples have higher assault rates than either married or dating couples. Likewise, Nicky Ali Jackson, "Observational Experiences of Intrapersonal Conflict and Teenage Victimization: A Comparative Study Among Spouses and Cohabitors," *Journal of Family Violence*, Vol. 11, No. 3, (1996) shows that cohabiting couples are more likely to engage in violence, even accounting for prior violence in the individual's family of origin.

34 Brinig, Margaret and Douglas W. Allen. (2000). "'These Boots are Made for Walking:' Why Most Divorce Filers are Women," *American Law and Economics Review*, 2, pp. 155.

35 These paragraphs are based on reports archived at Ohio State University websites, including: http://pni.psychiatry.ohio-state.edu/jkg/ and http://pni.psychiatry.ohio-state.edu/jkg/articel.html and www.acs.ohio-state.edu/units/research/archive/hormones.htm. The major work cited is: Kiecolt-Glaser, J.K., Newton, T., Cacioppo, J.T., MacCallum, R.C., Glaser, R. & Malarkey, W.B. (1996). "Marital conflict and endrocine function: Are men really more physiologically affected than women?" *Journal of Consulting and Clinical Psychology*, 64, 324-332.

36 This is consistent with the findings reported by Braver op.cit.pp 121-2, that divorced men recover from their anger more quickly than do women.

5 The Framers' Idea of Marriage and Family

1 *John Adams Diary*, June 2, 1778.

2 John Adams to Mercy Warren. 16 Apr. 1776 Warren-Adams Letters 1:222-23 http://press-pubs.uchicago.edu/founders/documents/v1ch18s9.html.

3 Allan C. Carlson, *From Cottage to Workstation: The Family's Search for Harmony in the Industrial Age* 10-15 (1993).

4 See, e.g., Joseph J. Ellis, *Founding Brothers: The Revolutionary Generation* (2000).

5 *Ethics*, 1097b2-1097b21.

6 *Ethics*, 1104a14-1104a17.

7 George Washington, *First Inaugural Address* (1789).

8 Vernon L. Provencal, "The Family in Aristotle," 6 *Animus* (Memorial University of Newfoundland)(http://www.swgc.mun.ca/animus/2001vol6/provencal6.htm)(2001)

9 Id.

10 John Witte, Jr., *From Sacrament to Contract: Marriage, Religion and Law in the Western Tradition*, 22-23 (1997).

11 Id. at 70-71.

12 Id. at 186-189. Witte points out that Locke's theological views of marriage were at odds with his political views, but as noted above Americans combined the civil role of the family with a Christian view of its content.

13 John Locke, *Second Treatise on Government*, Section 56, quoted in Thomas West, "Vindicating John Locke: How a Seventeenth-Century Liberal Was Really a Social Conservative," Family Research Council, June 19, 2001, http://www.frc.org/get.cfm?i=WT01F1.

14 John Locke, *First Treatise on Government*, Section 59, quoted in West, id.

15 Thomas G. West, *Vindicating the Founders: Race, Sex, Class and Justice in the Origins of America*, 103 (1997).

16 Practical reasonableness (*phronesis*) was a fundamental good to Aristotle, as was the classical virtue of prudence, later emphasized by Christian morality. But in both cases, these virtues were related to the exercise of other virtues and subject to standards of good. Hume attempts to divorce utility from those other values.

17 David Hume, *An Enquiry Concerning the Principles of Morals*, Section III: Of Justice, Part I (1839).

18 Adam Smith, *The Theory of Moral Sentiments:* Section I: On the Sense of Propriety, Chapter 1: Of Sympathy (1759).

19 Montesquieu, *The Spirit of the Laws* (1748), Translated by Thomas Nugent, 1750.

20 Montesquieu, *The Spirit of the Laws*, Book 4, Chapter 5.

21 Genesis 1:1-10.

22 *Declaration of Independence* (1776).

23 George Washington, *First Inaugural Address* (1789).

24 Jack N. Rackove, *James Madison, Writings*, 30 (1999).

25 *The Federalist*, No. 10.

26 William Galston, "Liberal Virtues and the Formation of Civic Character," in Mary Ann Glendon and David Blankenhorn, *Seedbeds of Virtue: Sources of Competence, Character and Citizenship in American Society*, 42-51 (1995).

27 *The Federalist*, No. 55.

28 George Washington, *Thanksgiving Day Proclamation* (1789).

29 Allan Carlson, "Toward a Theory of the Autonomous Family, The Second Natural Bond," http://www.profam.org/pub/fia/fia_1604.htm?search=family%20virtue.

6 *The Family and the Laws*

1 For an interesting commentary on Williams and his understanding of this problem of the church and the polity, see Mark DeWolfe Howe, *The Garden and the Wilderness*, especially ch. 1.

2 See Leon Kass, "Regarding Daughters and Sisters: The Rape of Dinah," *Commentary* (April 1992), pp. 29-38.

3 Allan Bloom, *Love and Friendship* (New York: Simon & Schuster, 1993), p. 243

4 See PETER MELZER v. BOARD OF EDUCATION OF THE CITY SCHOOL DISTRICT OF THE CITY OF NEW YORK, CAROL A. GRESSER, IRENE IMPELLIZZERI, VICTOR GOTBAUM, MICHAEL J. PETRIDES, LUIS O. REYES, NINFA SEGARRA, DENNIS M. WALCOTT, 196 F. Supp. 2d 229 (2002).

5 See my own testimony before the Subcommittee on the Constitution of the House Committee on the Judiciary (May 15, 1996).

6 "Declaration on the Admission of Women to the Ministerial Priesthood," *Sacred Congregation for the Doctrine of the Faith* (1976), Vatican II documents, pp. 331-45.

7 One can anticipate readily the objection that many people have remarried, found a more enduring second marriage, and retain a sense of loyalty or commitment to the children springing from both marriages. Our current experience casts up more examples of these cases, and more evidence of these claims, than anything supplied in my own childhood fifty years ago. And yet the strains are also manifest, and it is equally plain that these sense of deprivation, or that sense of something diminished, felt so palpably by the children, would be even deeper if a man sought to preserve both families at once under a condition of polygamy. The experience may merely tell us just why plural marriages, or serial marriages, can be felt and grasped at once as an impaired version of the very idea of marriage.

8 See *The Republic*, 592b.

7 *Marriage, Morality, and Rationality*

1 James Q. Wilson, *The Marriage Problem: How Culture Has Weakened Families* (New York: HarperCollins Publishers, 2002).

2 James Q. Wilson, "Marriage, Evolution, and the Enlightenment" (lecture, American Enterprise Institute, Washington, D.C., May 3, 1999), http://www.aei.org/news/newsID.10370/news_detail.asp (accessed August 11, 2004).

3 Wilson, *The Marriage Problem*, 19.

4   Wilson, "Marriage, Evolution, and the Enlightenment," para. 11. Wilson develops this idea in Chapter 2 of *The Marriage Problem*.

5   Ibid.

6   Ibid. Wilson expressed this idea in different language in *The Marriage Problem*, 29-30.

7   Wilson, *The Marriage Problem*, 69.

8   Ibid., 69-75.

9   Ibid., 69.

10   Ibid., 7.

11   Ibid., 41.

12   Ibid., 69.

13   Ibid., 83.

14   Ibid., 84-85.

15   Ibid., 86.

16   Ibid., 86-87.

17   Wilson, "Marriage, Evolution, and the Enlightenment," para. 35.

18   Ibid.

19   Ibid., para. 29.

20   Wilson, *The Marriage Problem*, 88.

21   A majority of the members of the United States Supreme Court appear to have adopted this view. See *Lawrence v. Texas*, 539 U.S. 558 (2003).

22   Wilson, "Marriage, Evolution, and the Enlightenment," para. 40.

23   Ibid., para. 42.

24   This point is carefully and insightfully explained by John Finnis in chapter one of his *Natural Law and Natural Rights* (Oxford: Clarendon Press, 1980).

25   H.L.A. Hart, *The Concept of Law* (Oxford: Clarendon Press, 1961), 78.

26   Finnis, *Natural Law*, ch. 1.

27   Alasdair MacIntyre, *Whose Justice? Which Rationality?* (Notre Dame, Ind.: University of Notre Dame Press, 1988), 367.

28   "If divorce becomes easier, a lot of prosperous men will leave their spouses and marry a trophy wife." Wilson, *The Marriage Problem*, 15. On the contributions of wives to the success of their husbands, see ibid., 18.

29   Ibid., 4.

30   On illegitimacy, see Robert D. Plotnick, "The Effect of Social Policies on Teenage Pregnancy and Childbearing," *Families in Society: The Journal of Contemporary Human Services* 74 (1993) 324-28. On cohabitation, see Wilson, *The Marriage Problem*, 100-01. On illegitimacy, see *The Marriage Problem*, 131-34.

31   The list of prominent politicians and other public figures who have been thus exposed over the past forty years is depressingly lengthy. I will assume that the reader neither needs nor desires to have the names on the list rehearsed here.

32 David Hume, *A Treatise on Human Nature* (1740), Book 2, pt. 3, iii.

33 See, e.g., Finnis, *Natural Law*, 95-97.

34 I will not repeat those arguments in any detail here. I have set them out at length against the best contemporary defense of the Humean view known to me—the case made by Australian philosopher Jeffrey Goldsworthy—in the first chapter of my book *In Defense of Natural Law* (Oxford University Press, 2000).

35 Richard Posner, *Sex and Reason* (Cambridge, Mass.: Harvard University Press, 1992).

36 See Germain Grisez, "The Christian Family as Fulfillment of Sacramental Marriage," *Studies in Christian Ethics* 9.1 (Spring 1996) 23-33.

37 Hadley Arkes, "Questions of Principle, Not Predictions," *Georgetown Law Journal* 84 (1995) 321-27.

38 Ibid.

39 Ibid.

40 John Finnis, "Law, Morality, and 'Sexual Orientation,'" *Notre Dame Law Review* 69 (1994) 1049, 1066.

41 See St. Augustine, *De bono conjugali* (9.9).

42 See Robert P. George and Gerald V. Bradley, "Marriage and the Liberal Imagination," Georgetown Law Journal 84 (1995) 301, 307-09.

43 Ibid.

44 See, e.g., Leon Kass, "Cloning and the Posthuman Future," chap. 5 in *Life, Liberty, and the Defense of Dignity* (San Francisco: Encounter Books, 2002).

45 George and Bradley, "Marriage," supra, note 42.

46 See, for example, Stephen Macedo, "Homosexuality and the Conservative Mind," *Georgetown Law Journal* 84 (1995) 26, 278.

47 Ibid.

48 Richard Posner, *The Problematics of Moral and Legal Theory* (Cambridge, Mass.: Harvard University Press, 1999) 77.

49 Ibid., n. 143.

50 Grisez, "The Christian Family," supra, note 36.

51 Grisez proposed this thought experiment in a conversation with the author.

52 Finnis, "Law, Morality, and 'Sexual Orientation,'" supra, note 40, 1066.

53 Robert P. George, "Can Sex Be Reasonable?" *Columbia Law Review* 93.1 (April 1993) 783-94.

54 Macedo, "Homosexuality," supra, note 46, 279.

55 Ibid., 278.

56 Ibid., 280.

57 John Finnis, "Law, Morality, and 'Sexual Orientation,'" in Jon Corvino (ed.), *Same Sex: Debating the Ethics, Science, and Culture of Homosexuality* (Totowa, New Jersey: Rowman and Littlefield, 1997), sec. 5.

58 Ibid.

59 Of course, a man and woman engaging in sexual intercourse can employ means of contraception to ensure that the conditions of reproduction do not obtain. Can contracepted

sex acts be reproductive in type? The question is difficult. People who share the general understanding of marriage and marital acts defended in this article are not of one mind as to the answer. An act of contraception, though performed to facilitate a desired act of sexual intercourse by reducing the odds that the act will result in conception where conception is not desired, is distinct from the act of sexual intercourse it facilitates. So some people believe that the question of the morality of contraception is independent of the question whether an act of sexual intercourse fulfills the behavioral conditions of reproduction. Those who believe that contraception can be morally justified for purposes of timing or spacing pregnancies generally also believe that spouses who employ means of contraception for these purposes do not vitiate the marital quality of their acts of sexual intercourse. I am inclined to the opposing view. Where one has deliberately frustrated the possibility of conception, it is not clear to me how one can say that an act of sexual intercourse is reproductive in type.

60 See, e.g., Macedo, "Homosexuality," supra, note 46, 278 and 280.

61 Andrew Koppelman, *The Gay Rights Question in Contemporary American Law*, 86-88 University of Chicago Press (July 1, 2002).

62 Ibid.

63 Ibid., 88.

64 See Peter Kurth's review of Michael Warner's book *The Trouble With Normal, Salon*, December 8, 1999, http://www.salon.com/books/feature/1999/12/08/warner/print.html (accessed August 11, 2004).

65 For example, Michelangelo Signorile proposes support for same-sex "marriage" as a "middle ground" on the way to abolishing the "moral codes" of what he condemns as an "archaic" institution. "A middle ground might be to fight for same-sex marriage and its benefits and then, once granted, redefine the institution of marriage completely, to demand the right to marry not as a way of adhering to society's moral codes, but rather to debunk a myth and radically alter an archaic institution." Michelangelo Signorile, "Bridal Wave," *OUT* magazine, December/January 1994, 161. Signorile makes his contempt for traditional moral codes clear. In discussing the "raunchy, impersonal atmosphere" of sex in public parks and bathrooms: "There's nothing morally wrong with this—and I say that as someone who has certainly had my share of hot public sex, beginning when I was a teenager and well into my adulthood." Signorile, "Nostalgia Trip," *The Gay and Lesbian Review* 5.2 (Spring 1998) 27.

  Another prominent campaigner for same-sex "marriage," Gabriel Rotello, similarly contemns the norm of sexual exclusivity: "Let me simply say that I have no moral objection to promiscuity, provided it doesn't lead to massive epidemics of fatal diseases. I enjoyed the 70's, I didn't think there was anything morally wrong with the lifestyle of the baths. I believe that for many people, promiscuity can be meaningful, liberating and fun." Rotello, "This is Sexual Ecology," *The Gay and Lesbian Review* 5.2 (Spring 1998) 24.

66 These are honest and clear-eyed defenders of the same-sex "marriage" who are candid

enough to admit that its adoption means the abandonment of any rational basis for a commitment to monogamy. For example, Princeton University historian Hendrik Hartog, a supporter of same-sex "marriage," recently observed that "there is a conservative question that lots of people ask: If you allow gay marriage, don't you have to allow polygamy as well? and I think the answer is yes. If you say people have a right to happiness and they have a right to form unions that will make them happy, then you may have to allow more than two people to form unions, as long as you are vigilant to prevent coercion and to insist on the competence of those who would make such decisions." "A Moment With Hendrik Hartog," *Princeton Alumni Weekly*, May 12, 2004, http://www.princeton.edu/~paw/archive_new/PAW03-04/14-0512/moment.html. Hartog's point obviously applies not only to polygamy, but also to polyamory and, indeed, any form of consensual adult sexual union.

67 Frederick Elliston, "In Defense of Promiscuity," in Robert M. Stewart (ed.), *Philosophical Perspectives on Sex and Love* (New York: Oxford University Press 1995), 146-58, at 152-53.

68 Andrew Sullivan, letter to the editor, *Salon*, December 15, 1999, http://www.salon.com/letters/1999/12/15/sullivan (accessed August 23, 2004). In his letter, Sullivan responded to Peter Kurth's criticisms in Kurth's review of Michael Warner's book *The Trouble with Normal*. Sullivan said: "In my most recent book, *Love Undetectable*, I defended the beauty and mystery and spirituality of sex, including anonymous sex."

69 Stephen Macedo, "Reply to Critics," *Georgetown Law Journal* 84 (1995) 329, 335.

70 Joseph Raz, *The Morality of Freedom* (Oxford: Clarendon Press, 1986) 162.

8 *Soft Despotism and Same-Sex Marriage*

1 For a thorough discussion of competing conceptions of marriage and their development from the 12th Century to the present day, see John Witte, Fr., *From Sacrament to Contract: Marriage, Religion, and Law in the Western Tradition* (Westminister John Knox Press, 1997).

2 For arguments of this nature in favor of same-sex marriage, see Evan Wolfson, *Why Marriage Matters: America, Equality, and Gay People's Right to Marry* (Simon & Schuster, 2004). See also the contributions of those in favor of same-sex marriage in Lyn D. Wardle et al., eds., *Marriage and Same-Sex Unions: A Debate* (Praeger, 2003) and Andrew Sullivan, ed., *Same-Sex Marriage: Pro and Con: A Reader* (Vintage Books, 1997).

3 See generally *Griswold v. Connecticut*, 381 U.S. 479 (1965) (right of married people to use contraception; extended to unmarried couples on equal protection grounds in *Eisenstadt v. Baird*, 405 U.S. 438 (1972)); *Roe v. Wade*, 410 U.S. 113 (1973) (right to abortion; upheld although reshaped in *Planned Parenthood of Southeastern Pa. v. Casey*, 505 U.S. 833 (1992)); and *Lawrence v. Texas*, 123 S. Ct. 2472 (2003) (right to engage in sexual relations with consenting adults, including homosexual conduct).

4   To date, one state has imposed same-sex marriage by judicial decree in the United States. That state is Massachusetts. See *Goodridge v. Massachusetts Dept. of Health*, 440 Mass. (2003). This case was decided just five months after the Supreme Court found that the constitution protects the right of consenting adults to engage in sodomy. See *Lawrence*, supra. In 1999, Vermont's Supreme Court stipulated that Vermont must extend to same-sex couples seeking marriage the same benefits made available to married couples. *Baker v. Vermont*, 1999 Vt. Lexis 406 (1999). Vermont's legislature responded in 2000 by creating civil unions for same-sex couples.

5   Hegel is among the first philosophers to develop the notion of "civil society." For Hegel, civil society was social order that includes what would otherwise be described as market relations, but which excludes the family and the state. See generally, G.W.F. Hegel, *The Philosophy of Right*, trans. S.W. Dyde (Prometheus, 1996) s. 161-260, p. 164-249. More recently, sociologists employing the concept of civil society have focused less on market relations, and more on other voluntary associations, especially religious organizations. See for eg. Robert Wuthnow, *Christianity and Civil Society: The Contemporary Debate* (Trinity Press, 1996). Civil society has been regarded from such a broad array of perspectives in recent scholarly works that its meaning has morphed considerably from Hegel's usage, and at times is in need of firmer definition. See generally, Michael Walzer, ed., *Toward a Global Civil Society* (Berghahn Books, 1997) and Simone Chambers & Will Kymlicka, eds., *Alternative Conceptions of Civil Society* (Princeton University Press, 2001). Here, the term "civil society" is self consciously used broadly: civil society is understood as *any* form of social order that can exist independently of the state. This conception has the merit of being both clear and comprehensive.

6   Such a criticism has been raised, for example, by legal pluralists. The anthropological concept of a "semi autonomous social field," introduced by Sally Falk Moore, is an attempt to speak of social order that is largely independent of the state. Sally Falk Moore, "Law and Social Change: The Semi-Autonomous Social Field as an Appropriate Subject of Study," *Law & Society Review* (Summer 1973) 719-746. See also John Griffiths, "What is Legal Pluralism?" (1986) nr. 24 *Journal of Legal Pluralism* 1-55.

7   Mary Douglas, *How Institutions Think* (Syracuse University Press, 1986) at 46.

8   For a trenchant criticism of the inadequacy of economics and politics in dealing with many social problems, including those affecting family life, see Alan Wolfe, *Whose Keeper? Social Science and Moral Obligation* (University of California Press, 1989).

9   The due process clause of the 14th Amendment supports this interpretation, and it is on liberty grounds that the court in *Lawrence*, supra, found a Texas law banning sodomy to be unconstitutional. This line of reasoning parallels the Court's substantive due process approach to property rights in the early 20th Century. See e.g. *Lochner v. New York*, 198 U.S. 45 (1905). A laissez-faire philosophy, which trusts in the goodness of individual choices and/or which equates goodness with choice, is common to these strains of jurisprudence.

10 In this respect, Susan Moller Okin was on the mark in her criticism of Nozick's *Anarchy, State and Utopia*. See Susan Moller Okin, *Justice, Gender and the Family* (Basic Books, 1991).

11 The most respectable defense of libertarianism in recent times is Robert Nozick's *Anarchy, State and Utopia* (Basic Books, 1977). He explicitly adopts a Lockean framework in his account of property rights, and hence market relations.

12 Alan Brinkley, *American History: A Survey* (McGraw-Hill, 2003) at 127 and 140.

13 For example, the inconsistencies between the *Fundamental Constitutions of Carolina of 1669*, which Locke is reputed to have written, and his *Second Treatise of Government*, are numerous and glaring. Most troubling among these inconsistencies is that the former legalizes slavery, while the latter repudiates the legitimacy of slavery, regarding it as a state of war between the slave and the slaveholder.

14 John Locke, *Second Treatise of Government* (Hackett Publishing Co., 1980) c. VII, s. 78, p. 43.

15 Locke, supra, c. VII, s. 82, p. 44.

16 Locke, supra, c. VI, s. 52, p. 30.

17 Locke, supra, c. VI, s. 67, p. 37.

18 Locke, supra, c. VI, s. 67, p. 37

19 Locke, supra, c. VI, s. 65, p. 35-36.

20 Locke, supra, c. IX, s. 123, p. 65-66.

21 Locke, supra, c. V, s. 27, p. 19.

22 Locke, supra, c. II, s. 6, p. 9.

23 Locke, supra, c. V, s. 40-42, p. 25-26.

24 Locke, supra, c. II, s. 4-6, p. 8-9.

25 Locke, supra, c. VI, s. 55, p. 31.

26 Locke, supra, c. VI, s. 63, p. 35.

27 Locke, supra, c. VI, s. 60, p. 33-34.

28 Locke, supra, c. IX, s. 123, p. 65-66.

29 Locke, supra, c. IX, s. 124-127, p. 66-67.

30 Locke, supra, c. XIX, s. 199, p. 101.

31 Locke, supra, c. XV, s. 170-171, p. 88-89.

32 Locke, supra, c. VIII, s. 118, p. 63.

33 A pre-political institution is *not* simply a natural form of social order; it is more fundamentally a *normative* order. State regulation of pre-political institutions is frequently permissible and/or desirable. However, state interventions that undermine or erode the constitutive norms of a pre-political institution are necessarily destructive to that institution, given that the institution is first and foremost normative.

34 The denial that the potential for procreation justifies marriage was central to the Court's reasoning in *Goodridge v. Massachusetts Department of Health*, supra, creating a right for same-sex couples to marry.

35 On the centrality of sex to marriage, see Robert P. George, *The Clash of Orthodoxies: Laws,*

Religion and Morality in Crisis (ISI Books, 2001) at 75-89. See also Gerard Bradley and Robert P. George, "Marriage and the Liberal Imagination," (1995) 84 *Georgetown Law Journal* 301.

36 The role of same-sex marriage in protecting children was also relied upon in *Goodridge*, supra.

37 The fact that social tragedy arises from the demise of marriage has been amply documented. See generally Sara McLanahan and Gary Sandefur, *Growing Up with a Single Parent: What Hurts, What Helps* (Harvard University Press, 1994); Barbara Dafoe Whitehead, *The Divorce Culture* (Alfred A. Knopf, 1997); Judith S. Wallerstein et. al., *Unexpected Legacy of Divorce* (Hyperion, 2000); James Q. Wilson, *The Marriage Problem: How Our Culture Has Weakened Families* (Harper Collins, 2002);.

38 Studies of single parents rearing children disproportionately include mature African American women, perhaps grandmothers, raising one daughter, often with special needs, within an extended network of support. See Joan F. Shireman and P.R. Johnson, "Single Parent Adoptions: A Longitudinal Study" (1985) 7:4 Children and Youth Services Review 321-334; Victor Groze and James A. Rosenthal, "Single Parents and their Adopted Children: A Psychosocial Analysis," (1991) 72:2 Families in Society 67-77.

39 The cautious approach of the 11th Circuit Court of Appeals in upholding a prohibition against adoption by homosexuals is reasonable, so long as such children can be placed with other loving families. See *Lofton v. Department of Children and Family* 358 F.3d 804 (11th Circuit, 2004).

40 See generally Leon Kass, "The Wisdom of Repugnance" in Leon Kass and James Q. Wilson, *Ethics of Human Cloning* (Aei Pr, 1998).

41 Studies on the effects of same-sex marriage suffer from a number of flaws, including a lack of longitudinal studies, a lack of representative sampling and control groups, and prejudgment on the merits. See, eg. Judith Stacy and Timothy J. Biblarz, "Does the Sexual Orientation of Parents Matter?" (April, 2001) 66 *American Sociological Review* 159-183.

42 Alexis de Tocqueville, *Democracy in America*, trans. George Lawrence (Harper, 1988) at 692.

43 Tocqueville, supra, at 667-668.

44 Tocqueville, supra, at 509-517.

45 Tocqueville, supra, at 241-245.

46 See supra, note 3.

47 As expressed by the Supreme Court, "At the heart of liberty is the right to define one's own concept of existence, of meaning, of the universe, and of the mystery of human life." *Planned Parenthood of Southeastern Pa. v. Casey*, 505 U.S. 833 at 851 (1992).

48 Tocqueville, supra, writes, "I think that extreme centralization of political power ultimately enervates society and thus, in the end, weakens the government too. But I do not deny that with the power of society thus centralized, great undertakings can be carried through at a given time and for a specific purpose [ie. war]." (p. 677). See also p. 701: "It would

seem that sovereigns now only seek to do great things with men. I wish that they would try a little more to make men great, that they should attach less importance to the work and more to the workman, that they should constantly remember that a nation cannot long remain great if each man is individually weak, and that no one has yet devised a form of society or a political combination which can make a people energetic when it is composed of citizens who are flabby and feeble."

49 See, for example, William Eskeridge, Jr., *The Case for Same-Sex Marriage: From Sexual Liberty to Civilized Commitment* (Free Press, 1996). See also Andrew Sullivan, "Here Comes the Groom: A Conservative Case for Gay Marriage," *New Republic* (Aug. 28, 1989).

50 Recent developments in Canada substantiate this observation. In Canada, where 6 provinces and 1 territory have embraced same-sex marriage through judicial fiat over the past three years, Parliament has also very recently revised the Criminal Code to protect gays and lesbians from hate speech. See Criminal Code R.S. 1985, c. C-46 s.318(4) and s. 319; 2004, c. 14, s.1-2. Canada's Parliament, with the approval of the Canadian Supreme Court in *Reference Re Same-Sex Marriage* (2004) SCC 79, is preparing to redefine marriage so as to permit same-sex unions across the nation.

51 Again, the Canadian experience is telling. In the case of *Trinity Western University v. British Columbia College of Teachers* [2001] 1 SCR 772, BCCT refused to grant full accreditation for a teaching program to a Christian University because the University upheld the tenet of its religious faith that homosexuality is immoral. While adjudging that the BCCT had arrived at the wrong result in this case, the Canadian Supreme Court noted that it would be impermissible for a teacher to discriminate against students because of sexual orientation. Accordingly, a teacher who expresses disapproval of homosexuality in the classroom would risk losing her job as well as being prosecuted under a provincial Human Rights Act and/or under federal criminal law for engaging in hate speech.

   Also troubling is the case of *Chamberlain v. Surrey School District* (2002) SCC 86, wherein the Canadian Supreme Court adjudged the decision of a School Board that refused to allow books depicting same-sex couples to be used in kindergarten and grade 1 classrooms to be unreasonable. See also Daniel Cere, "Supreme Court Supplants Parents" *Montreal Gazette* (December 30, 2002).

52 Gunilla Ringback Weitoft et al., "Mortality, Severe Morbidity, and Injury in Children Living with Single Parents in Sweden: A Population-Based Study" Vol. 361 *Lancet* 289; Stanley Kurtz, "The End of Marriage in Scandinavia" *Weekly Standard*, Volume 9, Issue 20 (02/02/2004).

53 See generally, Philip Reynolds, *Marriage in the Western Church: The Christianization of Marriage during the Patristic and Early Medieval Periods* (Brill Academic Pub., 2001).

54 Tocqueville, supra, at 287-294.

55 See, for example, Mark S. Prancer and Michael W. Pratt, "Social and Family Determinants of Community Service Involvement in Canadian Youth," in Miranda Yates et

al., *Roots of Civic Identity: International Perspectives of Community Service and Activism in Youth* (Cambridge, 1999); James Youniss et al., "Religion, Community Service, and Identity in American Youth" 22 *Journal of Adolescence* (1999) 243-253.

56 See, for example, David B. Larson, Byron R. Johnson, and John J. DiIulio, "Religion: The Forgotten Factor in Cutting Youth Crime and Saving At-Risk Urban Youth" found at www.manhattan-institute.org/html/jpr-98-2.htm.

57 *Engel v. Vitale*, 370 U.S. 421 421 (1962); *Wallace v. Jaffree*, 472 U.S. 38 (1985); *Lee v. Weisman*, 505 U.S. 577 (1992); *Santa Fe Independent School District v. Doe*, 530 U.S. 290 (2000).

58 As Justice Scalia pronounced in *Oregon v. Smith*, 494 U.S. 872 (1990): "The free exercise of religion means, first and foremost, the right to believe and profess whatever religious doctrine one desires."

59 As Tocqueville, supra, writes: "Despotism, by its very nature suspicious, sees the isolation of men as the best guarantee of its own permanence. So it usually does all it can to isolate them." (p.509) "I maintain that there is only one effective remedy against the evils which equality may cause, and that is political liberty." (p. 513) "But among democratic peoples all the citizens are independent and weak. They can do hardly anything for themselves, and none of them is in a position to force his fellows to help him. They would all therefore find themselves helpless if they did not learn to help each other voluntarily." (p. 514).

60 In extolling the importance of religion in democratic regimes, Tocqueville, supra, observes, "Every religion places the object of man's desires outside and beyond worldly goods and naturally lifts the soul to regions far above the realm of the senses. Every religion also imposes on each man some obligations toward mankind, to be performed in common with the rest of mankind, and so draws him away, from time to time, from thinking about himself" (p. 444-445).

61 Subsidiarity is thus antithetical to communism, which when applied to the realm of the family, results in the abolition of marriage. John Finnis, *Natural Law and Natural Rights* (Oxford University Press, 198) at 144-147.

8 *(How) Does Marriage Protect Child Well-Being*

1 William J. Doherty, et al., 2002. *Why Marriage Matters: Twenty-One Conclusions from the Social Sciences* (New York: Institute for American Values): 8-9 (co-authors include William J. Doherty, William A. Galston, Norval D. Glenn, John Gottman, Barbara Markey, Howard J. Markman, Steven Nock, David Popenoe, Gloria G. Rodriguez, Isabel V. Sawhill, Scott M. Stanley, Linda J. Waite, and Judith Wallerstein) ("Marriage exists in virtually every known human society. . . . At least since the beginning of recorded history, in all the flourishing varieties of human cultures documented by anthropologists, marriage has been a universal human institution. As a virtually universal human idea, marriage is about the reproduction of children, families, and society. . . . marriage across societies is a publicly acknowledged and supported sexual union which creates kinship

obligations and sharing or resources between men, women, and the children that their sexual union may produce."); see also Peter Lubin & Dwight Duncan, *Follow the Footnote or The Advocate as Historian of Same-sex Marriage*, 47 *Cath. U. L. Rev.* 1271 (1998).

2   Margo Wilson and Martin Daly, 2004. "Marital Cooperation and Conflict" in Charles Crawford and Catherine Salmon (eds.), *Evolutionary Psychology, Public Policy and Personal Decision*, (Mahwah, NJ: Lawrence Erlbaum Associates): 203 (emphases added). (cited in Daniel Cere and Douglas Farrow (eds.), 2004. *Divorcing Marriage: Unveiling the Dangers in Canada's New Social Experiment* (Montreal: McGill-Queen's University Press): 24). See also Katherine K. Young and Paul Nathanson, 2004. "The Future of an Experiment," in Daniel Cere and Douglas Farrow (eds.), *Divorcing Marriage: Unveiling the Dangers in Canada's New Social Experiment* (Montreal: McGill-Queen's University Press): 45 ("Comparative research on the worldviews of both small-scale societies and those of world religions, both Western and Eastern, reveal a pattern: Marriage has universal, nearly universal, and variable features. Its *universal* features include the fact that marriage is a) supported by authority and incentives; b) recognizes the interdependence of men and women; c) has a public, or communal, dimension; d) defines eligible partners; e) encourages procreation under specific conditions; and f) provides mutual support not only between men and women but also between them and children.").

3   For the latter argument see Maggie Gallagher, 2005. "(How) Will Gay Marriage Weaken Marriage as a Social Institution?: A Reply to Andrew Koppelman," *U. St. Thomas L. Rev.* (forthcoming).

4   See, e.g., Paul Amato and Alan Booth, 1997. *A Generation At Risk: Growing Up in an Era of Family Upheaval* (Cambridge, MA: Harvard University Press); Linda J. Waite and Maggie Gallagher, 2000. *The Case for Marriage: Why Married People are Happier, Healthier and Better-Off Financially* (New York: Doubleday); Sara McLanahan and Gary Sandefur, 1994. *Growing Up With a Single Parent: What Hurts, What Helps* (Cambridge, MA: Harvard University Press).

5   William J. Doherty, et al., 2002. *Why Marriage Matters: Twenty-One Conclusions from the Social Sciences* (New York: Institute for American Values): 6.

6   Id. at 18.

7   Kristin Anderson Moore, et al., 2002. "Marriage from a Child's Perspective: How Does Family Structure Affect Children and What Can We Do About It?", *Child Trends Research Brief* (Washington, D.C.: Child Trends) (June): 1 (available at http://www.childtrends.org/PDF/MarriageRB602.pdf). This research brief on family structure does not compare outcomes for children in same-sex couple households to children in other types of families.

8   Mary Parke, 2003. "Are Married Parents Really Better for Children? What Research Says About the Effects of Family Structure on Child Well-Being," *CLASP Policy Brief* no. 3 (Washington, D.C.: Center for Law and Social Policy) (May): 6. These are findings about the family structure debate in general. On the question of sexual orientation and parenting, the brief summarizes the social science this way: "Although the research on

these families has limitations, the findings are consistent: children raised by same-sex parents are no more likely to exhibit poor outcomes than children raised by divorced heterosexual parents. Since many children raised by gay or lesbian parents have undergone the divorce of their parents, researchers have considered the most appropriate comparison group to be children of heterosexual divorced parents. Children of gay or lesbian parents do not look different from their counterparts raised in heterosexual divorced families regarding school performance, behavior problems, emotional problems, early pregnancy, or difficulties finding employment. However, as previously indicated, children of divorce are at higher risk for many of these problems than children of married parents." Id. at 5.

9   See, e.g., E. Mavis Heatherington & John Kelly, 2002. *For Better or For Worse–Divorce Reconsidered* (New York: W. W. Norton & Co.).

10   "What is Needed to Defend the Bipartisan Defense of Marriage Act of 1996?": Hearing Before the Subcommittee on the Constitution, Civil Rights and Property Rights of the Senate Comm. on the Judiciary, 108th Cong., Sept. 4, 2003 (written statement of Prof. Judith Stacey, Ph.D., Department of Sociology, New York University).

11   In 1995, the American Psychological Association (APA) issued a statement indicating that, based upon the available scientific data, children raised by lesbian and gay parents are not "disadvantaged in any significant respect relative to the children of heterosexual parents." American Psychological Association, *Lesbian and Gay Parenting: A Resource for Psychologists* (1995) (available at www.apa.org/pi/parent.html). The American Academy of Pediatrics (AAP) issued a similar policy statement, concluding "that the weight of evidence gathered during several decades using diverse samples and methodologies is persuasive in demonstrating that there is no systematic difference between gay and nongay parents in emotional health, parenting skills, and attitudes towards parenting." American Academy of Pediatrics, 2002. "Coparent or Second-Parent Adoption by Same-Sex Parents," *Pediatrics* 109(2): 339-340 (February) (available at http://aappolicy. aappublications.org/cgi/content/full/pediatrics;109/2/339. Stanford University Law Professor Michael Wald made this assertion in his analysis of Proposition 22, a proposed initiative statute which would define marriage as the union of one man and one woman under California law. Assessing the claim that "it is better for children to be raised by two opposite-sex married parents," the author points to social science research and concludes baldly, "[T]he evidence does not support these claims." Michael S. Wald, 1999. "Same-Sex Couples: Marriage, Families, and Children: An Analysis of Proposition 22, The Knight Initiative" (Stanford, The Stanford Institute for Research on Women and Gender & The Stanford Center on Adolescence): 11. Wald also summarized, "Some opponents of same-sex couple marriage contend that it is harmful for children to be raised by gay or lesbian parents. Again, there is a large body of research available to assess this claim." Id. at vi (citing a statement from the American Psychological Association).

12   Mary L. Bonauto, 2003. "Civil Marriage as a Locus of Civil Rights Struggles," *Human Rights* (Summer): 3, 7.

13   Evan Wolfson, 2003. "Enough Marriage to Share: A Response to Maggie Gallagher,"

in Lynn Wardle, et al. (eds.), *Marriage and Same-Sex Unions: A Debate* (Westport, CT: Praeger): 25, 26-27.

14 For these reasons, see www.marriagedebate.com, or Maggie Gallagher, 2005. "(How) Will Gay Marriage Weaken Marriage as a Social Institution?: A Reply to Andrew Koppelman," *U. St. Thomas L. Rev.* (forthcoming) (available from the author at maggie@imapp.org).

15 American Academy of Pediatrics, 2002. "Coparent or Second-Parent Adoption by Same-Sex Parents," *Pediatrics* 109(2) (February): 339-340 (available at http://aappolicy.aappublications.org/cgi/content/full/pediatrics;109/2/339); Judith Stacey and Timothy Biblarz, 2001. "(How) Does The Sexual Orientation of Parents Matter?," *American Sociological Review* 66: 159-183; C. Patterson, 2000. "Family Relationships of Lesbians and Gay Men," *Journal of Marriage and Family* 62: 1052-1069; M. Kirkpatrick, 1997. "Clinical Implications of Lesbian Mother Studies," *Journal of Homosexuality* 14 (1/2): 201-211; American Psychological Association, 1995. *Lesbian and Gay Parenting: A Resource for Psychologists* (available at www.apa.org/pi/parent.html); C. Patterson, 1995. "Lesbian Mothers, Gay Fathers and Their Children," in A. R. D'Augelli & C. Patterson, *Lesbian, Gay and Bisexual Identities Across the Lifespan: Psychological Perspectives*: 262-290; C. Patterson, 1992. "Children of Lesbian and Gay Parents," *Child Development* 63: 1025-1042; G.D. Green & F.W. Bozett, 1991. "Lesbian Mothers and Gay Fathers," in J.C. Gonsiorek & J. D. Weinrich eds., *Homosexuality: Research Implications for Public Policy*; J.J. Bigner & F.W. Bozett, 1990. "Parenting by Gay Fathers," *Marriage and Family Review* 14 (3/4): 155-175; J.S. Gottman, "Children of Gay and Lesbian Parents," *Marriage and Family Review* 14 (3/4): 177-196; F.W. Bozett, 1989. "Gay Fathers: A Review of Literature," *Journal of Homosexuality* 18 (1/2): 137-162; D. Cramer, 1986. "Gay Parents and Their Children: A Review of Research and Practical Implications," *Journal of Counseling and Development* 64: 504-507.

16 Diana Baumrind, 1995. "Commentary on Sexual Orientation: Research and Social Policy Implications," *Developmental Psychology* 31 (No. 1): 130; Affidavit of Stephen Lowell Nock, *Halpern v. Attorney General of Canada*, No. 684/00 (Ont. Sup. Ct. of Justice); Robert Lerner & Althea K. Nagai, 2001. *No Basis: What the Studies Don't Tell Us About Same-Sex Parenting* (Washington, D.C.: Marriage Law Project). In addition, Judith Stacey and Timothy Biblarz, while generally supportive of same-sex parenting, acknowledge important methodological limitations in existing research. Judith Stacey and Timothy Biblarz, 2001. "(How) Does The Sexual Orientation of Parents Matter?," *American Sociological Review* 66: 159-183. For example the authors acknowledge that "there are no studies of child development based on random, representative samples of [same-sex couple headed] families." *Id.* at 166.

17 Nock Aff. ¶ 3, *Halpern v. Attorney General of Canada*, No. 684/00 (Ont. Sup. Ct. of Justice) (copies available from the Institute for Marriage and Public Policy; info@imapp.org). In 1995, prominent Berkeley sociologist Diana Baumrind reviewed various parenting

studies, including the work of Charlotte Patterson and David Flaks. Diana Baumrind, 1995. "Commentary on Sexual Orientation: Research and Social Policy Implications," *Developmental Psychology* 31(1): 130. In her review, Professor Baumrind evaluated, among other things, the claim that children of homosexual parents suffered no adverse outcomes, and were no more likely to develop a homosexual sexual orientation than were children not raised in such homes. Problems Baumrind found in the research she reviewed included the use of small, self-selected convenience samples, reliance on self-report instruments, and biased study populations consisting of disproportionately privileged, educated, and well-off parents. Due to these flaws, Baumrind questioned the conclusions on both "theoretical and empirical grounds." Id. at 133-134. Another review, prepared by Robert Lerner and Althea Nagai in 2001, looked at 49 separate parenting studies before concluding that "the methods used in these studies are so flawed that the studies prove nothing." Robert Lerner & Althea K. Nagai, 2001. *No Basis: What the Studies Don't Tell Us About Same-Sex Parenting* (Washington, D.C.: Marriage Law Project): 6.

18 Judith Stacey and Timothy Biblarz, 2001. "(How) Does The Sexual Orientation of Parents Matter?", *American Sociological Review* 66:159, 166. A recent widely publicized study by Jennifer Wainright, Stephen Russell and Charlotte Patterson provides perhaps the one apparent exception. The study analyzes data from the Add-Health survey, a nationally representative sample of 12,000 teens. The authors identify 44 teens who are living with a mother and a same-sex partner, and conclude that there are no statistically significant differences between these teens and a matched comparison sample of teens living with a mother who lives with opposite-sex partner. The study does not however, identify teens raised from birth by two same-sex partners and compare them to intact married (or cohabiting) families. The authors do not report what proportion of teens living with a mother who has a male partner in the home are in intact marriages versus remarriages or living with cohabiting mothers (both of which are risk factors for child well-being). And because the number of teens living with a same-sex partnered mother is so small, differences between the two groups would have to be unusually large in order to become statistically significant. For example, despite well-established differences in adolescent male and female rates of depression, this study found no significant difference in depression rates by gender either, probably as a result of the small sample size (The study identified a non-significant trend towards higher levels of anxiety and depression in adolescents raised by moms who have same-sex partners.) Wainright, Russell & Patterson, 2004. "Psychosocial Adjustment, School Outcomes, and Romantic Relationships of Adolescents with Same-Sex Parents," *Child Development* 75(6) (December): 1886-1898, 1892.

19 Charlotte J. Patterson et al., 2000. "Children of Lesbian and Gay Parents: Research, Law and Policy," in Bette L. Bottoms et al., eds., *Children and the Law: Social Science and Policy* 10-11 (available from lead author at cjp@virginia.edu); see also Charlotte J. Patterson, 2000. "Family Relationships of Lesbians and Gay Men," *Journal of Marriage and Family* 62: 1052-1069.

20 Golombok, S., Tasker, F., & Murray, C., 1997. "Children Raised in Fatherless Families from Infancy: Family Relationships and the Socioemotional Development of Children of Lesbian and Single Heterosexual Mothers," *Journal of Child Psychology and Psychiatry* 38: 783-791, 788. In 1981, Kirkpatrick, Smith and Roy examined 20 children (ages 5-12) of divorced lesbians moms and 20 children of heterosexual single moms. While they did not find an effect by orientation, they did find one by "early father loss." "In general, we found that the children who gave a response suggestive of gender problems were more likely to have in common a history of some physical difficulty early in life than to have in common mothers with a particular sexual orientation. Also these children were more likely to have been separated from their fathers early in their lives (*i.e.*, at three years of age or earlier). However, those parents who had separated early in the child's life had more often been engaged in a chaotic relationship than those who stayed together longer. While those children with any sign suggestive of gender difficulty were more likely to have early father loss, there were as many children in both groups with early father loss who had no indication of gender difficulty. Most children in both groups clearly mourned the loss of their fathers. The younger groups especially sought out interactions with father figures." Kirkpatrick, M., Smith, C. & Roy, R., 1981. "Lesbian mothers and their children," *American Journal of Orthopsychiatry* 51: 545-551, 549.

21 Golombok, S., Tasker, F., & Murray, C., 1997. "Children raised in fatherless families from infancy: Family relationships and the socioemotional development of children of lesbian and single heterosexual mothers," *Journal of Child Psychology and Psychiatry* 38: 783-791, 788.

22 See, e.g., Liz Seaton, "The Debate over the Denial of Marriage Rights and Benefits to Same-Sex Couples and Their Children," 4 *MARGINS L.J.* 127 (2004).

23 Mary L. Bonauto, "Denying Marriage Rights is Unconstitutional," 19 *Maine Bar Journal* 78, 84 (2004) (quoting *Goodridge v. Dept. of Publ. Health*, 798 N.E.2d 941, 964 (Mass. 2003)).

24 *Goodridge v. Dept. of Publ. Health*, 798 N.E.2d 941, 954 (Mass. 2003) ("Simply put, the government creates civil marriage.").

25 Richard Lacayo, "For Better or For Worse?" *Time Magazine*, March 8, 2004, at 26 ("[President George Bush and Senator John Kerry] both oppose gay marriage and would oppose extending the 1,138 federal rights and privileges to gay couples, but support the right of states to grant civil unions."); see also, Dennis M. Mahoney, "Ex-Local Minister Calls Gay Marriages Just," *Columbus Dispatch*, April 2, 2004, at 04E ("'There are over 1,000 benefits that come with civil marriage that are recognized by state and federal government that we don't have access to,' [Rev. Kay Greenleaf] said."); Chuanpis Santilukka, "Same-Sex Benefits Key to Marriage Debate," *St. Cloud Times*, March 24, 2004, at 1A; Evelyn Nieves & Jim VandeHei, "Kerry Backs Benefits for Legally United Gays," *Washington Post*, March 4, 2004, at A6; Dean E. Murphy, "For a Day, Same-Sex Pairs Get a Warm Reception," *The New York Times*, Feb. 23, 2004, at A14 (quoting a woman who with her

lesbian partner, had recently obtained a marriage license in San Francisco); Marriage Equality USA, 1,049 *Federal Rights*, available at http://www.marriageequality.org/facts. php?page=1049_federal.

26 For a more direct critique of the idea that most couples get legal benefits from marriage, *see* Joshua K. Baker, 2004. "1000 Federal Benefits of Marriage? An Analysis of the 1997 GAO Report," *iMAPP Policy Brief* (Washington, D.C.: Institute for Marriage and Public Policy) (May 26) (available at www.imapp.org); Maggie Gallagher, 2005. "(How) Will Gay Marriage Weaken Marriage as a Social Institution?: A Reply to Andrew Koppelman," *U. St. Thomas L. Rev.* (forthcoming).

27 Kristin Anderson Moore, et al., 2002. "Marriage from a Child's Perspective: How Does Family Structure Affect Children and What Can We Do About It?", *Child Trends Research Brief* (Washington, D.C.: Child Trends) (June): 1 (available at http://www. childtrends.org/PDF/MarriageRB602.pdf). This research brief on family structure does not compare outcomes for children in same-sex couple households to children in other types of families ("Children in single-parent families, children born to unmarried mothers, and children in stepfamilies or cohabiting relationships face higher risks of poor outcomes.... There is thus value for children in promoting strong, stable marriages between biological parents.").

28 See, e.g., *Levy v. Louisiana*, 391 U.S. 68 (1968) (ruling that state may not exclude illegitimate children from standing to sue for wrongful death of a parent); *Weber v. Aetna Casualty & Surety Co.*, 406 U.S. 164 (1972) (ruling that illegitimate children may not be excluded from recovery of workers' compensation benefits upon the death of a parent); *Gomez v. Perez*, 409 U.S. 535 (1973) (ruling that a state may not deny illegitimate children the right to parental support); *Trimble v. Gordon*, 430 U.S. 762 (1977) (right of an illegitimate child to inherit from unwed father); *Mills v. Habluetzel*, 456 U.S. 91 (1982) (requiring that illegitimate children be given a bona fide opportunity to prove paternity in seeking parental support).

29 See Joshua K. Baker, 2004. "1000 Federal Benefits of Marriage? An Analysis of the 1997 GAO Report," *iMAPP Policy Brief* (Washington, D.C.: Institute for Marriage and Public Policy) (May 26) (available at www.imapp.org); C. Eugene Steuerle & Adam Carasso, forthcoming 2005. "The Hefty Tax on Marriage Vows Facing Most Households with Children," *Focus on Children*.

30 Sixty percent of babies born out of wedlock are born to solo moms; about 4 in 10 are born to cohabiting parents. Bumpass and Lu, 2000. "Trends in Cohabitation and Implications for Children's Family Contexts in the United States," *Population Studies* 54: 19-41.

31 Studies show that 2 out of 3 children born out of wedlock have nonresident fathers at birth. This percentage climbs as children grow older (though some couples eventually marry). See, e.g., McLanahan, et al., 1998. "Unwed Fathers and Fragile Families," *Center for Research on Child Wellbeing, Working Paper* #98-12 (March): 7. An Urban Institute policy brief explains the impact: "Parents who do not live with their children are unlikely

to be highly involved in their children's lives." Elaine Sorensen & Chava Zibman, 2000. *To What Extent Do Children Benefit from Child Support?* The Urban Institute (January): 8. According to the National Survey of America's Families, one in three (34%) children with a nonresident parent saw that parent on a weekly basis in 1997. Another 38 percent saw their nonresident parent at least once during the year, though not on a weekly basis. Fully 28 percent of children with a nonresident parent had *no* contact with that parent during the course of the year. *Id.* Another review of several national surveys found that, by their mothers' estimates, roughly 40% of children with nonresident fathers saw their father once a month, while nearly the same number did not see their father at all in a given year. Wendy D. Manning & Pamela J. Smock, 1999. "New Families and Non-Resident Father-Child Visitation," *Social Forces* (September) 78(1): 87-116, at 89. See also Valerie King, 1994. "Variations in the Consequences of Nonresident Father Involvement for Children's Well-Being," *Journal of Marriage and Family* 56: 963 (finding half of children with nonresident fathers see their fathers only once a year, if at all, while just 21 percent see their fathers on a weekly basis).

32   The single greatest predictor of contraceptive efficacy, for example, is motivation of the user. Most methods of regulating births (including Natural Family Planning) are reasonably effective in highly motivated users.

33   Katherine Edin & Joanna Reed, forthcoming 2005. "Marriage Among the Disadvantaged," *Focus on Children*.

34   For a discussion of the signaling and channeling functions of marriage, see Maggie Gallagher, *What is Marriage For?*, 62 La. L. Rev. 773 (2002); Maggie Gallagher, *Rites, Rights, and Social Institutions: Why and How Should the Law Support Marriage?* 18 Notre Dame J.L. Ethics & Pub. Pol'y 225 (2004).

35   Thomas G. O'Connor, et al., 1999. "Frequency and Predictors of Relationship Dissolution in a Community Sample in England," *Journal of Family Psychology* 13(3): 436-449.

36   Adultery is disfavored in law in 24 states. See Jonathan Turley, "Of Lust and the Law," *Washington Post*, Sept. 5, 2004, at B01.

37   For a review of this literature see Linda Waite and Maggie Gallagher, 2000. *The Case for Marriage: Why Married People are Happier, Healthier, and Better-Off Financially* (New York: Doubleday): 78-96.

38   For a discussion of the literature on marriage and domestic violence, see for example, Linda Waite and Maggie Gallagher, 2000. *The Case for Marriage: Why Married People are Happier, Healthier, and Better-Off Financially* (New York: Doubleday): 150-160.

39   See, e.g., David Popenoe, 1996. *Life Without Father: Compelling New Evidence that Fatherhood and Marriage are Indispensable for the Good of Children and Society* (Cambridge MA: Harvard University Press); Ross D. Parke, 1996. *Fatherhood* (Cambridge, MA: Harvard University Press).

40   Commission on Children at Risk, 2003. *Hardwired to Connect: The New Scientific Case for Authoritative Communities* (New York: Institute for American Values): 23.

41 Id at 23-24.

42 Id. at 24.

43 Commission on Children at Risk, 2003. *Hardwired to Connect: The New Scientific Case for Authoritative Communities* (YMCA, Dartmouth Medical School, Institute for American Values): 23-25, 24.

44 Cynthia Harper and Sara McLanahan, 1998. "Father Absence and Youth Incarceration," (paper presented at the annual meeting of the American Sociological Association (San Francisco) (August).

45 Andrew J. Cherlin, et al., 1995. "Parental Divorce in Childhood and Demographic Outcomes in Young Adulthood," *Demography* 32: 299-318.

46 Martin Daly and Margo Wilson, 1996. "Evolutionary Psychology and Marital Conflict: The Relevance of Stepchildren," in David M. Buss and Neil M. Malmuth (eds.), *Sex, Power, Conflict: Evolutionary and Feminist Perspectives*, (Oxford: Oxford University Press): 9-28.

47 Martin Daly and Margo Wilson, 1985. "Child Abuse and Other Risks of Not Living with Both Parents," *Ethology and Sociobiology* 6: 197-210.

10 *The Current Crisis in Marriage Law*

1 Katherine Shaw Spaht, *Beyond Baehr: Strengthening The Definition of Marriage*, 12 B.Y.U. J. P. L. 277, 278 (1998).

2 Id. "Past generations did not necessarily require a legally binding definition of marriage, for people who are instructed in the tenets of Christian morality have an instinctive understanding of what the word means. The received model of Christian marriage is grounded in universal truths, natural orders, and enduring moral boundaries.... As a unique institution, Christian marriage has traditionally been defined by three elements: 1) sexual complementarity, the 'ordering' purpose of which is procreation; 2) mutual faithfulness; and 3) 'the special bond of permanence conferred by God as a "sacrament," [Catholic] a gift of grace.' [Protestant view of Marriage as a covenant, a special source of grace]." "The latter a quote from David Orgon Coolidge, *Same-Sex Marriage? Baehr v. Miike and the Meaning of Marriage*, 38 S. Tex. L. Rev. 1, 31 (1997).

3 *Baker v. Nelson*, 191 N.W. 2d 185 (Minn. 1972).

4 Id. Spaht, supra note 1 at 278. See also *Developments in the Law: The Law of Marriage and Family*, 116 Harv. L. Rev.1997 (2003).

5 Carl E. Schneider, *Moral Discourse and the Transformation of American Family Law*, 83 Mich. L. Rev. 1803 (1985). See also Carl E. Schneider, *Marriage, Morals and the Law: No-Fault Divorce and Moral Discourse*, 1994 Utah L.Rev. 501 and Daniel Cere, A Report to the Nation from the Council on Family Law (discussion of close relationship theory) (Institution for American Values, 2005) (on file with author).

6 Paul Johnson, *Intellectuals* (Harper Perennial 1988).

7 See generally Mary Somerville Jones, *An Historical Geography of Changing Divorce Law in the United States* (1978); Ira Mark Ellman, Paul M. Kurtz, Elizabeth Scott, *Family Law: Cases, Text, Problems* 3-52 (3rd ed. 1998); Harry D. Krause, Linda D. Elrod, Marsha Garrison, J. Thomas Oldham, *Family Law: Cases, Comments, and Questions* 4-34(5th ed. 2003); Walter Wadlington and Raymond C. O'Brien, *Domestic Relations: Cases and Materials* 1-122 (5th ed. 2002); Roderick Phillips, *Untying the Knot: A Short History of Divorce* (1991). See also Shaakirrah R. Sanders, *The Cyclical Nature of Divorce in the Western Legal Tradition* 50 Loy. L. Rev. 407 (2004).

8 Katherine Shaw Spaht, *The Last One Hundred Years: The Incredible Retreat of Law from the Regulation of Marriage*, 63 La. L. Rev. 243 (2003). See also Shankirrah R. Sanders, *The Cyclical Nature of Divorce in Western Legal Tradition*, 50 Loy. L. Rev. 407 (2004). Louisiana was the only state significantly influenced by Catholic doctrine.

9 Homer H. Clark, Jr. *Cases and Problems on Domestic Relations* 4 (St. Paul, Minn.: West Pub. Co. 1980).

10 Id. at 7.

11 Id.

12 Id. at 8: "The strength of the English influence may be measured by the fact that South Carolina had no general divorce statute at all until 1942, and that New York's statute limited divorce to the ground of adultery from 1787 to 1966." Anglicans did retain "canon law divorce while Protestants amended it more substantially."

13 Id. At first in states which prohibited divorce by general laws a spouse could obtain a divorce by act of the legislature.

14 Id.

15 William R. Corbett, *A Somewhat Modest Proposal to Prevent Adultery and Save Families: Two Old Torts Looking for a New Career*, 33 Ariz. L. J. 987 (2001).

16 See Spaht supra note 8 at 247: "Other states [other than Louisiana] chose different 'legal' mechanisms as barriers around the marriage relationship, such as the alienation of affection action; but all had legal barriers to protect marriage from external threats." In Louisiana by denying the adulterer the right to marry his accomplice, the law removed one incentive for seduction.

17 Spaht, supra note 8 at 294.

18 Id. at 294.

19 Clark, supra note 9 at 8: "By the 1860's and 1870's some western states had even begun to reach out for divorce business from the eastern states and the now familiar American institution of migratory divorce appeared." See *Williams* v. *North Carolina*, 317 U. S. 287 (1942), which initiated the phenomenon labeled "migratory divorce."

20 Id. at 9. For a particularized history from the vantage point of the women's movement, see Herma Hill Kay, *From the Second Sex to the Joint Venture: An Overview of Women's Rights and Family Law in the United States During the Twentieth Century*, 88 Cal. L. Rev.2017 (2000).

21 Id.

22 Id.:"The drive for uniformity produced a uniform act which was only enacted in three states."

23 Id. The attempt to enact a constitutional amendment continued for more than fifty years: "It is difficult to imagine what sort of a divorce law might have received Congressional approval if the constitutional amendment had passed, but in all likelihood it would have been more restrictive than the statutes of many states."

24 Id. at 10.

25 *Williams v. North Carolina*, 317 U.S. 287 (1942) (residents of North Carolina traveled to Nevada to obtain divorces from their spouses which according to the Court was permissible as long as the North Carolina residents established a "domicile" in Nevada first as required by the full faith and credit clause of the U.S. Constitution).

26 Clark, supra note 9 at 10.

27 Id. at 11.

28 Id. at 247-50, 268-75. Spaht, note 8 supra.

29 Katherine Shaw Spaht, *A Proposal: Legal Re-Regulation of the Content of Marriage*, 18 Notre Dame J. L., Ethics, & Pub. P. 243, 246 (2004).

30 Harry Cohen, Note, 24 Tul. L. Rev. 501 (1950); Margaret P. Brinig, *Rings and Promises*, 6 J.L. Ec. & Org. 203 (1990).

31 Spaht, supra note 8.

32 Id.

33 John Witte, Jr. *From Sacrament to Contract: Marriage, Religion, and Law in the Western Tradition* (1997), in which the author argues that the legal rules for entrance into and exit from marriage should be equally restrictive or equally lax.

34 Spaht, supra note 8 at 248.

35 Carl E. Schneider, *The Channelling Function in Family Law*, 20 Hofstra L. Rev. 495 (1992).

36 Spaht, supra note 8 at 248.

37 Id.

38 Clark, supra note 9 at 12.

39 Id. See also Herbert Jacob, *The Silent Revolution* (1988) and Judy Parejko, *Stolen Vows: The Illusion of No-Fault Divorce and the Rise of the American Divorce Industry* (2002) (a fascinating examination of the reality behind California's no-fault divorce legislation which includes the personal interest of a chairman of the powerful Judiciary Committee and the interests of attorneys to be served by the "no-fault" divorce legislation).

40 Id.

41 Schneider, supra note 5 at 1803.

42 Id.

43 Yet, as Carl Schneider explains the privacy promoted by psychological discourse is not related to "secrecy," but instead to the ability to behave as one chooses without governmental or legal constraint. See Schneider, supra note 5 at 1850-51.

44 Thirty-one states combine a "no-fault" ground for divorce with traditional fault grounds: Alabama, Alaska, Arkansas, Connecticut, Georgia, Idaho, Illinois, Indiana, Louisiana,

Maine, Maryland, Massachusetts, Mississippi, Missouri, Nevada, New Hampshire, New Jersey, New Mexico, New York, North Carolina, North Dakota, Ohio, Oklahoma, Pennsylvania, Rhode Island, South Carolina, South Dakota, Tennessee, Texas, Utah, Vermont, Virginia, and West Virginia. Linda D. Elrod and Robert G. Spector, *A Review of the Year in Family Law: State Courts React to Troxel,* 35 Fam. L. Q. 620, chart 4: Grounds for Divorce....(2002).

45　There are seventeen states with a "no-fault" ground as the exclusive ground for divorce: Arizona, California, Colorado, Delaware, District of Columbia, Florida, Hawaii, Iowa, Kentucky, Michigan, Minnesota, Montana, Nebraska, Oregon, Washington, Wisconsin, and Wyoming. See Linda D. Elrod and Robert G. Spector, *A Review of the Year in Family Law: State Courts React to Troxel,* 35 Fam. L. Q 620, chart 4: Grounds for Divorce....(2002).

46　"At one time, the public purposes of marriage law, for better and/or for worse, were etched with crystal clarity into the law. American law vigorously and with great articulateness promoted the relationship between sex, fertility, and marriage, by attempting to regulate virtually all sexual conduct in order (a) to minimize the possibility that children will be produced outside of marriage, and (at one time) (b) to maximize the likelihood that marriages will produce children." Maggie Gallagher, *Rites, Rights, and Social Institutions: Why and How Should the Law Support Marriage,* 18 Notre Dame J.L., Ethics & Pub. P. 225, 233-34 (2003).

47　Francis Cardinal George, "Law and Culture," Dedication Address at Ave Maria School of Law (Mar. 21, 2002), 1 Ave Maria L. Rev. 1, 13 (2003).

48　Id. at 16-17. See also Schneider supra note 5.

49　The United States Constitution does not give the federal government jurisdiction to legislate or to adjudicate on marriage. This jurisdiction is reserved to the states under the Tenth Amendment to the United States Constitution.

50　U.S. Const. amend. XIV.

51　125 U.S. 190 (1888)(considering constitutionality of divorce granted by legislative act as it was in all states prior to enactment of divorce under the general law and constitutionality of the effect of divorce on wife and her rights concerning certain property). "Marriage, as creating the most important relation in life, as having more to do with the morals and civilization of a people than any other institution, has always been subject to the control of the legislature." Id. at 205. In explaining that marriage is more than a mere contract, the Supreme Court stated: "The relation once formed, the law steps in and holds the parties to various obligations and liabilities. It is an institution, in the maintenance of which in its purity the public is deeply interested for it is the foundation of the family and of society, without which there would be neither civilization nor progress." Id. at 211.

52　381 U.S. 479 (1965), cited in *Lawrence v. Texas,* note 58 infra, as the most pertinent.

53　Conn. Gen. Stat. Sec. 43-32 and 54-196 (1958): "Any person who uses any drug, medicinal article or instrument for the purpose of preventing conception shall be fined not less than fifty dollars or imprisoned not less than sixty days nor more than one year or be both fined and imprisoned." "Any person who assists, abets, counsels, causes, hires or commands another to commit any offense may be prosecuted and punished as if he were the principal offender."

54 381 U.S. at 482.

55 Id.

56 Id. at 486.

57 Id.

58 *Lawrence v. Texas*, 539 U.S. 558, 564-65, 123 S.Ct. 2472, 2476-77 (2003).

59 388 U.S. 1 (1967).

60 "The sentence imposed for the violation of the statute was a one-year jail sentence or suspension of sentence for 25 years on the condition that the Lovings leave the state and not return to Virginia together for 25 years." Id. at 1819.

61 Id. at 1823.

62 Id.

63 Id. at 1824.

64 Id. at 1824 (citing *Skinner v. Oklahoma*, 316 U.S. 535, 541 (1942)) Emphasis added.

65 Gallagher, supra note 46 at 231-32: "What is 'older than the Bill of Rights,' to use the language of *Griswold*, is not a right to marry, but marriage itself as a social institution."

66 Arguably, the use was not deliberate since the case of *Skinner v. Oklahoma*, 316 U.S. 535, 62 S. Ct. 1110 (1942) was cited for the proposition. In addition, the opinion cited *Maynard v. Hill*, note 51 supra.

67 434 U.S. 374, 98 S.Ct. 673 (1978).

68 "At issue in this case is the constitutionality of a Wisconsin statute, Wis. Stat. § 245.10(1),(4), (5) (1973), which provides that members of a certain class of Wisconsin residents may not marry, within the State or elsewhere, without first obtaining a court order granting permission to marry. The class is defined by the statute to include any 'Wisconsin resident having minor issue not in his custody and which he is under obligation to support by any court order or judgment.' The statute specifies that court permission cannot be granted unless the marriage applicant submits proof of compliance with the support obligation and, in addition, demonstrates that the children covered by the support order 'are not then and are not likely thereafter to become public charges.' No marriage license may lawfully be issued in Wisconsin to a person covered by the statute, except upon court order; any marriage entered into without compliance with § 245.10 is declared void; and persons acquiring marriage licenses in violation of the section are subject to criminal penalties." Id. at 675.

69 "[R]easonable regulations that do not significantly interfere with decisions to enter into the marital relationship may legitimately be imposed." Id. at 681.

70 Id. at 679.

71 414 U.S. 632, 639-640, 94 S.Ct. 791, 796 (1974).

72 Id. at 384, 98 S.Ct. at 680.

73 Id. at 387, 98 S.Ct. at 681.

74 482 U.S. 78 (1987).

75 "The attributes described as sufficient to constitute the core of the "right to marry" include…(3) "the *expectation* that marriage will be fully consummated'…." What remains of the traditional model of marriage is a hint of sexual complementarity conveyed by the word 'consummated,' but without reference to the ordering purpose of procreation." Emphasis added. Spaht, supra note 1 at 280-81 (quoting from the *Turner* case at 96).

76 Schneider, supra note 5.

77 *Turner v. Safley*, note 74 supra.

78 478 U.S. 186, 194-95 (1986): "Nor are we inclined to take a more expansive view of our authority to discover new fundamental rights imbedded in the Due Process Clause.…There should be, therefore, great resistance to expand the substantive reach of those clauses, particularly if it requires redefining the category, or rights deemed to be fundamental."

79 Justice Marshall writing for the majority in *Zablocki v. Redhail*, supra note 64 at 384, 98 S.Ct. At 680 (1978) quoted from *Carey v. Population Services International*, 431 U.S. 678, 97 S.Ct. 2010 (1977): " 'While the outer limits of [the right of personal privacy] have not been marked by the Court, it is clear that among the decisions that an individual may make without unjustified government interference are personal decisions 'relating to marriage.'"

80 491 U.S. 110, 109 S.Ct. 2333 (1989).

81 Under the common law and in Louisiana (which retains the civil law), the husband of the mother at the time of conception or birth is presumed to be the father of the child.

82 491 U.S. at 148 n.6, 109 S.Ct. at 2355 n.6 (1989).

83 521 U.S. 702, 117 S.Ct. 2258 (1997).

84 505 U.S. 833, 112 S.Ct. 2791 (1992).

85 517 U.S. 620, 116 S.Ct. 1620 (1996). See Steven D. Smith, *Conciliating Hatred*, *First Things* 17-22 (June/July 2004).

86 410 U.S. 113, 93 S.Ct. 705 (1973).

87 505 U.S. at 851, 112 S.Ct.at 2481. Justice Scalia referred to this language as *dicta* in his dissenting opinion in *Lawrence v. Texas*, 123 S.Ct. at 2472 (2003).

88 517 U.S. at 634-635, 116 S. Ct. at 1628-29. See also Steven D. Smith, *Conciliating Hatred*, *First Things* 17-22 (June/July 2004) (classifies this Supreme Court jurisprudence as "evil-motives" jurisprudence; legislation is unconstitutional because the motive of those proposing and passing it is evil).

89 539 U.S. 558, 123 S. Ct. 2472 (2003).

90 "*Bowers* was not correct when it was decided, and it is not correct today. It ought not to remain binding precedent. *Bowers v. Hardwick* should be and now is overruled." Id. at 2484.

91 Id. at 2484.

92 Justice Kennedy in distinguishing this case from others that might arise in the future emphasized that *Lawrence* did not involve minors, "persons who might be injured or coerced or who are situated in relationships where consent might not easily be refused." Nor did the case "involve public conduct or prostitution." Id. at 2484.

93 Id. at 562 , 123 S.Ct. at 2475 (Emphasis added.). "The instant case involves liberty of the person both in its spatial and more transcendent dimensions."

94 Failing to characterize the right to homosexual sodomy as a fundamental right means that the Court applied the "rational basis" level of scrutiny to the Texas statute. Generally, when rational basis scrutiny is applied there is great deference to the state interest–both its legitimacy (the reason why the legislation was enacted) and its relationship to the interest sought to be protected (means chosen reasonably related to accomplishment of the purpose). Texas received no such deference.

95 *Lawrence,* supra note 89 at 2482.

96 Id. "The stigma this criminal statute imposes, moreover, is not trivial [even though it is a Class C misdemeanor]."

97 Id. at 2488-2498, 2490. "This reasoning leaves on pretty shaky grounds state laws limiting marriage to opposite-sex couples." Id. at 2496.

98 "To the extent *Bowers* relied on values we share with a wider civilization, it should be noted that the reasoning and holding in *Bowers* have been rejected elsewhere. The European Court of Human Rights has followed not *Bowers* but its own decision in *Dudgeon v. United Kingdom*....Other nations, too, have taken action consistent with an affirmation of the protected right of homosexual adults to engage in intimate, consensual conduct....The right the petitioners seek in this case has been accepted as an integral part of human freedom in many other countries...." Id. at 575, 123 S.Ct. at 2483.

99 See Stanley Kurtz, *The End of Marriage in Scandinavia: the conservative case for same-sex marriage falls apart, Weekly Standard* 26 (Feb. 2, 2004). See also discussion in text at notes 165-69 infra.

100 See *Spain Clears the Way for Gay Marriage, NYTimes Int'l* A2 (Oct. 2, 2004); Marlise Simons, *Church and State Clash, Noisily, in Spain, NY Times Int'l* A3 (Oct. 4, 2004). The Canadian Supreme Court has ruled that same-sex "marriage" is not unconstitutional, clearing the way for the Canadian Parliament to enact national legislation legally recognizing same-sex "marriage:" See critique of that opinion in Bruce Stein, *Wash. Times* (http://washingtontimes.com/commentary/20041213-084740-8718r.htm). In *Fourie Bonthurys v. Minister & Director of Home Affairs,* S. Afr. S. Ct., No. 232/2003 (11/30/04), 31 F.L.R. 1068 (12/7/04), the South African Supreme Court redefined "marriage" under the common law to include same-sex unions, citing the constitution's equality guarantee (prohibiting discrimination on the ground of sexual orientation).

101 *Lawrence,* supra note 89 at 568, 123 S.Ct. at 2484.

102 Id. at 567, 123 S.Ct. at 2478. See also Justice Sandra Day O'Connor's concurring opinion: "That this law as applied to private, consensual conduct is unconstitutional under

the Equal Protection Clause does not mean that other laws distinguishing between heterosexuals and homosexuals would similarly fail under rational basis review. Texas cannot assert any legitimate state interest here, such as tradition, security, or preserving the traditional institution of marriage. Unlike the moral disapproval of same-sex relations—the asserted state interest in this case—other reasons exist to promote the institution of marriage beyond mere moral disapproval of an excluded group." Id. at 2488.

103 Id. at 562, 123 S.Ct. at 2475.

104 *Planned Parenthood of Southeastern Pa. v. Casey*, 505 U.S. 833, 851 (1992).

105 Id.

106 *Lawrence*, supra note 89 at 571, 123 S.Ct. at 2480.

107 Id. "Not surprisingly, Justice O'Connor's separate opinion, like so many of her other opinions which lack logical rigor, seeks to distinguish good and acceptable laws that 'preserve the traditions of society' from those bad and unacceptable laws that 'express moral disapproval.'" Spaht, supra note 8 at 258 (quoting from O'Connor's concurring opinion in *Lawrence* note 89 supra at 2488).

108 Id. at 2486-89.

109 Gallagher, supra note 46 at 226.

110 The use of "civil" as an adjective preceding *marriage* appeared in *Goodridge v. Department of Health*, 440 Mass. 309, 798 N.E. 2d 941 (2003) because it appears in the Massachusetts statute. The language of the statute is familiar because it appears in many states' statutes. "Simply put, the government creates civil marriage. In Massachusetts, civil marriage is, and since pre-Colonial days has been precisely what its name implies: a wholly secular institution." Id. at 321, 798 N.E.2d at 954.

　　The dichotomy between "civil" and "religious" marriage as it has existed in Europe is a recent rhetorical device in the United States. The strict separation between "civil" jurisdiction over matters of *marriage* and religious authority over *marriage* in Europe and in England involved the civil government's wresting of jurisdiction over marriage from the Catholic Church, and in England the ecclesiastical courts, a triumph ultimately completed in Europe with the French Revolution. Western European countries such as France and Spain recognize only a "civil" marriage but it is customary to also have a "religious" ceremony, too. In the United States religious authorities are recognized by most states as civil officiants for the purpose of celebrating a marriage that will be recognized under "civil" laws.

　　See Midge Decter, *Civil Unions: Compromise or Surrender?* 33 *Imprimis* #11 (Nov. 2004): "Today what is being called 'civil marriage' is a kind of trick of language, a term used as a political euphemism for surrendering to the most recent demand of the homosexual rights movement."

111 See discussion in text at notes 74-77, supra.

112 744 A.2d 864 (Vt. 1999).

113 *Goodridge v. Department of Public Health*, 440 Mass. 309, 798 N.E.2d 941 (2003).

114 74 Haw. 530, 852 P.Ed. 44 (1993). See also subsequent litigation in Hawaii in *Baehr v.*

Miike, 80 Haw. 341, 910 P.2d 112 (1996) and *Baehr v. Miike*, 950 P.2d 1235 (C.C. Haw. 1997).

115 1998 WL 88743 (Feb 27, 1998).

116 Haw. Const. art. 1, §23; Alaska Const. art. 1, §25. The Hawaii Constitution grants power "to reserve marriage to opposite-sex couples," and the Legislature exercises that power by reserving marriage to heterosexual couples.

117 28 U.S.C. §1738 C (1996), 1 U.S.C .§7 (1996).

118 Only Connecticut, Massachusetts, New Jersey, New Mexico, New York, and Rhode Island do not have state statutory or constitutional language preserving traditional marriage. http://www. Heritage. Org/Research/Family/Marriage 50 States.cfm. Seventeen states have language in their state constitutions, and in three states (Massachusetts, Wisconsin, and Tennessee) the legislature has approved a constitutional amendment but it must be approved again before it appears on the ballot in November, 2006. Id.

119 See earlier discussion in text at notes 38-45 supra.

120 Vt. Const. Ch. 1, art. 7 (government for the people; they may change it).

121 Gallagher, supra note 46 at 227.

122 *Baker*, supra note 112 at 224-29, 744 A.2d at 886-89.

123 Id. at 221-22, 744 A.2d at 884.

124 Id. at 228, 744 A.2d at 888-89. "The State's interest in extending official recognition and legal protection to the professed commitment of two individuals to a lasting relationship of mutual affection is predicated on the belief that legal support of a couple's commitment provides stability for the individuals, their family, and the broader community."

125 The same technique was used subsequently in *Goodridge*, note 113 supra at 344, 798 N.E.2d at 970: "Entry of judgment shall be stayed for 180 days to permit the Legislature to take such action as it may deem appropriate in light of this opinion."

126 See note 123 supra. Gallagher, supra note 46 at 227: "Marriage in this view consists of an individual right to access certain material legal benefits."

127 *Goodridge*, note 113 supra at 328, 798 N.E.2d at 959: "That the Massachusetts Constitution is in some instances more protective of individual liberty interests than is the Federal Constitution is not surprising. Fundamental to the vigor of our Federal system of government is that state courts are absolutely free to interpret state constitutional provisions to accord greater protection to individual rights than do similar provisions of the United States Constitution."

128 Bolder because in the *Baker* case the Vermont Court gave the legislature the option of creating an alternate status to that of marriage, as long as it provided the same benefits and protections to same-sex couples as those afforded to married couples.

129 Opinions of the Justices to the Senate, 802 N.E.2d 565 (Mass. 2004).

130 Vt. St. Ann. Tit. 18 §5169 (2000).

131 William C. Duncan, *The State Interests in Marriage*, 2 Ave Maria L. Rev. 153 (2004).

132 *Baehr v. Lewin*, 852 P.2d 44 (Haw. 1993).

133 *Brause v. Bureau of Vital Statistics*, 1998 WL 88743 (Alaska Super. 2/27/1998). See also

Brause v. State of Alaska DHS, 21 P.3d 357 (Alaska Super. 4/17/2001).

134 Hi. Const. art. 1, §23; Ak. Const. art. 1, §25. See Kevin G. Clarkson, *The Alaska Marriage Amendment: The People's Choice on the Last Frontier*, 16 Alaska L. Rev. 213 (1999). See note 116 supra.

135 Vt. Const. Ch. II, §72 (amending constitution).

136 Ma. Const. Amend. 48, Initiative, Part IV, Legislative action on Proposed Constitutional Amendments, 1-5.

137 *Goodridge*, note 113 supra at 328, 798 N.E.2d at 958 n.17: "Recently the United States Supreme Court has reaffirmed that the Constitution prohibits a State from wielding its formidable power to regulate conduct in a manner that demeans basic human dignity, even though that statutory discrimination may enjoy broad public support. The Court struck down a statute criminalizing sodomy...."

138 Karen S. Peterson, *Love and the Law: A Reality Check, USA Today*, Dec. 4, 2002, at D8 (discussing reactions to the report). See also Gallagher, supra note 46 at 229: "It is worth looking at in some detail, because of the ALI's character as a mainstream legal body and because the *Principles of the Law of Family Dissolution* represent the culmination of ten years of work by eminent family law scholars and divorce lawyers."

139 Herma Hill Kay, *From the Second Sex to the Joint Venture: An Overview of Women's Rights and Family Law in the United States During the Twentieth Century*, 88 Calif. L. Rev. 2017 (2000).

140 Id.

141 Id. at 2089: "At first glance, the joint venture may seem to be the exact antithesis of a stable relationship and therefore poorly suited as a conceptualization of an enterprise that typically involves the rearing of children." Described by Kay as "the most attractive aspect" of the joint venture analogy, renewal involves a decision by the couple "whether the venture should be continued to the next stage," always with the "recognition that either spouse is free to terminate the undertaking." Id. at 2090.

142 See note 143 infra.

143 Id. at 62: "...the imposition of external standards (community consensus) on an intimate relationship may risk inappropriate, and possibly *even unconstitutional intrusion on marital privacy....* Because marital relationships do vary, important privacy norms can be violated if the law imposes liability after the marriage for conduct that was within the bounds of the marriage as the spouses then understood it. This means that an external standard should only reach conduct that is highly unlikely to have been part of any couple's mutual understanding, or that is sufficiently malevolent to justify overriding these privacy norms."

144 Gallagher, supra note 46 at 229, 231.

145 *The Principles of the Law of Family Dissolution: Analysis and Recommendations* §6.02 comment a: "Domestic partners fail to marry for diverse reasons. Among others, some have been unhappy in prior marriages and therefore wish to avoid the *form* of marriage even as they enjoy its *substance* with a domestic partner....In all these cases, the absence

of *formal* marriage may have little or no bearing on the character of the parties' domestic relationship and on the equitable considerations that underlie claims between lawful spouses at the dissolution of a marriage."

146 *The Principles of the Law of Family Dissolution: Analysis and Recommendations* §§ 6.01-06 (American Law Inst. 2000), available at http://www.ali.org [hereinafter, *Principles*].

147 Id. at § 6.02.

148 Gallagher, supra note 46 at 229.

149 David Orgon Coolidge, *Widening the Lens: Chapter 6 of the ALI Principles, Hawaii and Vermont*, 4 J.L. & Fam. Stud. 79 (2002) (discussing "civil union" law of Vermont and the "reciprocal beneficiaries" law of Hawaii). "Chapter 6 of the *Principles* was developed over many years by a corps of elite law professors." Id. at 85.

150 Id. at 79.

151 "The new report is intended to set guidelines for individual judges and state legislatures, says co-author Ira Mark Ellman, a law professor at Arizona State University and editor of the report. The project addresses the 'sense of unfairness' that the couples feel when a judicial decision 'is decided by the luck of the draw, who the judge is,' he says. And more couples will settle out of court if they know a decision is predictable, he says." Peterson, supra note 138.

152 Gallagher, supra note 46 at 231: "By emphasizing the rights of adults, it intrinsically devalues the interest of children and the community in marriage...[I]t undermines the very norms of commitment it rhetorically upholds. It logically calls into question the notion of family law itself. If the purpose of marriage and family law is to affirm neutrally the multiplicity of adult emotional choices, because individual declarations of intimacy are sacred matters in which the state has no right to interfere, then the question becomes: why do we have laws about marriage at all?"

153 See *Baker*, supra note 112 at 225, 744 A.2d at 886-87, where the court surveys the alternative legal statuses established elsewhere including in Europe.

154 Haw. Rev. Stat. Ann. §572C-1-7 (Michie 1999). The reciprocal beneficiary relationship that parties may enter is not limited to those who have a sexual relationship, only those who cannot marry. Either party may end the relationship and it ends automatically if one party marries. "The Hawaii law contrasts dramatically with the Vermont Civil Unions Act, passed in 2000, which addresses both formation and dissolution. The Vermont Act is based on marriage and the shift from non-marital to marital is virtually complete. Only same-sex couples are eligible, but the coverage broadens dramatically." Coolidge, supra note 2 at 81.

155 Charles Murray, *Marriage-Lite*, The Pub. Int. 31 (Summer, 2004); Jonathan Rauch, *Gay Marriage: Why Gay Marriage is Good for Gays, Good for Straights, and Good for America* (2004); and William Eskridge, *The Case for Same Sex Marriage* (1996).

156 Coolidge, supra note 2 at 85.

157 *Largess v. Supreme Judicial Court of the State of Massachusetts*, 373 F. 2d 219 (1st Cir. 2004), cert. denied, _____ U.S. _____ 2004 WL 2184961 (Nov. 29, 2004). See http://www.ny-

times.com/aponline/national/AP-Scotus-Gay-Marriage.html. See also Jennifer Peter, *Months after marriage, gays start divorcing, The Advocate,* 22A (Dec. 11, 2004).

158　For example, in France the law recognizes the *pacte civil de solidarite or PAC,* which requires registration in court of two individuals who desire to be afforded certain of the rights and privileges of marriage. Fr. Civ. Code arts. 515-1 to 515-7 (No. 99-944, Nov. 15, 1999, J.O. Nov. 16, 1999, at 169559). See Sarah Lyall, *In Europe, Lovers Now Propose: Marry Me, a Little, NY Times Int'l* 3A (Feb. 15, 2004).

159　Coolidge, supra note 2 at 89.

160　Id. at 88 n.56.

161　"...at least some of the advocates are honest enough to admit that they intend to transform marriage—*re-imagine* marriage. That re-imagining of marriage consists of questioning not simply the historical and universal requirement of sexual complementarity, but also the shared common understandings of the marital obligation of fidelity, of the manner in which married persons organize their property relationships, and of the other restrictions regulating entry into marriage. After all, once sexual complementarity, the most fundamental of assumptions about marriage, is purged from the legal institution it becomes difficult to argue justification for any other traditional moral view of marriage." Spaht, supra note 8 at 243-44.

162　Coolidge, supra note 2 at 88 n. 6.

163　Id. See William N. Eskridge, Jr., *The Emerging Menu of Quasi-Marriage Options: Why Traditionalists Should Favor Same-Sex Marriage* (July 7, 2000) at http://www.writ.news. findlaw.com/commentary/2000707_eskridge.html (last visited on Apr. 1, 2003) (rejecting the notion that couples should be able to choose the level of commitment they prefer from a "menu" of options); *The Case for Same-Sex Marriage* (1996). Jonathan Rausch, *Gay Marriage: Why It is Good for Gays, Good for Straights, and Good for America* (NY Times Books 2004).

164　Jonathan Rauch, *Gay Marriage: Why Its Good for Gays, Good for Straights, and Good for America* 47-49 (NY Times Books 2004). Emphasis added.

165　See Stanley Kurtz, *The End of Marriage in Scandinavia: the conservative case for same-sex marriage falls apart, Weekly Standard* 31(Feb. 15, 2004). His article has provoked two rejoinders thus far: 1. M.V. Lee Badgett, *Will Providing Marriage Rights to Same-Sex Couples Undermine Heterosexual Marriage? Evidence from Scandinavia and the Netherlands,* prepared for the Council on Contemporary Families and the Gay and Lesbian Strategic Studies at the University of Massachusetts Amherst (http://www. iglss.org/media/files/briefing.pdf) The report accuses Kurtz of "consistent misuse and misinterpretation of data." 2. William Eskridge, Jr., Darren R. Spedale, and Hans Ytterberg, Nordic Bliss? *Scandinavian Registered Partnership and the Same-Sex Marriage Debate,* http://www.bepress.com/ils/iss5/. He has responded to the rejoinder, Stanley Kurtz, *Despite a Challenge, the Evidence Stands: Marriage is in Decline in The Netherlands* (http://www.nationalreview.com/kurtz/kurtz200407210936.asp). In England, the civil partnership bill affords gays and lesbians the right to form unions and obtain some of the rights of married couples. See http://news.scotsman.com/latest.cfm?Id+3771386.

166 Maggie Gallagher, iMAPP Policy Brief (May 3, 2004) (www.imapp.org), quoting from Gunnar Anderson, et al., 2004, *Divorce-Risk Patterns in Same-Sex "Marriages" in Norway and Sweden,* presented at the 2004 annual meeting of the Population Association of America (http://paa2004.princeton,edu/download.sap?submissionID=40208).

167 Patrick Fagan and Grace Smith, *The Transatlantic Divide on Marriage: Dutch Data and the U.S. Debate on Same Sex Unions,* Web Memo #577 (Sept.29,2004) (http://www.heritage.org/Research/Family/wm577.cfm?renderforprint+1) citing Masha Antokoskaia and Katharina Boele-Woelki, *Dutch Family Law in the 21ˢᵗ Century: Trend-Setting and Straggling Behind at the Same Time,* Netherlands Comparative Law Asso. (June 28, 2004).

168 See note 158 supra. The French *pacte civil de solidarite* or *PAC* requires registration in court of two individuals who desire to be afforded certain of the rights and privileges of marriage. The two individuals need not prove a sexual relationship. Heterosexual couples have increasingly rejected marriage and simply registered as a *PAC*. One of the couples interviewed by the *New York Times* reporter, Sarah Lyall, *In Europe, Lovers Now Propose: Marry Me, a Little, NYTimes Int'l* 3A (Sun. Feb. 15, 2004) described being "PAC'ed" as different from conventional marriage, "but a *light approximation* of it." The heterosexual couples described the *PAC* as "the perfect halfway house"–"an intermediate way between no commitment and a wedding." Why not a wedding? "…I'm too scared to get married [even though she and her boyfriend already have a child]." Another commented that she feared a long-term commitment, and a *PAC* can be dissolved by one member with three months' notice and few legal complications.

169 Id. "Even in a culture that makes full use of contraceptive and abortion technology, half of all pregnancies are unintended and one-third of our children are born outside of marriage." Gallagher, supra note 46 at 241.

170 Rauch, supra note 164.

171 Rauch, supra note 164 at 47-48: "Give the benefits to committed partners of whatever gender. Give them to seniors and their caregivers. Maybe even give them to–here it comes–groups [a reference to polyamory movement]. The alternatives-to-marriage movement wants the government to stop picking and choosing among relationships and lifestyles. Domestic-partnership programs are a foot in the door.…Wouldn't it be nice if there were a halfway house…? A way to get health insurance without having to say, 'till death us do part'?"

172 Cal. Fam. Code §297.5 (rights, protections and benefits; responsibilities, obligations, and duties under law).

173 Charles Murray, *Marriage-Lite, Pub. Int.* 31 (summer, 2004).

174 Id. at 32.

175 See Gallagher, supra note 46.

176 Murray, supra note 173 at 32.

177 Id. at 34.

178   See Maggie Gallagher, *Rites, Rights and Social Institutions: Why and How Should the Law Support Marriage?* 18 Notre Dame J. L., Ethics & Pub. P. 225, 231 (2004).

179   See Duncan, supra note 131; Lynn D. Wardle, *"Multiply and Replenish": Considering Same-Sex Marriage in Light of State Interests in Marital Procreation*, 24 Harv. J.L. & Pub. Pol'y 771 (2000-01).

180   Carl E. Schneider, *The Channelling Function of Law*, 20 Hofstra L. Rev. 495 (1992). See also Gallagher, supra note 46 at 237: "Law has a communicative function as well as a punitive function. Marriage is inherently a normative institution. It consists of preferring a certain type of relationship to others: one that is public, exclusive, and (in intention) permanent."

181   Gallagher, supra note 46 at 235-36.

182   Rauch, supra note 164 at 89.

183   La. Const. art. XII, § 15. For other examples, *see* provisions cited in note 190 infra. See also FOCUS ON MARRIAGE-BALLOT WATCH (Initiative & Referendum Institute No. 8, October 2004) (http://www.iandrinstatitute.org/BW%202004-8%20(Marriage). pdf.).

184   Louisiana is an example of such a state, *see* La. Const. art. XIII, §1(B) (prohibits multiple objects in a constitutional amendment unless the amendment revises an entire article of the constitution).

185   "Gay" activists are correct in identifying divorce as the gravest threat to marriage but that threat has existed for almost 200 years and cannot now be identified as a contemporary threat except in an individual, pragmatic sense.

186   Rauch, supra note 164 at 90. "It is even possible (although I wouldn't give the odds) that, a generation from now, legal marriage might seem not so much prestigious as anachronistic."

187   See Bruce C. Hafen, *The Constitutional Status of Marriage, Kinship, and Sexual Privacy–Balancing the Individual and Social Interests*, 81 Mich. L. Rev. 463 (1982-1983).

188   *What Next for the Marriage Movement*, a statement authored by over one hundred forty signatories and published by the Institute for American Values.

189   In addition to the state provisions contained in note190 infra, Hawaii, Alaska (see note 134 supra), Missouri, Mo. Const. Art. 1, §33; Oklahoma, Okla. Const. Art. II, §35; Michigan, Mich. Const. Art. I, §25; Mississippi, Miss. Const. Art. I, §25; Oregon, "It is the policy of Oregon, and its political subdivisions that only a marriage between one man and one woman shall be valid or legally recognized as a marriage"; Montana, Mont. Const. art. XIII, §7; and Nevada, Nev. Const. Art. I, §21.

190   Nebraska, Neb. Const. Art. 1, §29; Louisiana, La. Const. Art. XII, §15; Utah, 2004 Utah Bal. Meas. 3 (State Net) (2004 H.J.R. 25, proposing the addition of a new sec. 9 to Art. 1 of the Utah Const.); Wisconsin, 2003 Wis. Assem. J.R. 66 (State Net) (proposing the addition of a new 13 to Art. 13 of the Wis. Const.); Kentucky, 2004 Ky. Bal. Meas. 1 (State Net) (2005 S.B. 245, proposing the addition of a new sec. 233 A to the Ken.

Const.); Arkansas, 2004 Ark. Bal. Meas. 4 (State Net) (citizen-generated initiative, the placement of which in the Ark. Const. is yet to be determined); North Dakota, 2004 N.D. Bal. Meas. 3 (State Net) (citizen-generated initiative, proposing the addition of a "new section" to Art. 11 of the N.D. Const.); Ohio, Ohio Bal. Meas. 2 (State Net) (citizen-generated initiative, proposing the addition of a new sec. 11 to Art. 15 of the Ohio Const.); Georgia, Ga. Const. art. 1, §4 (2004). See also 31 Fam. L. R. 1022 (11-9-04).

Massachusetts addresses both subjects in its proposed constitutional amendment which denies recognition of same-sex "marriage" but creates civil unions for same-sex couples with identical rights and obligations of married persons. HB 3190 (Mar. 29, 2004).

191 *Lawrence v. Texas*, 123 S.Ct. at 2472, 2479-81 (2003).

192 Brad Knickerbocker, "Political battles over gay marriage still spreading," *Christian Science Monitor* (Nov. 29, 2004) (http://www.csmonitor.com/2004/1129/p01s04-USSC.html).

Jeffrey Rosen, *Courting Disaster*, NY Times Mag. 29-30, 30 (12/5/04) writes: "Both of these special-interest groups [social conservatives and liberal egalitarians] are bound to fail in their efforts to persuade courts to reverse their political defeats because courts rarely impose values that a majority of the country rejects. And on the few occasions when they have tried in the past, they have usually provoked a swift and democratic rebuke."

193 S. J. Res. 30.

194 See http://www.boston.com/news/nation/articles/2004/11/18/bishopsokinitiativeon-marriage/.FoundingoftheMarriageLawFoundationinUtah. *http://www.Larktheherald. com/modules.php?p=modload&name=News&file=article&sId=40554&mode=thread & order=0&thold=0*

Activists hope to pass as many as twenty more in the next two years. Anthony Glassman, GayPeople's chronicle, *http://www.gaypeopleschronicle.com/stories04/November/ 04Nov19/04Nov19-stl.htm.*

195 But see Leslie Eaton, *A New Push to Loosen New York's Divorce Law*, NY Times (Nov. 30, 2004).

11 *Marriage, the Poor, and the Commonweal*

1 Nancy F. Cott. 2000. *Public Vows: A History of Marriage and the Nation*. New Haven: Yale University Press. p. 2.

2 C. Eugene Steurle. 1995. "Tax Credits and Family Values." *The Responsive Community* 5: 3.

3 Cott, *Public Vows*, pp. 19-21, and Mary Ann Glendon and David Blankenhorn, eds., 1995, *Seedbeds of Virtue*. Lanham, MD: Madison Books.

4 For the economic, psychological, and health benefits of marriage for adults, see Linda Waite and Maggie Gallagher. 2000. *The Case for Marriage*. New York: Doubleday. For

the social and economic benefits of marriage to children, see Sara McLanahan and Gary Sandefur. 1994. *Growing Up with a Single Parent*. Cambridge, MA: Harvard University Press.

5   Steven L. Nock. 1998. *Marriage in Men's Lives*. New York: Oxford.

6   Nock, *Marriage in Men's Lives*, and Robert Putnam. 2001. *Bowling Alone*. New York: Simon and Schuster. Pp. 73, 94.

7   Isabel V. Sawhill. 1999. "Families at Risk." In H. Aaron and R. Reischauer, *Setting National Priorities: the* 2000 *Election and Beyond*. Washington, DC: Brookings Institution; and, David Popenoe. 1996. *Life Without Father*. New York: Simon and Schuster. Pp. 9, 13.

8   Paula Roberts. 2004. "I Can't Give You Anything But Love: Would Poor Couples with Children Be Better Off Economically if They Married?" *CLASP Policy Brief* 5. Washington, DC: Center for Law and Social Policy. Pp. 4-7.

9   Sara McLanahan. 1997. "Parent Absence or Poverty: Which Matters More?" In G. Duncan and J. Brooks-Gunn, *Consequences of Growing Up Poor*. New York: Russell Sage. P. 47.

10   Sawhill, 1999.

11   Steven L. Nock. 2000. "The Divorce of Marriage and Parenthood." *Journal of Marriage and Family Therapy* 22: 245-263, 2000. Charles Murray. *The Emerging British Underclass*. London: The IEA Health and Welfare Unit, 1990.

12   Robert Michael. "An Economic Perspective on Sex, Marriage, and the Family in Contemporary United States." In S. Tipton and J. Witte, eds., *The Modern American Family in Interdisciplinary Perspective*. New York: Columbia University Press, forthcoming.

13   George Akerlof, Janet L. Yellen, and Michael L. Katz. 1996. "An Analysis of Out-of-Wedlock Childbearing in the United States." *The Quarterly Journal of Economics* CXI: 277-317. George A. Akerlof. 1998. "Men Without Children." *The Economic Journal* 108: 287-309.

14   Akerlof et al., p. 279.

15   Ibid., p. 309.

16   Ibid., p. 313.

17   Akerlof, p. 289.

18   David Ellwood and Christopher Jencks. "The Spread of Single-Parent Families in the United States Since 1960." In D. Moynihan, L. Rainwater, and T. Smeeding, eds., *The Future of the Family* . New York: Russell Sage, forthcoming.

19   Sara McLanahan and Gary Sandefur. 1994. *Growing up with a Single Parent*. Cambridge, MA: Harvard University Press. p. 29.

20   Ibid., p. 41.

21   Ibid., p. 53.

22   Cynthia C. Harper and Sara S. McLanahan. 1998. "Father Absence and Youth Incarceration." Annual Meeting of the American Sociological Association (San Francisco).

23 McLanahan and Sandefur, p. 71.

24 Ibid, p. 38.

25 Sawhill, 1999, p. 103.

26 Ibid, p. 108.

27 David Popenoe and Barbara Dafoe Whitehead, *The State of Our Unions:* 2004. New Brunswick, NJ: *The National Marriage Project*, 2004.

Contributors

HADLEY ARKES is Edward N. Ney Professor of Jurisprudence and American Institutions at Amherst College. He has written five books with Princeton University press: *Bureaucracy, the Marshall Plan, and the National Interest* (1972), *The Philosopher in the City* (1981), *First Things* (1986), *Beyond the Constitution* (1990), and *The Return of George Sutherland* (1994). His most recent book, *Natural Rights and the Right to Choose*, was published by Cambridge University Press in September 2002.

DON BROWNING is Alexander Campbell Professor Emeritus of Religious Ethics and the Social Sciences at the University of Chicago Divinity School. He has interests in the relation of religious thought to the social sciences, specifically in the way theological ethics may employ sociology, psychology, and the social scientific study of religion. A student of psychology, he has special interests in psychoanalysis, self-psychology, object-relations theory, and evolutionary psychology, and has written on the cultural, theological, and ethical analysis of the modern psychologies. He is an ordained minister of the Christian Church (Disciples of Christ).

JEAN BETHKE ELSHTAIN is Laura Spellman Rockefeller Professor of Social and Political Ethics at the University of Chicago and the Thomas and Dorothy Leavy Chair in the Foundations of American Freedom at Georgetown University. A political philosopher whose task has been to show the connections between our political and ethical convictions, Professor Elshtain is author or co-author of over twenty books and four hundred articles. Her books include *Just War against Terror: The Burden of American Power in a Violent World*, *Democracy on Trial*, and *Public Man, Private Woman: Women in Social and Political Thought*. She is a senior fellow of the Witherspoon Institute.

DAVID F. FORTE is Charles R. Emrick Jr.–Calfee, Halter & Griswold Endowed Professor of Law at Cleveland State University. Professor Forte served as chief counsel to the United States Delegation to the United Nations in 1985-86 and has been a Liberty Fund Fellow, a National Endowment to the Humanities Fellow, an Ohio Humanities Scholar, a Bradley Resident Scholar at the Heritage Foundation, and a Salvatori Fellow at the Free Congress Foundation. He has taught at Skidmore College and, since joining the Cleveland faculty, has written and lectured on a wide range of topics, including international law, comparative law, Constitutional law, Islamic Law, medical ethics, natural law, and jurisprudence.

MAGGIE GALLAGHER is president of the Institute for Marriage and Public Policy, whose mission is research and public education on ways that law and public policy can strengthen marriage as a social institution. A nationally syndicated columnist, Ms. Gallagher is the author of three books on marriage and the principal drafter of *The Marriage Movement: A Statement of Principles*. Her most recent book (co-authored with University of Chicago Professor Linda J. Waite) is *The Case for Marriage: Why Married People are Happier, Healthier, and Better-Off Financially*, which summarizes the social science evidence on the benefits of marriage for men, women, and children. She received her A.B. from Yale University.

ROBERT P. GEORGE is McCormick Professor of Jurisprudence and director of the James Madison Program in American Ideals and Institutions at Princeton University. He is the author of *Making Men Moral: Civil Liberties and Public Morality* (1993) and *In Defense of Natural Law* (1999), and editor of *Natural Law Theory: Contemporary Essays* (1992), *The Autonomy of Law: Essays on Legal Positivism* (1996), and *Natural Law, Liberalism, and Morality* (1996), all published by Oxford University Press. His most recent book is *The Clash of Orthodoxies*, published by ISI Books. Professor George currently serves on the President's

Council on Bioethics. From 1993-98 he served as a presidential appointee to the United States Commission on Civil Rights. He is a former Judicial Fellow at the Supreme Court of the United States, where he received the 1990 Justice Tom C. Clark Award. He is general editor of New Forum Books, a Princeton University Press series of interdisciplinary works in law, culture, and politics. He is a senior fellow of the Witherspoon Institute.

HAROLD JAMES is professor of history at Princeton University. He served as a member of the Independent Commission of Experts investigating the political and economic links of Switzerland with Nazi Germany and of commissions to examine the roles of Deutsche Bank and Dresdner Bank. He is also chairman of the editorial board of *World Politics* and is a member of the executive committee of Princeton's Institute for Regional and International Studies. He has authored many books, including *The End of Globalization: Lessons from the Great Depression*, *The Deutsche Bank and the Nazi Economic War against the Jews*, and *Europe Reborn: A History 1914-2000*. In addition, he co-authored a history of the commercial bank Deutsche Bank, which won the *Financial Times* Global Business Book Award in 1996.

ELIZABETH MARQUARDT is an affiliate scholar at the Institute for American Values in New York City. Her writings have appeared in the *New York Times*, *Washington Post*, *Christian Science Monitor*, and elsewhere. Her book, based on a new, national study, is *Between Two Worlds: The Inner Lives of Children of Divorce* (Crown).

JENNIFER ROBACK MORSE has been a research fellow at the Hoover Institution, Stanford University, since 1997. Her most recent book is *Smart Sex: Finding Life-Long Love in a Hook-Up World* (Spence, 2005). Her previous book, *Love and Economics: Why the Laissez-Faire Family Doesn't Work* (Spence, 2001), shows why the family is the necessary building block for a free society and why so many modern attempted substitutes for the family do not work. Her scholarly articles have appeared in the *Journal of Political Economy*, *Economic Inquiry*, the *Journal of Economic History*, the *University of Chicago Law Review*, and the *Harvard Journal of Law and Public Policy*, among other publications.

ROGER SCRUTON is professor of philosophy at the University of Buckingham. He is also a writer, a journalist, a political activist (founder of the Conservative

Philosophy Group), an editor (from 1982-2000, editor of the *Salisbury Review*), a publisher (founder and director of Claridge Press), a composer (whose opera *The Minister* received its world premier four years ago, and was most recently performed by Lot 18 in Oxford, 1998), and a broadcaster (who has presented two full documentaries and many short programs on television, as well as taking part in radio presentations and discussions; recently a regular contributor to BBC's popular *Moral Maze*).

KATHERINE SHAW SPAHT is Jules F. and Frances L. Landry Professor of Law at Louisiana State University. Her areas of specialization are family law, community property law, and successions and donations. As the drafter of Louisiana's covenant marriage statue and subsequent amendments to the law in 1999, 2001, and 2004, Spaht has written extensively on that subject, as well as Louisiana's community property system and its unique law of forced heirship. Her articles include "Covenant Marriage and the Law of Conflict of Law," "Louisiana's Covenant Marriage: Social Analysis and Legal Implication," "For the Sake of the Children: Recapturing the Meaning of Marriage," and "Why Covenant Marriage May Prove Effective as a Response to the Culture of Divorce."

SEANA SUGRUE is associate professor and chairman of the department of political science at Ave Maria University. Prior to joining Ave Maria University, she served as founding associate director of the James Madison Program in American Ideals and Institutions at Princeton University. She has taught in the fields of law and political theory at Princeton and McGill. Her research interests include the role of law and civic institutions in the formation of a just society, and pro-life concerns.

W. BRADFORD WILCOX is assistant professor of sociology at the University of Virginia. Prior to coming to the University of Virginia, he held research fellowships at Princeton University, Yale University, and the Brookings Institution. Mr. Wilcox's research focuses on the influence of religious belief and practice on marriage, cohabitation, parenting, and fatherhood. His first book, *Soft Patriarchs, New Men: How Christianity Shapes Fathers and Husbands* (Chicago, 2004), examines the ways in which the religious beliefs and practices of American Protestant men influence their approach to parenting, household labor, and marriage.

Index

A NOTE ON THE WITHERSPOON INSTITUTE

The essays in this volume were presented to an audience of scholars, journalists, public policy experts, and other professionals, at a conference at Princeton University sponsored by the Witherspoon Institute.

The Witherspoon Institute works to enhance public understanding of the political, moral, and philosophical principles of free and democratic societies. It also promotes the application of these principles to contemporary problems.

The institute is named for John Witherspoon, a leading member of the Continental Congress, a signer of the Declaration of Independence, the sixth president of Princeton University, and a mentor to James Madison. As important as these credentials and his other notable accomplishments are, however, Witherspoon's commitment to liberal education and his recognition of the dignity of human freedom—whether it be personal, political, or religious—inspires this institute's name.

In furtherance of its educational mission, the Witherspoon Institute supports a variety of scholarly activities. It sponsors research and teaching by means of a fellowship program; it organizes conferences, lectures, and colloquia; and it encourages and assists scholarly relations and collaborations among individuals sharing the institute's interest in the foundations of a free society. The Witherspoon Institute also serves as a resource for the media and other organizations seeking speakers and public comment on matters of concern to the institute and its associated scholars.

This book was designed and set into type
by Mitchell S. Muncy,
with cover design by Stephen J. Ott,
and printed and bound
by Bang Printing,
Brainerd, Minnesota.

The index is by IndExpert, Ft. Worth, Texas.

The text face is Adobe Caslon,
designed by Carol Twombly,
based on faces cut by William Caslon, London, in the 1730s,
and issued in digital form by Adobe Systems,
Mountain View, California, in 1989.

The paper is acid-free and is of archival quality.

45